Hollywood Heroes is the book I wish I h and timely. Frank and Zach convincing of some of the biggest superheroes toda Batman—point to our desire for an ult exemplified in the Christian worldview. If you want to think more deeply about the intersection of culture and faith (or if you just want an interesting read!), this book is for *you*.

> **SEAN McDOWELL, PhD,** apologetics professor at Biola University; author or coauthor of more than eighteen books, including *Chasing Love*

What a delightful book! *Hollywood Heroes* is the perfect primer for teens, tweens, or really anyone who might not normally be interested in spiritual conversations. I foresee a whole series of family movie nights and dinner conversations sprouting from this book.

> **HILLARY MORGAN FERRER,** founder and author of *Mama Bear Apologetics* books and ministry

I love this book because it shows what many Christians have been saying for years: Hollywood is making faith-based films but doesn't really know it! Frank and Zach Turek have written an exegesis of the superheroes we all know and love, helping us understand that beneath the costumes and superpowers—or even super weaknesses, as is the case of hobbits—these heroes represent the only Superhero who truly saves . . . Jesus. And what's more, this book sheds light on the foundational desire of every human heart. You see, just like they talk about in the book, the "hero gig" didn't come naturally to Tony Stark (aka Iron Man); it doesn't come naturally to us fallen sinners either. But what does come naturally to us is the need to be saved by someone more powerful and virtuous than we are. Our hearts crave it, yearn for it. *Hollywood Heroes* is your ticket to seeing how good-overcoming-evil is the grand narrative that sells out seats because it points to the Hero in the greatest story ever told, the gospel.

> **LAUREN GREEN,** Fox News channel's chief religion correspondent; author of *Lighthouse Faith*; host of *Lighthouse Faith* podcast

In *Hollywood Heroes*, Frank and Zach Turek remind us that the greatest story ever told has been told and retold countless times. Surprisingly, it's been told and retold within the framework of some of your favorite movies!

ANDY STANLEY, founder & senior pastor of North Point Ministries (where 10.5 million watch or listen every month)

Don't think for a minute that this book is only for superhero-movie fans or even for movie fans in general. I had only seen *one* of the movies Frank and Zach discuss and yet was enthralled by the unique worldview connections they made and the powerful insights they brought to light. I love that *Hollywood Heroes* captures the reader's imagination by showing and not simply telling—a rare achievement in apologetics. It's a creative, engaging, and fresh work that I highly recommend—to movie buffs and non–movie buffs alike!

NATASHA CRAIN, host of *The Natasha Crain Podcast*; author of four books, including *Faithfully Different*

Here's a unique, creative, and compelling treatment of a phenomenon that is especially relevant in our culture today. You'll be both entertained and enlightened by the provocative insights in these pages. Enjoy the journey—and apply the lessons to your life!

LEE STROBEL, *New York Times* bestselling author; founder of the Center for Evangelism and Applied Apologetics at Colorado Christian University

Hollywood heroes like Captain America, Iron Man, and even my friend the Greatest American Hero have, for generations, told us stories of truth and justice in service of the greater good. And now, thanks to Frank and Zach's brilliant work, we see how these Hollywood heroes reveal the Greatest Story Ever Told.

CONNIE SELLECCA, movie and TV actress in over thirty-five films and shows, including *The Greatest American Hero*

In this book, Frank and Zach Turek reveal an exciting and unique superhero allegory that produces a powerful weapon for sharing our faith!

JOHN TESH, Emmy-winning TV host; radio personality; Gold Album recording artist

Neil Gaiman, paraphrasing G. K. Chesterton, wrote, "Fairy tales are more than true—not because they tell us dragons exist, but because they tell us dragons can be beaten." Here Frank and Zach Turek give us a valuable resource to help us meet the Author of all stories as we explore the movies and stories that capture our imaginations.

MAX McLEAN, artistic director of Fellowship for Performing Arts; star of the movie *Most Reluctant Convert: The Untold Story of C. S. Lewis*

Nearly *half* of the world's top-grossing movies *of all time* involve superheroes of one kind or another. Think about that for a moment. What's behind our international, universal obsession with these fictional characters, and what does this fascination tell us about our shared longings and expectations? In *Hollywood Heroes*, Frank and Zach Turek open your eyes to what's been hidden in plain sight. Don't watch another superhero movie until you've read this book. *Hollywood Heroes* will help you leverage pop culture for the glory of God and turn Hollywood storytelling into an opportunity to share the gospel.

J. WARNER WALLACE, Dateline-featured cold-case detective; author of *Person of Interest* and *Cold-Case Christianity*

As a mom, I understand the concern many Christian parents have about the religious themes found in movies like Harry Potter and Star Wars. But as our kids mature and are exposed to culture, what if we could use those stories to teach discernment and initiate meaningful conversations about gospel truth? *Hollywood Heroes* will help you find on-ramps to sharing the gospel not only with your children but also with other people who might be resistant to religious language yet are enchanted by well-produced superhero films. My kids love the Marvel franchise, and I'll be using this book as a guide to help them understand why they are so drawn to those movies—and how their favorite heroes point to the Ultimate Hero, Jesus Christ.

ALISA CHILDERS, Dove-winning recording artist; author of *Another Gospel: A Lifelong Christian Seeks Truth in Response to Progressive Christianity*

Anyone who invests time in absorbing pop-cultural entertainment, whether academic or casual, knows that media creators regularly draw on each other's work. Such borrowing is so frequent that complaints about a creativity drain in Hollywood are common. And yet the impulse and propensity of Hollywood's content creators to borrow, emulate, and at times subvert the greatest story ever told— the story of the gospel—somehow gets overlooked by the masses. *Hollywood Heroes* addresses this oversight with readable insights and memorable illustrations and, in the process, guides readers into discerning truth from error from unexpected sources. Just as God used J. R. R. Tolkien to awaken the heart and mind of C. S. Lewis to the fact that the biblical story was "the myth that was true," so Frank and Zach Turek are His instruments to awaken the massive fanbases of today's Hollywood megahits. The similarities are not contrived. Good storytelling maps to good storytelling. And under the providence of God, the most popular stories of modern pop culture can't help but mime the Ultimate Story and its Hero, Jesus.

DR. MICHAEL S. HEISER, executive director and professor at AWKNG School of Theology; host of *The Naked Bible Podcast*

As an avid movie buff, I really enjoyed discovering how heroes from movies I've seen so many times teach us important lessons about our faith. If you are looking to learn how to identify parallels between the silver screen and the Word of God, *Hollywood Heroes* is a great resource and a fun read!

ALLEN PARR, host of the YouTube sensation *The BEAT with Allen Parr*

The world is intensely fascinated by Hollywood. Wildly popular actors set trends, create fashions, and (tragically) reproduce millions after their own kind. But *Hollywood Heroes* uncovers a positive side to that which is so often negative. This powerful book has the potential to reach many with the gospel. Buy it, read it, then pass it on to unsaved loved ones, friends, and neighbors.

RAY COMFORT, author; evangelist; host of thousands of person-on-the-street videos at LivingWaters.com

Father-and-son team Frank and Zach Turek are the new Batman and Robin of apologetics, presenting a vigorous gospel message against the background of Hollywood superheroes. As they state, "Hollywood heroes help us yearn for what Jesus will do to finally set things right when He comes again." Exactly! Reading this book feels like watching an action movie: It keeps your attention; it is passionate and powerful; and in the end, the good guy—the ultimate Savior and Deliverer, infinitely more perfect than Captain America and incomparably more powerful than Harry Potter—triumphs gloriously. Get a copy for yourself and for your movie-loving friends.

DR. MICHAEL L. BROWN, host of the *Line of Fire* broadcast; author of several books, including *The Silencing of the Lambs*

All good stories point to the One True Story of a God who rescues humanity through the life, death, and resurrection of Jesus. In their delightful new book, Frank Turek and Zach Turek take the reader on a fast-paced yet thoughtful tour of popular superhero stories, revealing what they teach us about the truth of the Bible and the meaning of our lives. *Hollywood Heroes* will change how I view movies and discuss them with my superhero-loving kids.

JEFF MYERS, PhD, author; president of Summit Ministries

I've got to hand it to Frank and his son Zach for writing *Hollywood Heroes*. I love how the Tureks use people's fixation of superheroes to their advantage by revealing the Ultimate Hero. And no, it's not Captain America. It's Jesus Christ! *Hollywood Heroes* is a gripping book that is sure to capture your imagination as you discover the powerful truths and victorious nature of Jesus amid the battle between good and evil.

JASON JIMENEZ, president of STAND STRONG Ministries; bestselling author; cohost of the Challenging Conversations series in *I Don't Have Enough Faith to Be an Atheist* podcast

Humanity doesn't lack heroes; it lacks *the right kind* of heroes. In their book *Hollywood Heroes*, this father–son duo takes us to the silver screen to learn from heroes and villains. In this apologetic creative script, Frank and Zach Turek equip readers to watch film more Christianly while also leading us to the One who trumps all Hollywood heroes: our heavenly Hero, the Lord Jesus Christ. If you are looking for a fun and exciting way to learn apologetics, then this book is for you.

BOBBY CONWAY, founder and host of One-Minute Apologist

An excellent contribution toward helping us understand how Christianity makes sense of our deepest desires and intuitions. The book is written at a lay level, but that doesn't compromise the rich philosophical analysis from Frank and Zach Turek as they unpack the stories of the heroes who have captivated our attention for so many generations. They masterfully wrap their deep intellectual insights and carefully reasoned arguments into an easy-to-digest description of how the elements that we love in these hero stories are a reflection of the Greatest Story Ever Told: what God did to redeem a broken humanity. There is something for everyone in this book.

JON McCRAY, host of the popular YouTube channel *Whaddo You Meme??*

HOLLYWOOD
HEROES

HOW YOUR
FAVORITE MOVIES
REVEAL GOD

Frank Turek and Zach Turek

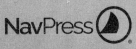

A NavPress resource published in alliance
with Tyndale House Publishers

NavPress is the publishing ministry of The Navigators, an international Christian organization and leader in personal spiritual development. NavPress is committed to helping people grow spiritually and enjoy lives of meaning and hope through personal and group resources that are biblically rooted, culturally relevant, and highly practical.

For more information, visit NavPress.com.

Hollywood Heroes: How Your Favorite Movies Reveal God

Copyright © 2022 by Frank Turek and Zach Turek. All rights reserved.

A NavPress resource published in alliance with Tyndale House Publishers

NavPress and the NavPress logo are registered trademarks of NavPress, The Navigators, Colorado Springs, CO. *Tyndale* is a registered trademark of Tyndale House Publishers. Absence of ® in connection with marks of NavPress or other parties does not indicate an absence of registration of those marks.

The Team:

David Zimmerman, Acquisitions Editor; Erin Healy, Developmental Editor; John Greco, Copy Editor; Olivia Eldredge, Operations Manager; Matthew James Gillespie, Designer

Cover photograph of superhero copyright © choreograph/Depositphotos. All rights reserved.

Author photo by Frank Turek copyright © 2021. All rights reserved.

The authors are represented by Ambassador Literary Agency, Nashville, TN.

Some of the anecdotal illustrations in this book are true to life and are included with the permission of the persons involved. All other illustrations are composites of real situations, and any resemblance to people living or dead is purely coincidental.

For information about special discounts for bulk purchases, please contact Tyndale House Publishers at csresponse@tyndale.com, or call 1-855-277-9400.

ISBN 978-1-64158-351-0

Printed in the United States of America

28   27   26   25   24   23   22
7   6   5   4   3   2

CONTENTS

PREFACE

To Get the Most out of This Book, Watch These Movies

Most of the characters we cover in this book have more than ten hours of screen time, and many of the comic book heroes have histories that date back to the 1940s. That's a lot of content for us to cover in a short book like this, so we've written with an underlying assumption that the backstory of each character is at least passingly familiar to most readers.

This list of movies is not exhaustive. (For example, you'll notice that some of the Batman movies from the 1990s are missing.) That's because we've only listed the movies we spent time writing about. For the best experience with this book, we recommend that you watch some or all of these movies ahead of time—keeping in mind that some are not appropriate for viewers of all ages. If watching the movies is not appropriate or possible, *Hollywood Heroes* is written in such a way that you or your kids don't actually have to watch the movies to enjoy this book and profit from it (see Natasha Crain's endorsement).

Our own experience has been that these movies and characters are not only fun, but they can also help us discover important truths about God, ourselves, and our future. Thanks for joining us on this adventure!

CAPTAIN AMERICA:

Captain America: The First Avenger	July 22, 2011
The Avengers	May 4, 2012
Captain America: The Winter Soldier	April 4, 2014
Avengers: Age of Ultron	May 1, 2015

Captain America: Civil War	May 6, 2016
Avengers: Infinity War	April 27, 2018
Avengers: Endgame	April 26, 2019

IRON MAN:

Iron Man	May 2, 2008
Iron Man 2	May 7, 2010
Captain America: The First Avenger[1]	July 22, 2011
The Avengers	May 4, 2012
Iron Man 3	May 3, 2013
Avengers: Age of Ultron	May 1, 2015
Captain America: Civil War	May 6, 2016
Spider-Man: Homecoming	July 7, 2017
Avengers: Infinity War	April 27, 2018
Avengers: Endgame	April 26, 2019
Spider-Man: Far from Home	July 2, 2019

HARRY POTTER:

Harry Potter and the Philosopher's Stone	November 10, 2001
Harry Potter and the Chamber of Secrets	November 15, 2002
Harry Potter and the Prisoner of Azkaban	May 31, 2004
Harry Potter and the Goblet of Fire	November 18, 2005
Harry Potter and the Order of the Phoenix	July 11, 2007
Harry Potter and the Half-Blood Prince	July 15, 2009
Harry Potter and the Deathly Hallows—Part 1	November 19, 2010
Harry Potter and the Deathly Hallows—Part 2	July 15, 2011

STAR WARS:

Episode IV—A New Hope	May 25, 1977
Episode V—The Empire Strikes Back	May 21, 1980
Episode VI—Return of the Jedi	May 25, 1983
Episode I—The Phantom Menace	May 19, 1999
Episode II—Attack of the Clones	May 16, 2002
Episode III—Revenge of the Sith	May 19, 2005
Episode VII—The Force Awakens	December 18, 2015
Episode VIII—The Last Jedi	December 15, 2017
Episode IX—The Rise of Skywalker	December 20, 2019

THE LORD OF THE RINGS:

The Fellowship of the Ring	December 19, 2001
The Two Towers	December 18, 2002
The Return of the King	December 17, 2003

PREFACE

BATMAN:

Batman	June 23, 1989
Batman Returns	June 19, 1992
Batman Begins	June 25, 2005
The Dark Knight	July 18, 2008
The Dark Knight Rises	July 20, 2012
Batman v Superman: Dawn of Justice	March 25, 2016
Justice League	November 17, 2017
Zack Snyder's Justice League[2]	March 18, 2021

WONDER WOMAN:

Batman v Superman: Dawn of Justice	March 25, 2016
Wonder Woman	June 2, 2017
Justice League	November 17, 2017
Wonder Woman 1984	December 25, 2020
Zack Snyder's Justice League	March 18, 2021

INTRODUCTION

Looking Death in the Face

SEPTEMBER 29, 2006, Ramadi, Iraq: US Navy SEAL Michael Monsoor and his team are under attack from AK-47 fire and a rocket-propelled grenade. But they're not sure where the enemy is.

As an Mk 48 machine gunner in SEAL Team 3, Monsoor normally operates from the front of Delta platoon, which means he's often the first to take fire. He does that while carrying a hundred pounds of gear in temperatures that exceed 100°F. Since arriving in Iraq in April, Monsoor and his team, which includes "American Sniper" Chris Kyle, have killed 84 insurgents, but not without casualties of their own.

A few months back, Petty Officer Monsoor saw a teammate wounded and pinned down under withering enemy fire. "With complete disregard for his own safety," said witnesses, Monsoor ran straight into the gunfire, bullets ricocheting off the ground at his feet, in order to save his teammate. While suppressing the enemy with his machine gun in one arm, Monsoor used his other arm to drag his injured teammate back to an evacuation vehicle. His bravery that day would eventually win him the Silver Star.

Today in a violent, terrorist-infested neighborhood in Ramadi, it's looking like Monsoor will need that kind of bravery again.

He's on the roof of a building with two other Navy SEALS. Insurgents on the ground have blocked off the streets in Ramadi, and there's someone in the town mosque yelling over the loudspeakers, "Kill the Americans!"

Monsoor takes a position in front of a doorway to the roof and between his two SEAL teammates, who are in the prone firing position near his feet. There's a lull in the gunfire, and the three men scan the streets looking for the enemy.

Suddenly, from an unseen position, an insurgent on the ground throws a grenade that hits Monsoor in the chest and falls to his feet. Given the time the throw took, Monsoor knows he can't grab it and throw it back. He has only a split second to make a decision. If he leaps through the doorway behind him to save himself, his two Navy SEAL teammates will surely die.

Monsoor yells, "Grenade!" Then, instead of jumping backward to save himself, Monsoor jumps *forward*, chest first, onto the grenade.

It detonates.

Thirty minutes later, twenty-five-year-old Michael Monsoor is dead. His two Navy SEAL teammates survive because Monsoor's body muffled the blast.

At Monsoor's funeral, one of his teammates said, "Mikey looked death in the face that day and said, 'You will not take my friends. I will go in their stead.'"

I'd never seen a president cry until April 8, 2008. That's when President George W. Bush invited Michael Monsoor's parents into the White House to give them their son's Medal of Honor. With tears streaming down his face and his voice quivering, the president read the citation. It ended this way:

Although only he could have escaped the blast, Petty Officer Monsoor chose instead to protect his teammates. Instantly and without regard for his own safety, he threw himself onto the grenade to absorb the force of the explosion with his body, saving the lives of his two teammates. By his undaunted courage, fighting spirit, and unwavering devotion to duty in the face of certain death, Petty Officer Monsoor gallantly gave his life for his country, thereby reflecting great credit upon himself and upholding the highest traditions of the United States Naval Service.[1]

Since then, Garden Grove High School, Monsoor's alma mater in Garden Grove, California, has named their new football stadium the Michael A. Monsoor Memorial Stadium. The golden trident of the Navy SEALs dominates the fifty-yard line. And in January 2019, the United States Navy commissioned the USS *Michael Monsoor*, one of the newest and deadliest guided missile destroyers in the fleet.

As the president said, Michael Monsoor died for his country. But as his surviving teammate said, Monsoor didn't just die for his country; with the grenade at his feet, Michael Monsoor chose to die for his friends. Most Medal of Honor winners who live to tell about it express the same sentiment: I couldn't let my buddies die. I love them. They would have done the same for me.

Love of country isn't the primary motivation for heroics in battle; rather, it's the love of friends. As Jesus said before His crucifixion, "Greater love has no one than this: to lay down one's life for one's friends" (John 15:13).

Everyone—regardless of their religious or cultural beliefs—recognizes that sacrificing yourself to save someone else is one of the most powerful and beautiful forms of love.

That's why Michael Monsoor was a real-life hero. It's also why nearly all the heroes we love in the movies are willing to sacrifice themselves to save those threatened by evil.

Such acts of brave sacrifice are God-like—literally. Just over two thousand years ago, God took on a human nature and then allowed Himself to be sacrificed in order to save billions of people threatened by evil. In the movies, the hero normally rescues innocent people from some kind of external evil. In this real world, God does that and more. He also rescues guilty people from *their own* evil—even evil directed at God Himself.

Later, we'll see what Jesus actually did and why He did it. But first, we need to give you a pre-mission brief because, whether you know it or not, you're in a war for the souls of every human being, including your own. We're all looking death in the face, and we need to take action now before it's too late. This war is unseen, but its effects are not. They can be seen in our behavior and in the headlines every day. Allow us to explain.

The Unseen Realm

If there's one thing every person knows, regardless of their religious beliefs, it's that this world is messed up; things aren't the way they are supposed to be. The world is broken, and so are we. Even the best lives and best relationships are a struggle. No matter how good we have it, something is still missing, something is not quite right. We tell ourselves the next job, relationship, accomplishment, accolade, or paycheck will fix it all, but they never do. On top of that, no matter how rich you are or how many people love you, pain, suffering, and death come to all of us.

We all long for liberation from our bondage to decay and into a life of bliss. But no matter how hard we try, we can't find what we're looking for here. Maybe that should be a clue that there is something beyond us. As C. S. Lewis famously put it, "If we find ourselves with a desire that nothing in this world can satisfy, the most probable explanation is that we were made for another world."[2]

We are indeed made for another world. But the spiritual battle going on in this world may prevent us from getting there. We're speaking of the unseen realm of spiritual warfare that has existed from the beginning of time and continues to this day. And we are all participants in it whether we know it or not. (In fact, the spiritual forces of darkness would rather keep us ignorant of it.)

That's what the Bible teaches, as our friend and Bible scholar Dr. Michael Heiser makes clear in his bestselling book *The Unseen Realm*.[3] Christians have always believed in spiritual warfare, but some today relegate the spiritual battle to Bible times because it contradicts their modern sensibilities.

Especially startling for modern Christians is the teaching that God has a heavenly divine council that oversees the nations.[4] When God confuses the language of the people at Babel, He places over them members of this divine council, but these "sons of God" rebel against the one true God and lead the people of their nations to worship them instead of Him. Following the Babel incident, as recorded in Genesis 12, God promises Abraham that He will bless all of the nations on earth through him. This starts the long process of God winning back the nations through one nation, Israel, from which the one Savior of the world, Jesus, will come.

Notice that when Jesus gives His disciples the Great Commission, He says, "Therefore go and make disciples of all *nations*" (Matthew 28:19, emphasis added). Notice further that when the Great Commission officially kicks off at Pentecost (Acts 2), the reversal of Babel occurs. Instead of people being separated by languages, suddenly people from all over the known world—with many different languages—could understand the apostles. And the nations that begin to be reconciled at Pentecost mirror the nations separated at Babel! (Despite being authored by forty different people over 1,500 years, the interconnectedness and symmetry of the Bible are amazing.)

What does this mean for us today? An overview of the biblical story—which is the story of reality[5]—will help us understand our mission. Think of the unfolding plan of God in five phases represented by the acronym **CRIME.**

Creation: God creates the world and all living things. He makes us in His image.

Rebellion: The creation becomes degraded and dangerous after Satan, humans, and the divine council all rebel.

Intervention: God intervenes to save us by coming as Jesus, our sinless substitute who takes our deserved punishment upon Himself. He is resurrected from the dead, proving He's God and showing His message can be trusted.

Mission: Our mission now is to show earthly rebels the good news Jesus has accomplished and to make disciples of all nations before the King returns. But we have opposition from rebels in the unseen realm.

Eternity: Jesus returns as King, quarantines the remaining rebels, and restores creation so those who love God can enjoy Him, His creation, and one another for eternity.

We mentioned that while much of this war is in the unseen realm, many of its effects are not. Every day we see the rebels making choices that either bring them closer to surrender or make them more entrenched in their rebellion. We even see those who have pledged allegiance to the King slipping back into their old habits of rebellion. As the apostle Paul put it, "Our struggle is not against flesh and blood, but against the rulers, against the authorities, against the powers of this dark world and against the spiritual forces of evil in the heavenly realms" (Ephesians 6:12).

Now, when you start talking about Satan and demons, modern people think you've lost your mind. That's unenlightened superstition, they will say.

"Frank and Zach. In this day and age, you don't really believe in demons, do you?"

Yes, for a number of reasons.

First, because Jesus did (and we just have a personal policy—if someone rises from the dead, we just trust whatever the guy says!). Second,

His apostles, who were confirmed by miracles, believed in them as well. And third, there's evidence that miracles occur today and that demons are active. Professor Craig Keener lays out the documentation in his meticulously researched two-volume set called *Miracles*.[6]

But even without reading Dr. Keener's convincing work, we can come to the same conclusion just by looking at the world around us. Here's why.

We all agree that this world isn't quite right, that things aren't the way they're supposed to be. Even atheists point out plenty of things they believe are wrong with the world. But if things aren't the way they are supposed to be, then there must be some objective "Supposer" (God) whose nature defines the way things are supposed to be. Otherwise, it would just be a matter of opinion that we ought to love one another and not murder, rape, or otherwise abuse one another. Those moral truths are not mere human opinions but are instead grounded in the nature of God, and we are supposed to obey them.

But *we don't obey them*, at least not perfectly. And our disobedience often seems to go beyond mere self-interest. We don't just do wrong to benefit ourselves; we often *enjoy* doing wrong beyond what is necessary to give us any advantage. It's as if there's some external force urging us on.

Think of the evil that's occurred in recent times: children are sold into sex slavery; dictators starve their people to benefit themselves; the terrorists who threw the grenade at Michael Monsoor are known to rape, behead, and sometimes even crucify women and children. In the last century, more than one hundred million people were slaughtered by atheistic leaders and Nazi regimes. Do we really think all of that malicious evil is solely the result of people just being selfish?

Even our own behavior in so-called civilized America provides a clue that demonic forces are real. Why else do many in our society now celebrate the killing of millions of unborn children in the name of convenience to the point where people are encouraged to "shout your abortion" and demand that the government pay for it? Why else do we have a personal desire for revenge against those who hurt us, one that goes beyond what's necessary for dispassionate justice? Why else do people "cancel" their fellow citizens simply for holding a different political opinion?

The truth is, human beings sometimes display a dark delight for malicious, gratuitous evil that should make it obvious there are demonic forces at work—forces that influence people to go mindlessly from selfish to cruel and even sadistic. (And those who don't commit crimes themselves are still fascinated with them. Look up a list of popular podcasts these days, and you'll almost always find shows about unsolved murders near the top of the list.)

So yes, not only does God exist, but demons exist too. And these spiritual forces are all involved in the war in the unseen realm, the effects of which can be seen in our world.

How will this war in the unseen realm impact your life? It depends on whose side you have chosen. When the rebellion is finally quelled, will you be lauded or condemned for the choice you made and how you conducted yourself in battle? The answer to that question will determine your destiny.

But wait. This raises important questions: Why is there evil at all? Why doesn't God just squash the rebels in the unseen realm? And what does all this have to do with Hollywood heroes?

What Good Is Evil?

I (Frank) had just finished my *I Don't Have Enough Faith to Be an Atheist* presentation at Wright State University when a young atheist approached the microphone with a trap disguised as a question. He said, "What would you think of a parent who told his child not to touch a loaded gun but then left him alone with it? The child then shot and killed himself."

I said, "That would be a bad parent."

He responded, "Okay, so let's replace the gun with an apple. God did the same thing to Adam and Eve. Doesn't that make God a bad parent?"

The young man seemed to have a good point. Why would an all-knowing, good God put the tree in the garden if He knew Adam and Eve would disobey Him? According to Christian theology, all the pain and suffering that we experience began with them. We're all now paying for the sin of Adam and Eve. How is that fair?

"Let's make sure the analogy works," I said. "In your analogy the parent represents God, right?"

"Right."

"Well, what if the parent had the power to resurrect the child? What if He gave the child a choice to be resurrected or not?"[7]

The young man paused. He could see that his analogy was flawed because it treated God as though He were a mere human being, powerless to correct a tragedy. Unlike a human parent, God can resurrect anyone who dies. And that's what Christianity teaches.

But the question still remains, why would an all-knowing, good God allow us to make such a mistake, even if He's going to one day right all wrongs?

The answer is: because love cannot exist without free choice. Yes, free choice allows for the possibility of evil, but it is the only way love can exist. Love must be freely given. It cannot be forced.

God could squash all evil, but He'd have to squash free will, too, which would make this a world devoid of choice and love. Satan would be put out of existence, but so would all of us because we do evil every day. (Instead of ending evil by taking away free will, God will nullify evil's effects by quarantining it. But we'll get to that later.)

Instead of questioning God for giving Adam and Eve the opportunity and ability to sin, we really should be thanking Him. If God hadn't granted us such freedoms, we would be nothing but moist robots, unable to love or experience meaningful relationships.

Suffering can also bring about good. For example, it can motivate us to make positive changes in our lives that also ripple forward to help ourselves and often countless others. Let's take an example from the world of superheroes.

When Peter Parker first learns he has special spider-like powers, he's more interested in using them for his own personal gain rather than serving others. This selfishness eventually bites him, big time. Think of the time Peter has the opportunity to easily stop a robbery that's happening right in front of him. Out of revenge, he chooses not to intervene, as the man who is being robbed had just conned Peter.

Peter thinks he got the con man back by letting the robber take his cash. But just a few minutes later he discovers that the escaping robber has carjacked and shot his beloved Uncle Ben. As a crying Peter sees his uncle labor through his final breaths on the sidewalk, the last words Ben spoke to him earlier that evening penetrate his soul: "With great power comes great responsibility." At that point, the superhero known as Spider-Man is born.

From then on, Spider-Man devotes his powers not to selfish pursuits but to the service of others. He goes on to save thousands of people. But without the murder of Uncle Ben, the Spider-Man we know would not exist.

What we're seeing here is a powerful phenomenon called "the ripple effect." That's the fact that every event in life, whether good or bad, is like a rock thrown into a pond—the ripples spread out and impact everything else in the pond. In the case of Peter Parker, the murder of one innocent man (his uncle) rippled forward to save thousands of lives later on. On a larger scale, the same can be said of the murder of Jesus. The murder of that innocent God-man brought immeasurable good to billions of people throughout history. And it continues to do so two thousand years later.

Sometimes we can see how tragedy ripples forward for good, but most of the time we can't. Since we are locked in time and have an extremely limited perspective, we simply can't trace how an act today ripples forward to impact billions of events and people over the centuries. But God can.

So, while we may not know why certain bad things happen, *we know why we don't know*. We're limited beings confined in time, which means we're simply not in a position to know what reasons God has for allowing bad things to happen. Since everything is connected, evil can and does often ripple forward to bring forth good. In fact, God guarantees it.[8]

It's not just that good can come from evil but that some greater goods cannot be achieved any other way. For example, suffering can draw us closer to God, wake us up to what is really important, and prod us to develop the kind of virtue that can only grow in the face of evil and hardship. In our fallen state, it's difficult to develop compassion unless there's suffering. A person can't develop perseverance unless there are obstacles to overcome. And there's no way to develop courage unless there's evil or danger to face. In other words, we can't get better unless we have opposition.

Think about children. What do you call children who get everything they want?

Spoiled.

What's spoiled about them?

Their character. You can't give children (or adults!) everything they want. If you do, you'll ruin them. Instead of developing character that defers to and honors others, giving children everything they want shrinks their souls and turns them into self-absorbed brats. They become like narcissistic, entitled celebrities, ready to throw a temper tantrum unless everything goes exactly their way. Without some opposition to our egos in the form of pain, suffering, and struggle, we would all become even more selfish and hellish than we already are.

If God had not given His creatures free choice, there would be no need for heroes and no possibility of growth. If there was no evil to fight and no virtue to develop, we wouldn't experience the deeper satisfaction of an expanded soul. Good times don't grow our character like bad times. The biblical character Job, who experienced horrific suffering, is a deeper and more virtuous person after his ordeal than before.

That's one reason a redeemed world is ultimately better than an innocent world. God actually achieves greater good by allowing the evil that comes from free choice than if He had merely made us like robots. Even the sinless Jesus learned obedience through suffering.[9] This world may be a terrible resort, but it's a great gym.[10]

God knows that love is worth the pain of evil, especially since He will one day end the effects of evil on the redeemed. Once the full number of people have accepted the free pass into His Kingdom provided by the sacrifice of His Son, Christ will come back and right all wrongs.[11] God will then quarantine evil in a place called hell.

In the meantime, while we're waiting for Christ to come, we're stuck in a world of trouble. Since it's not heaven yet, there is evil to fight, souls to be won, and growth to be achieved. Fictional stories from Hollywood can help us realize that.

Why US Marines Read Fiction

The Commandant of the United States Marine Corps periodically releases and updates a professional reading list for Marines of all ranks to further their professional development. On it you'll find all sorts of books on leadership, military history, time management, and a host of other topics. What you might also be surprised to find is that there are works of fiction on the list as well. Popular science-fiction novels like *Ender's Game*, *Starship Troopers*, and *Ready Player One* are on that list and for good reason. General Martin Dempsey, former chairman of the Joint Chiefs of Staff (the highest-ranking officer in all of the US armed forces) wrote that fiction creates "a mental laboratory [that] invites us to explore challenges and opportunities that we might otherwise overlook." In other words, fiction allows us to explore the world of possibility.

We have a habit of overlooking things that are seemingly impossible simply because we have never experienced them. In logic, this is called the anecdotal fallacy, where one draws a conclusion based on personal experience or isolated examples. How many times have you debated someone whose entire argument revolved around personal experience? They can't comprehend a different perspective because it has never happened to them. While that doesn't necessarily make their viewpoint wrong, it can lead to some potentially dangerous conclusions, particularly when they want to use their experience to make big personal decisions or to influence public policy.

Fiction helps us imagine worlds different from our own. It allows us to wonder what would happen if there was a worldwide pandemic even more destructive than COVID-19. Or what the world would look like after a nuclear holocaust. Or what types of technology would be useful in the space age.

Fiction gives us moral lessons as well. It allows us to experience scenarios that can be hard to replicate in the real world but are important to character development. How can we give people a lesson in courage when the majority of them will never fight in a battle? (After all, few people will ever be put in Michael Monsoor's position.) How do we show the potential terrors of government oppression when the majority of Americans have never experienced it? How can we develop understanding and empathy for those whose experiences are outside our own? Name your issue or scenario, fiction can help teach the ethics that pertain to it.

Fiction can implant theological lessons into our hearts in ways that mere commands and facts cannot. As the Bible itself teaches, stories—both imagined and true—are often the best way to teach virtues and theology.[12] That's why Jesus used parables, and it's why the Bible is one long factual story rather than a long series of merely factual statements.

Stories sometimes slip past the artificial barriers we put up to keep out ideas that may threaten our worldview. Stories appeal straight to the heart. As professor Gisela Kreglinger insightfully observes, "Avoiding overt 'God-talk' is an important strategy that Jesus employs. By luring the reader into thinking the parable is just about everyday life, the defense mechanisms of Jesus' religious audience are down, and they are tricked into an understanding of God that is at least surprising, but often shocking and seemingly unacceptable."[13] Indeed, it's hard to keep out something you don't see coming. As we'll see, our favorite movies can do the same thing.

Why Do We Love Hollywood Heroes?

Captain America, Iron Man, and the other heroes of the Marvel Universe are about to battle Thanos. Luke Skywalker crosses lightsabers with Darth Vader. Aragorn charges the overwhelming forces of Mordor. Batman confronts the Joker. Superman takes down Doomsday. Wonder Woman incinerates Ares. We are captivated. Why?

There's something that enthralls us about stories where human lives are put in danger, that depict a real struggle between good and evil, that show how love and dedication can ultimately overcome even the most hopeless of situations.

It's more than just entertainment. We may not realize it, but the stories and heroes that thrill us in the theater are simply amped up, fantasized versions of the struggle between good and evil that happens in real life. Some of it is in the unseen realm, and some of it we see clearly.

We long for "another world" that we were really made for, and we are enchanted by someone who will bring us there—someone who will fight evil and bring us safely to a world where there is no pain, suffering, or struggle. Hollywood heroes help us yearn for what Jesus will do to finally set things right when He comes again. If we love Hollywood heroes, we should also love Jesus because He is our Ultimate Hero.

We are also enchanted by virtue. Some people today may claim morals are relative, but they contradict that claim when they desperately want to see the bad guy get justice. They don't really think that murder, theft, and rape are just matters of opinion. Otherwise, why would they cheer when they see the villain get taken down by the courageous hero who risks his own life to save the innocent?

Whether on the big screen or in real life, we are naturally drawn to those who exhibit courage, self-control, wisdom, justice, faith, hope, and love. We intuitively know those virtues make them heroes. No one ever mistakes a cowardly, double-crossing, selfish cheat for a good guy, even if he occasionally does the right thing.

All of this assumes that human life really matters, that there's a right and wrong way to treat people, that there's a true purpose to life and an ultimate destiny for all of us. That's actually the Christian worldview.

So when we see heroes and villains battle it out in a well-crafted movie, we're seeing a dramatized version of reality. The heroes are involved in a high-stakes mission to save the world, and so are we. Christians are just trying to do it one person at a time. As Gandalf put it (one of the heroes we'll see from *The Lord of the Rings*), "All we have to decide is what to do with the time that is given us."

As we take a journey with Hollywood heroes such as Captain America, Iron Man, Gandalf, Batman, Wonder Woman, and many others, we'll learn from their successes and failures and see how their best qualities point to an ultimate hero beyond them. But before we take that journey, we have to make a critical distinction between God and superheroes.

God versus Superheroes

Atheist Richard Dawkins dismisses the God of the Bible as he dismisses a long list of other supposed gods. He writes, "I have found it an amusing strategy, when asked whether I am an atheist, to point out that the questioner is also an atheist when considering Zeus, Apollo, Amon Ra, Mithras, Baal, Thor, Wotan, the Golden Calf and the Flying Spaghetti Monster. I just go one god further."[14]

Is Dawkins right? Is the God of the Bible no different than the non-existent gods of mythology?

While there are some similarities that we'll see throughout this book, the God of the Bible and the gods of mythology are in completely different categories. In order to see this, let's define what Christians mean by "God."

When Christians say "God," we don't mean an old man on a cloud, a big angel, or a more powerful and bigger version of yourself (like a superhero). We are talking about the uncreated, eternal being who created all things and sustains all things. In other words, God didn't just create the universe, He keeps it going moment to moment.[15]

In order to grasp who God really is, set aside the word *God* for a minute and marinate on this question: Who is the Source and Sustainer of all things? Whoever that is, that's who Christians mean by "God."

The Source and Sustainer of all things is:

- *Self-existing*: not caused by another; the foundation of all being
- *Infinite*: unlimited; the completely maximized or actualized Being
- *Simple*: undivided in being; is not composed of parts
- *Immaterial*: spirit; not made of matter
- *Spaceless*: transcends space; isn't confined by space
- *Timeless*: transcends time; eternal, had no beginning and will have no end
- *Omnipotent*: all-powerful; can do whatever is logically possible
- *Omnipresent*: everywhere present
- *Omniscient*: all-knowing; knows all actual and possible states of affairs
- *Immutable*: changeless; the anchor and standard by which everything else is measured
- *Holy*: set apart; morally perfect; is perfectly just and loving
- *Personal*: has mind, emotion, and will; makes choices

These attributes exist in a unified and infinite way in the Source and Sustainer. You can discover them through evidence-based arguments and careful philosophical reasoning.[16] And they are confirmed by the biblical writers who, as we've explored and discussed elsewhere, are reliable sources.[17]

Contrast God's attributes with those Dawkins mentioned along with fictional superheroes. Superheroes do not have any of the infinite attributes of God—no finite being does or could. Since God is the only unlimited, infinite, infallible being, He is in a unique category. Everything else is finite or limited.

Superheroes, like humans, have some of the powers of God but only in a limited way. Whereas God has *all knowledge*, superheroes and humans have *some knowledge*. Whereas God is *all-powerful*, superheroes and humans have *some power*. In other words, our finite attributes are analogous to God's infinite attributes, but they are not exactly the same in degree or kind.

We can put it this way: superheroes are limited, created beings *inside* the universe, not the ultimate, infinite, uncreated Being who is *outside* the universe and sustains it every moment. Since God is the Source and Sustainer of all of creation, if any of the superheroes or finite "gods" that Dawkins listed actually existed, they would need to be created and sustained by God. In fact, Dawkins himself wouldn't be here without God.

Now, it is true that there are some similarities between God and the finite gods Dawkins mentions. And there's much we can learn about God from the superheroes we see in movies. While superheroes are myths, Jesus is the true "myth."

The True "Myth"

We are about to relive some of the most compelling stories ever shown on the big screen. We're going to see many parallels to the biblical account that will tell us about God and ourselves.

But let's be honest: the majority of these films' screenwriters probably didn't intentionally borrow parallels or ideas from the biblical accounts (though there are significant exceptions we'll mention). They unconsciously included those elements because sacrifice in the struggle to defeat evil is at the center of the story of reality, which is the Christian story.

As philosopher Peter Kreeft put it, "There are Christ figures everywhere in literature and life. This should not surprise us. For Christ was not an emergency afterthought or a freak from outer space, but the central point of the whole human story from the beginning in the Mind of its Author."[18]

Mythical Christ figures helped bring C. S. Lewis to Christianity. In 1931, when Lewis was on his spiritual journey from atheism to Christianity, he thought the story of Jesus was like a mythical pagan story of sacrifice. He admitted he was always moved by stories of gods sacrificing themselves *unless* they were in the Gospels. But his friend J. R. R. Tolkien, author of *The Lord of the Rings*, personally convinced Lewis that Christianity was the true "myth." Jesus Christ really sacrificed Himself and rose from the dead in order to accomplish the ultimate victory of good over evil. Lewis wrote:

> Now the story of Christ is simply a true myth: a myth working on us in the same way as the others, but with this tremendous difference that it really happened: and one must be content to accept it in the same way, remembering that it is God's myth where the others are men's myths: i.e. the Pagan stories are God expressing Himself through the minds of poets, using such images as He found there, while Christianity is God expressing Himself through what we call 'real things'.[19]

Lewis then spent much of his career providing evidence for the truth of Christianity. Christianity is literally the greatest story ever told, and it's true!

As revealed in the quote above, Lewis believed that God expressed Himself through the minds of ancient myth writers. Might God do the same through the minds of modern moviemakers? As ancient myths moved Lewis to understand the truth, can modern myths do the same for us?

What can we learn about God and ourselves from Captain America? From Iron Man? From *The Lord of the Rings*? *Star Wars*? Batman? Wonder Woman? Even the controversial Harry Potter? More than you might think. And we hope to enjoy ourselves as we relive some of these stories to learn from them.

Like Jesus, these heroes often look death in the face to save us. As we're about to see, the first one will even jump on a grenade for you.

1
CAPTAIN AMERICA

Black Widow: These guys come from legend. They're basically gods.
Captain America: There's only one God, ma'am,
and I'm pretty sure he doesn't dress like that.

THE AVENGERS (2012)

The First Avenger: His Power Is Goodness

IT'S HARD TO IMAGINE HOW one man could inflict such evil. Yet before
the true depths of Germany's murderous dictator were fully known,
one superhero was already on the case. Captain America took on Adolf
Hitler before the United States did.

In March 1941, about nine months before the US entered World
War II, the first Captain America comic book shows the Captain punch-
ing Hitler in the face. That's a fitting start, given the character's destiny.
If there's one thing that Captain America won't tolerate, it's a bully.

The idea behind the hero, according to co-creator Jack Kirby, was that
he needed to be passionate about freedom and possess "the character to
win and to triumph over evil. It is a simple formula, but very effective and
powerful." (Jack Kirby created Captain America with Joe Simon. In 1961,
Kirby became one of the founders of Marvel Comics, along with Stan Lee.)

In many ways, Captain America is Marvel's moral equivalent of

Superman—unyieldingly good even in the face of horrifying evil. But unlike some superheroes, Captain America was not born with his powers in the manner of, say, Superman or Thor. Neither is he reliant on money and technology to overcome his shortfalls in the superpower department like Batman or Iron Man. In fact, Cap's powers aren't even his most defining attribute. In terms of sheer power, he is greatly outclassed by other characters in the Marvel Cinematic Universe (hereafter referred to as the "MCU").

Instead of physical power, his moral character and devotion to his cause are his greatest assets. Even his choice of weapon reflects this: a shield—symbolic of the fact that he fights to protect others rather than for personal gain. We might say the Captain is trying to *defend* rather than *offend*.

This is ironic because when we are first introduced to Steve Rogers, it doesn't seem like he's strong enough to defend anything. He's a man who is so small and sickly that he is denied entry into the army during World War II.

In our day, this doesn't seem like a big deal. Most of us haven't experienced a draft or a time when a significant portion of the population was expected to serve. Since the end of the Vietnam War, the US military has been made up entirely of volunteers. But back during World War II, getting rejected from military service was almost unheard of, unless you had an extremely significant medical condition, which even then could sometimes be glossed over.

People felt they were being dishonorable if they didn't join. Many young boys lied about their age to join the service (the youngest recorded was 12 years old). Yet Steve Rogers is so weak he is turned down as a volunteer.

Not to be denied, Steve tries again at several different recruiting centers. At one, he finally finds a man who believes in him, Dr. Abraham Erskine. Steve is selected to take part in the Super Soldier program, though he doesn't know this initially. Dr. Erskine chooses Steve in large part because, having emigrated from Nazi Germany, the doctor knows what it's like to be bullied. He believes Steve wouldn't bully anyone, even as a super soldier.

Two key tests in *The First Avenger* show what Steve has to do to prove himself worthy.

The first is the "action test." While Steve is at boot camp, Colonel Chester Phillips begins to question why Dr. Erskine favors Steve over Hodge, another recruit who "looks the part" of a soldier: big, strong, and mean.

COL. CHESTER PHILLIPS: [*Looking over the men*] You're not REALLY thinking about picking Rogers, are you?

ABRAHAM ERSKINE: I wasn't just THINKING about it. He is a clear choice.

COL. CHESTER PHILLIPS: When you brought a ninety-pound asthmatic onto my army base, I let it slide. I thought maybe he'd be useful to you like a gerbil. Never thought you'd pick him. You put a needle in that kid's arm, it's gonna go right through him . . . [*Looking at Steve straining to do exercises*] Look at that. He's makin' me cry.

ABRAHAM ERSKINE: I am looking for qualities beyond the physical.

COL. CHESTER PHILLIPS: Do you know how long it took to set up this project? Of all the groveling I had to do in front of Senator What's-his-name's committee?

ABRAHAM ERSKINE: Yes, I'm well aware of your efforts.

COL. CHESTER PHILLIPS: Then throw me a bone. Hodge passed every test we gave him. He's big, he's fast, he obeys orders—he's a soldier.

ABRAHAM ERSKINE: He's a bully.

COL. CHESTER PHILLIPS: You don't win wars with niceness, doctor. You win wars with guts. [*The Colonel then pulls the pin of a grenade and throws it among the recruits*] . . . GRENADE!

Once the dust clears, it becomes clear that Dr. Erskine is right. Steve is the one who, like Michael Monsoor, willingly dives on the grenade to save his squad, while Hodge runs away and hides behind a truck.

The second test for Steve is mental. Dr. Erskine wants to know what kind of man Steve is. Is he blinded by hate or is he standing up for those who don't have the ability to defend themselves?

ABRAHAM ERSKINE: Do you want to kill Nazis?

STEVE ROGERS: Is this a test?

ABRAHAM ERSKINE: Yes.

STEVE ROGERS: I don't want to kill anyone. I don't like bullies; I don't care where they're from.

Steve passes this test as well, leading Dr. Erskine to make a statement that really defines what makes Captain America so special.

ABRAHAM ERSKINE: Whatever happens tomorrow you must promise me one thing. That you will stay who you are. *Not a perfect soldier, but a good man* (emphasis ours).

This line, probably more than any other, defines Captain America as a character. In fact, unlike most superheroes and despite being around for almost eighty years, Captain America is unique in the sense that as a character he is static—he undergoes almost no moral change over the course of his story arc.

While the word *static* often has a negative connotation when it comes to storytelling, for the character of Captain America, this is the entire point. The same ninety-pound Steve Rogers we meet in *The First Avenger*, the would-be soldier who is too small and sickly to enlist in the army, is the same guy duking it out with the supreme villain Thanos in *Avengers: Infinity War* and *Endgame*. Steve Rogers is a moral hero the whole time. The Super Soldier program just gave him the physical tools to do the job.

The only thing he doesn't seem to like is the uniform: "You know, for the longest time I dreamed about coming overseas and being on the front lines. Serving my country. I finally get everything I wanted, and I'm wearing tights."

He Experiences No Moral Change

What do we mean by "no moral change," and why is that significant? In most stories, characters experience conflict that challenges them morally.

For example, in the *Star Wars* series, the Force is divided into light and dark sides, making it easy for us to understand the moral progression of its characters. We see Anakin Skywalker kill children at the end of *Revenge of the Sith*, and we understand that this is him falling to the dark side. Conversely, we see Luke Skywalker redeem his father (spoiler alert! Darth Vader) at the end of *Return of the Jedi*. Luke resists the temptation to kill him in cold blood, and thus stays on the path of the light side. As an audience, we can easily see that each character ends up at a point on the moral spectrum different from where they started.

Moral conflict allows an author or director to advance the plot in a way that enchants the audience. If the story started with "And they lived happily ever after," most people wouldn't be interested, would they? Moral conflict forms the basis for almost every story ever told. Without it, there is almost no way to move the plot from one place to another.

Oftentimes this conflict is internal to a character—meaning they undergo some type of moral change that drives the plot forward. This then allows the character to respond to external moral conflict, which forces them to take action based on the lessons they have learned. In other words, they have to save themselves before they can save anyone else.

Tony Stark, who eventually becomes Iron Man (and is the subject of our next chapter), is a good example of this. Tony is rich, confident, flashy, and has a quip for everything. But he's morally conflicted. Tony begins the first *Iron Man* movie as an arrogant and essentially amoral but genius arms dealer. After being captured by terrorists and seeing that his inventions are being used for evil, he undergoes a significant internal moral change that sets him on the path of becoming Iron Man.

Once Tony exorcises his personal demons, he is then free to do all the hero stuff that comes after—save the day, get the girl, and return to his glamorous life. The Tony Stark we see fighting Thanos alone on Titan at the end of *Infinity War* is starkly different from the one we see selling missiles at the start of *Iron Man*. He's undergone significant moral change.

Now, as we mentioned, this kind of dramatic life and moral change doesn't apply to Steve Rogers. There's really not much internal moral conflict to be worried about. His moral compass is consistent, and it points outward, not inward. He's always had himself figured out; it's everyone else he needs to save.

Enlisting in the army wasn't just his duty as an American but a deeply personal moral obligation—he literally couldn't live with himself if he didn't.

In this way, Captain America is about as close as Marvel comes to an "ideal" superhero. The audience is never worried he will make the wrong decision, even when he goes against some of the other heroes as he does in *Civil War*. Instead, we are left to wonder how he will get himself and his friends out of the mess created when he makes the right choice. He's a guy who doesn't cut corners—ever.

Rather than a moral journey, we are instead treated to stories of Cap's dedication, bravery, and commitment to his principles—often in the face of overwhelming odds—and how he selflessly helps his team overcome the bad guys. That's why, when the Avengers can't figure out what to do, they look to Cap to lead them, trusting he will always make the right decision.

After all, they can't look to Tony Stark for consistent leadership. As we'll discuss later, Tony is a visionary, but he often acts emotionally and impulsively. Steve, on the other hand, is timelessly right and true. His heroism is woven into the core of his being, not something that evolved over time. Tony Stark's path to goodness saves him from himself, while Steve Rogers' goodness reflexively saves others because he just *is* good—goodness is his nature. For example, when Tony Stark curses during an intense battle, here's Steve's reflexive response:

STEVE ROGERS: Language!

TONY STARK: Wait a second. No one else is gonna deal with the fact that Cap just said "Language"?

STEVE ROGERS: I know. It just slipped out.

Steve also says things like:

"There are men laying down their lives. I got no right to do any less than them. That's what you don't understand. This isn't about me."

"The price of freedom is high. It always has been. And it's a price I'm willing to pay. And if I'm the only one, then so be it. But I'm willing to bet I'm not."

"For as long as I remember, I just wanted to do what was right."

In this way, Steve Rogers is much more like Jesus than other super-heroes. There's no moral conflict or change in Rogers or Jesus because their natures are good. Jesus is the standard of moral good in the real world, while Captain America is the standard of moral good in the fantasy world of superheroes.

Captain America's moral priorities are so integral to his nature that he's even willing to go against his own country if he thinks it's in the wrong. In *The Winter Soldier*, Cap begins to question the authority he once took for granted. It slowly becomes clear over the course of the movie that Hydra—the organization he fought against during World War II—has infiltrated S.H.I.E.L.D., the organization he now works for. When he is no longer sure he is fighting for the side with the moral high ground—and he can't get his country back onto that high ground—he shifts his allegiance to align with what is right and true. He continues to go down this path in *Civil War*, rebelling against the idea that a governing body should be able to control his ability to do what he thinks is right.

Christians are commanded to do the same. While we are to be good citizens, our first allegiance is to God. So if there is an irreconcilable conflict between our country and God—or even our friends and God—we are to take our cue from the apostles and "obey God rather than human beings" (Acts 5:29).

As admirable as Captain America is, there's still a great moral difference between Captain America and Jesus. Jesus is perfect—completely sinless. While Jesus' human nature grew in knowledge (Luke 2:52), He didn't need to grow out of bad behavior, because His nature was sinless from conception, and He maintained it throughout his life. That sinlessness was a requirement for Jesus to be our Savior. If He had sinned, then the punishment He took on the cross would have been for His own sins, not ours, and His sacrifice wouldn't have helped us.

The sinlessness of Jesus isn't just asserted as a theological fact; it was the consistent testimony of those who knew Him best. Both His enemies and those who followed Him closely for three years claimed they never saw Him sin.[1] (Can you imagine the people who know you best—your close friends or family—claiming you are completely without sin? Everyone who knows us at all knows we are far from perfect.)

We may think we're morally superior to some people we know. Unfortunately, other people are not our standard. When we contrast our behavior to the pure goodness of Christ, we know we fall far short and therefore need a Savior.

He's on a Team and in a Battle (Just Like You Are)

Every legendary team needs a captain who can help focus people with diverse personalities and gifts toward one goal. That's what Steve does as he transforms individuals into a team known as the Avengers. He is the foundation on which the rest of the team is built.

In the sports world, we might call him a "glue guy"—someone who makes the rest of the team better even if he doesn't always stand out individually. No one on the team is worried that he's only there for personal gain. Everyone trusts that Steve will stand firm and do what's right, regardless of the cost and whether or not he gets recognized.

"Captain" isn't just a title for Steve; it's a state of mind. He is *the Captain* of the Avengers. He's the guy everyone relies on to make the right choices at the most dangerous times. In the first *Avengers* movie, we see Iron Man asking Cap to direct the team as the Chitauri invasion begins:

IRON MAN: [*as the fight begins*] Call it, Captain!

CAPTAIN AMERICA: Alright, listen up. Until we can close that portal, our priority is containment. Barton, I want you on that roof, eyes on everything. Call out patterns and strays. Stark, you got the perimeter. Anything gets more than three blocks out, you turn it back or you turn it to ash.

HAWKEYE: [*to Iron Man*] Want to give me a lift?

IRON MAN: Right. Better clench up, Legolas.

[*Iron Man takes Hawkeye up to the roof*]

CAPTAIN AMERICA: Thor, you gotta try and bottleneck that portal. Slow 'em down. You got the lightning. Light them up.

[*Thor swings his hammer and flies off; Captain America turns to Black Widow*]

CAPTAIN AMERICA: You and me, we stay here on the ground, keep the fighting here. And Hulk?

[*the Hulk turns and glares at Cap*]

CAPTAIN AMERICA: Smash!

[*Hulk grins and leaps away*]

This is really the point at which they go from a bunch of individuals to a coherent team capable of defeating an entire alien invasion—and it's in large part because Cap sees how they fit together, despite their differences and personality conflicts. He is able to get them to work as a unit for a cause larger than all of them. This allows the team to go from saving the world in the first *Avengers* movie to saving the entire universe in *Endgame*.

By the time we get to *Endgame*, audiences have been waiting ten years to hear the famous comic book phrase "Avengers, assemble!" (You can watch clips on YouTube of people seeing that iconic moment in theaters. The cheering gets so loud you'd think their team had just won the Super Bowl!) Finally, when all the pieces are on the chessboard—all of the dead Avengers have been resurrected by the Infinity Gauntlet and Thanos has brought his entire army to reclaim it—there's no question about who's going to give the famous order. The man in charge is Captain America.

Compare this team with the one gathered by the ultimate leader: Jesus. When Jesus ascended to heaven, He left his eleven remaining disciples to carry out His mission to the entire world. The Eleven were often dimwitted, scared, and skeptical—some of them even had doubts while Jesus was standing right in front of them (Matthew 28:17). This did not seem like a good plan!

But Jesus knew what He was doing. Each of the apostles He chose had gifts that, together, allowed them to ignite what turned out to be the most successful movement in human history. This movement had no army or navy. Yet, with the Spirit's help, they converted the Roman Empire and much of the world to Christianity through peaceful means, despite severe persecution that took several of their lives.

Today, Christianity lives on through a worldwide body of believers comprising individuals who each have different gifts and abilities. Just as no superhero can do it all, no Christian can do it all. Like the Avengers, we need one another to fight evil and rescue people from death.

But how are we supposed to do that? The apostle Paul says each of us is to be like a fighter training for a fight, like a runner running to win and like a soldier willing to endure suffering to please his commanding officer.[2] He put it most vividly in his letter to the church at Ephesus when he wrote:

> Finally, be strong in the Lord and in his mighty power. Put on the full armor of God, so that you can take your stand against the devil's schemes. For our struggle is not against flesh and blood, but against the rulers, against the authorities, against the powers of this dark world and against the spiritual forces of evil in the heavenly realms. Therefore put on the full armor of God, so that when the day of evil comes, you may be able to stand your ground, and after you have done everything, to stand. Stand firm then, with the belt of truth buckled around your waist, with the breastplate of righteousness in place, and with your feet fitted with the readiness that comes from the gospel of peace. In addition to all this, take up the shield of faith, with which you can extinguish all the flaming arrows of the evil one. Take the helmet of salvation and the sword of the Spirit, which is the word of God.
>
> And pray in the Spirit on all occasions with all kinds of prayers and requests. With this in mind, be alert and always keep on praying for all the Lord's people.
>
> EPHESIANS 6:10-18

Wow! You can almost see Cap suiting up against the forces of evil here (or Tony Stark stepping into his Iron Man armor). The shield imagery here is especially fitting for Cap. In fact, this entire passage fits him to a T.

And it's supposed to fit us to a T as well. Christianity is not just fire insurance. It's not just about avoiding hell and getting into heaven. We shouldn't be lounging around waiting for our bodies to break down so we can be admitted into heaven. We're supposed to be spiritual warriors for Christ, invading enemy territory and rescuing as many as possible by inviting them into God's Kingdom.

This is where the entire superhero storyline is most like our lives today. We are all involved in a cosmic battle in the unseen, spiritual realm for the survival of a Kingdom.[3] We are not fighting against other people ("flesh and blood"), but against the dark forces that tempt us and others to rebellion (incredibly, a rebellion against the very one who loves us enough to die for us).

Our only offensive weapons in this battle are prayer, truth, and the Word of God—"the sword of the Spirit." Those are exactly the weapons Jesus used when He was tempted by Satan. So we need to make them our daily weapons as well.

These are weapons all of us can access. They do not require telepathic powers, superhuman strength, or the ability to fly. Captain America doesn't have many of those powers either. In fact, that's one of the reasons we find ourselves rooting for him so much—he's a lot more like us than most of the other superheroes. His relative weakness makes him relatable to us mere mortals. Since Cap can't just zap his enemies, the outcomes of his confrontations are nearly always in doubt. Sort of like ours. Steve suffers losses all the time, but he always gets back up to fight for what he believes is right.

That "Avengers, assemble!" quote we mentioned above was pretty iconic, but rewind the movie by about three minutes from that spot and you'll see another iconic scene. It shows Captain America getting back to his feet to stand alone against the army of Thanos. It looks like this in the screenplay:

Steve stares at Thanos and his army. And even in the face of such overwhelming odds . . . he gets to his feet.

Thanos stares, almost sad, as Steve tightens the broken shield on his arm . . . AND STARTS WALKING TOWARD HIM.

One man against thousands. All alone.

Jesus wasn't the strongest guy in the room either. When the eternal divine Jesus took on a human nature and came to earth, He gave up His divine privileges.[4] In other words, God in human flesh wasn't even as strong as Superman—He came to earth with His divine hands tied behind His back!

Jesus' strength, like Captain America's, is moral. That's why Jesus and Captain America serve as relatable examples for all people everywhere. After all, who can perform the physical feats of the superheroes? None of us can. But all of us have the ability to carry out God's will with the help of the Spirit. We just have to be willing to use the weapons He's given us.

When we use those weapons, we affect the ultimate battle taking place in the spiritual realm. The outcome is not in doubt—God's Kingdom will triumph, and the gates of hell will not prevail against it. But what is in doubt (not to God but to us) is who will be in His Kingdom.

Will you be there?

You have to make a choice. If you haven't consciously chosen Jesus, you've already made a choice. He said, "Whoever is not with me is against me" (Matthew 12:30).

The good news is that admission to the eternal Kingdom is free. You just have to pledge allegiance to the right side.

He Sacrifices, and Not Just for His Friends

As we've mentioned, Thanos is the evil character behind most of the chaos unleashed in the MCU during the *Infinity Saga*, which encompasses all of the movies from the original *Iron Man* to *Avengers: Endgame*. Thanos believes that the total amount of resources in the universe is finite and that an extreme form of population control—killing half of the life forms in the universe—is necessary in order to make it livable for the rest. Otherwise, overpopulation will slowly destroy life as we know it.

To do this, he plans to unite all six Infinity Stones, which control various aspects of existence. Once he has all of the Infinity Stones, he'll be able to accomplish his goal with a snap of his fingers: half of the life in the universe will be obliterated. All twenty-two movies in the MCU to this point play a part in building up to the storyline in which Thanos attempts to do this in *Infinity War* and *Endgame*.

Standing against him are the Avengers, led in large part by Captain America. Allowing even one innocent person to die goes against everything Cap stands for. He would rather fight to the bitter end than sacrifice the life of one innocent being. We see him do this over and over again with different levels of sacrifice. Let's look at three of them.

The first level of sacrifice is Cap's refusal to take the easy way out to preserve himself. In *Infinity War*, he won't allow Vision (another super-hero) to sacrifice himself in order to destroy the Mind Stone (which is a part of Vision). If Vision were to die, it would be impossible for Thanos to assemble all six Infinity Stones. But Cap won't allow it, despite the likelihood of endangering himself.

Cap says, "We don't trade lives." He does this knowing that if Thanos can obtain the stone, it may cost him his own life as well as the lives of countless others.

It's admirable to protect someone when doing so might hurt you later. But there's a higher level of sacrifice when, in order to protect someone, you face immediate danger.

That's the second level of sacrifice Captain America displays. We see it in *Civil War*, when Cap stands up to Iron Man after Iron Man discovers that Bucky (a.k.a. The Winter Soldier and Cap's best friend growing up) was responsible for murdering Tony's parents. Despite knowing Bucky was brainwashed when he committed the murders, Tony is hell-bent on revenge. But Cap has compassion for his friend. He declares to Bucky, "I'm with you until the end of the line"—a line paying tribute to their friendship during World War II.

STEVE ROGERS: [*about Bucky*] He's my friend.

TONY STARK: So was I. [*beats up Steve some more . . .*] Stay down. Final warning.

[*Steve stands up again . . .*]

STEVE ROGERS: I could do this all day.

Cap continues to protect Bucky by taking the full force of Iron Man's fury.

Jesus does the same thing for us. The Father's perfect justice demands that you be punished for your sin, but Jesus has compassion and agrees to take the fury for you. Jesus will never leave you or forsake you, no matter what you do now or in the future. Like Captain America, Jesus urges you to trust in Him, follow Him, and do good to others, but He's not going to abandon you because of your bad behavior. (In fact, it's precisely because of your bad behavior that you need Him. If any of us were perfect, we wouldn't need a Savior!)

Most of us can at least understand why someone would be willing to sacrifice Himself for those He loves. Michael Monsoor gave us a real-life depiction of this with a story so gripping that no one in Hollywood could have written it better. But what about sacrificing yourself for people you've never met?

That's the third level of sacrifice we see from Captain America. At the end of *The First Avenger*, Cap finds himself in an impossible situation. He's on a plane loaded with nuclear weapons set on auto-pilot for his home city, New York. He must choose either to bail out of the plane, knowing that millions of people will die, or to put the plane into the Arctic Ocean before it explodes. Cap chooses the latter, sacrificing his life and the chance to spend it with the woman he loves (though, by a trick of fate, he only winds up frozen in ice for seventy years).

Would you lay your life down for people you don't even know? Some say that soldiers do that. It's true that people serve in the military to protect their country, but that's usually not why they give their lives on the battlefield. Most Medal of Honor winners who survive their heroism admit they braved death to save their buddies, not to save the faceless millions back home. It's an exceedingly rare person who truly dies for people he doesn't know.

Now, let's take the degree of sacrifice still higher: how many people do you know who would die for their *enemies*? That's the fourth and ultimate level of sacrifice that not even Steve Rogers would make. In fact, no superhero will die to save his enemies. And why would they?

But Jesus does.

All of us have been enemies of God at some point in our lives, yet Jesus laid down His life for us. As a murderous former enemy of Jesus, Paul put it this way: "Very rarely will anyone die for a righteous person, though for a good person someone might possibly dare to die. But God demonstrates his own love for us in this: While we were still sinners, Christ died for us" (Romans 5:7-8).

And the manner in which Jesus sacrificed Himself is beyond any earthly heroism. As the second person of the eternal Trinity, Jesus agreed to sacrifice Himself not in a split second but from eternity. He lived His entire life knowing that unspeakable torture awaited Him—that He would be "oppressed and afflicted" and "led like a lamb to the slaughter" (Isaiah 53:7). (Imagine that as a teenager you knew that in your early thirties you would be brutally tortured and crucified. Think of the agony and stress you would have been under had that been you.)

As much as we should admire real-world heroes like Michael Monsoor or fantasy heroes like Captain America, how much more should we be enamored with a hero who sacrificed Himself to save us—His enemies?

Captain America and You

One part of a story we especially enjoy is the epilogue—the "happily ever after" part. After all the work has been done and all the bad guys have been vanquished, we want to see who ends up marrying whom, whose story is finished, and whose story will continue. The creators of the Marvel Cinematic Universe have done a fine job ending a series as complicated as the *Infinity Saga* on a high note, especially for two of its flagship characters: Iron Man and Captain America.

Those two characters develop in opposite ways. *Endgame* producer Stephen McFeely put it this way:

> We figured out pretty early that . . . Tony and Steve were sort of on crisscrossing arcs. That Tony movie by movie was . . . becoming more selfless. And Steve was becoming a bit more self interested. . . . Tony becomes a complete person when he loses his life and Steve becomes a complete person when he gets one. We drove toward that.[5]

Audiences have seen Captain America (we'll talk about Iron Man in the next chapter) serve others faithfully over the years without hardly a thought for himself. Steve has stood by as others have fallen in love, started families, and led full lives. It seems like all he's done is move from one fight to another, one mission to the next, serving and sacrificing as only he can.

Finally, much like the apostle Paul, Cap knows his mission is over. He's ready to appoint his successor and move to the reward awaiting him.

So after Thanos is defeated in *Endgame* and the universe is restored, Cap is left with a final job—to go back through time and put the Infinity Stones back where they were taken from. He is sent back in time by the Hulk, the Falcon, and Bucky, who all expect him to reappear a few seconds later by using the time machine. When he doesn't, they realize that something is amiss. Bucky is the first to notice an older man sitting on a bench a few yards away. As they approach, they realize it's an older Steve Rogers.

"I put the stones back," Old Man Cap says. "And I thought maybe I should try some of that life Tony was telling me to get."

We're then treated to a clip of Cap dancing with the love of his life, Peggy Carter. He used the time machine to go back in time to get married and grow old with her—living out the life he was meant for but that his life of service wouldn't let him have. Steve returns to his friends only to pass on the mantle of Captain America to his successor—the Falcon—ensuring that his mission will carry on.[6]

This, again, is where the world of superheroes mirrors reality. Christians have a spiritual mission we need to pass on to others. But unlike Captain America, Jesus didn't pass on His mission to one guy. He passed it on to all of us. He gave His disciples the Great Commission to "go and make disciples of all nations, baptizing them in the name of the Father and of the Son and of the Holy Spirit, and teaching them to obey everything I have commanded you" (Matthew 28:19-20).

That command has been passed on and extends to us now. And it's no easy task. The most productive apostle, Paul, experienced resistance worthy of any superhero. He was whipped with thirty-nine lashes five times, beaten with rods three times, shipwrecked three times, pelted with stones and left for dead, and contended with danger daily.

He reveals, "I have been constantly on the move. I have been in danger from rivers, in danger from bandits, in danger from my fellow Jews, in danger from Gentiles; in danger in the city, in danger in the country, in danger at sea; and in danger from false believers. I have labored and toiled and have often gone without sleep; I have known hunger and thirst and have often gone without food; I have been cold and naked" (2 Corinthians 11:26-27). (And we think we're having a tough day when the Wi-Fi is slow or someone unfriends us on social media!)

But that's not the end of it. Paul and Jesus also promise that future followers of Christ will be persecuted as well. Jesus predicts, "If they persecuted me, they will persecute you also" (John 15:20). And Paul writes, "Everyone who wants to live a godly life in Christ Jesus will be persecuted" (2 Timothy 3:12).

That's why Paul, just before he's executed in Rome, warns Timothy, his successor, that the resistance will continue. "People will not put up with sound doctrine. Instead, to suit their own desires, they will gather around them a great number of teachers to say what their itching ears want to hear" (2 Timothy 4:3).

But resistance should not stop soldiers from carrying out their mission. Paul charges Timothy to push back against the resistance in order to save as many as possible: "Keep your head in all situations, endure hardship, do the work of an evangelist, discharge all the duties of your ministry" (2 Timothy 4:5).

Like Captain America, Paul knows that he can now rest and receive his reward: "I have fought the good fight, I have finished the race, I have kept the faith. Now there is in store for me the crown of righteousness, which the Lord, the righteous Judge, will award to me on that day— and not only to me, but also to all who have longed for his appearing" (2 Timothy 4:7-8).

That last part is for you and me. Paul knows you don't earn your way *into* the Kingdom, but you do earn rewards you'll receive once you get there. You earn them right now by "fighting the good fight" with the weapons God has given us: truth, prayer, and the Word of God.

Are you in the good fight? Since Christ hasn't come back yet to usher in eternity, now is not the time to hang it up. God has an *endgame*, and you're in it. God can still use you on his team to affect time and eternity. Are you in?

You're in whether you know it or not. The only question is, whose side are you on?

For Personal Reflection or Family/Small Group Discussion

1. What is the most attractive/unattractive characteristic of Captain America to you? Why?

2. Captain America and Iron Man make each other and their team better. Can you think of someone in your life who makes *you* better? Have you told them?

3. Captain America is other-focused—his moral compass compels him to help others. Who do you know who tends to be other-focused, and what do they do that helps them maintain that focus?

4. Captain America contributes to a team that has members with more gifts and abilities than he has. What gifts and abilities do you have to contribute to the world's most important team—the church?

5. Captain America shows allegiance to the truth over his government. When is it necessary for Christians to disobey their government peacefully?

2

IRON MAN

Apparently, I'm volatile, self-obsessed,
and don't play well with others.

TONY STARK

WHEN LOOKING AT TONY STARK, we think we want the life he has. Who wouldn't want to be as attractive, witty, and wealthy as he is? Tony is undeniably cool and has a wisecrack for every situation. Just look at his lines:

- *Upon first meeting Thor:* "Doth mother know you weareth her drapes?"
- *Responding to Nick Fury's recruitment pitch:* "I told you. I don't want to join your super-secret boy band."
- "Is it better to be feared or respected? I say, is it too much to ask for both?"
- *After regaining consciousness:* "What just happened? Please tell me nobody kissed me."
- *To the young Spider-Man:* "Don't do anything I would do, and definitely don't do anything I wouldn't do. There's a little gray area in there, and that's where you operate."

- *To Pepper*: "Don't say 'wind farm.' I'm already feeling gassy."
- *To his daughter*: "Go to bed, or I'll sell all your toys."

And there are many even better quips we'll get to.

Tony appears to be living life on his own terms, doing what he wants to do, when he wants to do it, and with whom he wants to do it. He's not answering to anyone but himself. In fact, if we were to follow our natural desires, we'd have to admit we are not only more like Tony Stark than Jesus, *we want to be* more like Tony Stark than Jesus!

That's the life we see from the outside. But all is not well with Tony on the inside. He's the smartest guy in the world and one of the richest. But no amount of money, power, or women can give him what he truly seeks. He has everything to live *with* and nothing to live *for*.

In many ways, Tony Stark is much more like us than Steve Rogers is. Steve doesn't require any moral development. Like Jesus, he's a morally sound servant from the beginning—he's always on the right side, and you never have to worry that he'll do the wrong thing.

Tony, on the other hand, has a lot of growing up to do. He starts out a self-absorbed playboy but is transformed from selfish to conflicted to a servant. That's why, as we'll see in this chapter, Tony Stark tells us more about ourselves than about God. His story, in many ways, is really ours.

Many people in America and other developed countries don't suffer from too much pain but too much pleasure. We think more pleasure will bring more contentment, purpose, and happiness, but that's just not the case. We need something else. Tony Stark will help us realize that. As with any good movie character, it all starts with casting.

The Real-Life Tony Stark

The movie transformation of Tony Stark from hedonist to hero is the result not only of good script writing but also of perfect casting. The Marvel Cinematic Universe has picked great stars that make the series so successful: Samuel L. Jackson as Nick Fury, Chris Evans as Captain America, and Chris Pratt as Star-Lord are among the prime examples. But one of them easily looms larger than all the rest, and it was one of the first: Robert Downey Jr. as Tony Stark, a.k.a. Iron Man.

Jon Favreau, who directed the first two *Iron Man* films and plays Tony's lovable security guy known as Happy Hogan, said that his choice of Downey was rejected several times by the producers. "Downey wasn't the most obvious choice," Favreau said, "but he understood what makes the character tick. He found a lot of his own life experience in Tony Stark."

"What life experience?" you ask. Let's put it this way: in the history of Hollywood, few, if any, actors have had as much in common with a character they played than Robert Downey Jr. has had with Tony Stark. To cite just a few similarities:

- Both had famous fathers—Downey's father was an actor, writer, and director. Tony Stark's father was part of the Manhattan Project, helped with the creation of Captain America, and was one of the founding members of S.H.I.E.L.D. (the intelligence agency run by Nick Fury).

- Both rose to fame early on in life—Downey acted in his father's films at an early age, and Stark was a child prodigy, graduating from MIT at age seventeen. He inherited his father's company at the age of twenty-one.

- Both had notable public missteps—Downey was nominated for an Academy Award for his role as Charlie Chaplin in *Chaplin* in 1992, but then spent much of the next decade in and out of legal trouble due to his persistent drug use (which started when his dad gave Jr. marijuana at age six!). He was arrested multiple times, fired from multiple film and television roles, and spent over a year in prison. Stark starts off the first *Iron Man* movie essentially as tabloid fodder, claiming to have slept with numerous women while also drinking and gambling to excess. ("Give me a scotch. I'm starving!") His alcohol use almost sinks him completely in *Iron Man 2*.

- Both recovered to do spectacular things. Sober since 2003, Downey is now the second-highest grossing box-office star of all time (both domestically and internationally). And Tony channeled his failures to create the Iron Man suit and become a servant who saves the world from evil.

Favreau put the parallels this way, "Everybody knew [Robert Downey Jr.] was talented. . . . Certainly by studying the Iron Man role and developing that script, I realized that the character seemed to line up with Robert in all the good and bad ways. And the story of Iron Man was really the story of Robert's career."[1]

Downey was so in touch with the character of Tony Stark that he often improvised his own dialogue, including the iconic "The truth is . . . I am Iron Man" line at the end of the first movie that changed the course of Marvel history (more on that later). The casting of Downey was critical to the success of the entire MCU franchise. As of this writing, there are a total of twenty-three movies in the MCU that have collectively grossed somewhere in the neighborhood of $22.5 billion with roughly fifty hours of total runtime.

But if they hadn't selected Robert Downey Jr. for *Iron Man*, they probably wouldn't have had the kind of success that enabled them to make the movies that followed it. This is another example of the ripple effect we mentioned in the introduction. The selection of Downey created a ripple effect of success that fueled the creation of the rest of the MCU movies. Fortunately, Robert Downey Jr. was there to make a big splash with *Iron Man* and send those good ripples forward for our enjoyment.

The Long Journey from Selfish to Selfless

When Stan Lee, Larry Lieber, Jack Kirby, and Don Heck created the comic *Iron Man* in 1963, they designed Tony Stark to be someone the culture might actually hate—the quintessential capitalist. Stan Lee explains why:

> I think I gave myself a dare. It was the height of the Cold War. The readers, the young readers, if there was one thing they hated, it was war, it was the military. . . . So I got a hero who represented that to the hundredth degree. He was a weapons manufacturer, he was providing weapons for the army, he was rich, he was an industrialist. . . . I thought it would be fun to take the kind of character that nobody would like, none of our readers would like, and shove him down their throats and make them like him. . . . And he became very popular.[2]

In the movies, Tony Stark starts out much the same way—a rich, capitalist playboy so self-absorbed that it's difficult to imagine him actually being a hero. If Tony Stark wrote a book, it would be *Ten Steps to Humility and How I Made It in Seven!*

Tony is told more than once that he only fights for himself. In *The Avengers*, Steve Rogers goes after Tony Stark for his selfishness.

STEVE ROGERS: Big man in a suit of armor. Take that off, what are you?

TONY STARK: A few things actually. Uh, genius, billionaire, playboy, philanthropist.

STEVE ROGERS: I know guys with none of that worth ten of you. I've seen the footage. The only thing you really fight for is yourself. You're not the guy to make the sacrifice play, to lay down on a wire and let the other guy crawl over you.

TONY STARK: I think I would just cut the wire.

STEVE ROGERS: Always a way out. . . . You know, you may not be a threat, but you better stop pretending to be a hero.

Tony actually admits that the "hero gig" doesn't come naturally to him. (But he does have a point: genius, billionaire, playboy, philanthropist!) The Tony Stark of the first movie is just a cool guy in a really impressive suit of armor. He's not a hero—yet. Tony has to mature, and to do that he'll get a big dose of the character-building catalyst known as adversity.

Robert Downey Jr. summed up the arc of the Tony Stark character this way: "For me the end of this run with Marvel is a complete one-eighty. It started off with someone who is absolutely self-centered, has more money than they can ever spend, is spiritually dead, and has no idea that they're about to go through a crucible that is going to put them into a position to be of service to their community."[3]

That one-eighty starts in the first MCU movie, *Iron Man*. That's where we see Tony coming to grips with the fact that his legacy is that of an amoral arms dealer. His company has gone behind his back to sell weapons to terrorists, and his business partner, Obadiah Stane, was the mastermind behind the attack in Afghanistan that nearly killed Tony with his own Stark Industries missile!

A badly wounded and unconscious Tony is saved by Yinsen, a surgeon, who inserts a device into Tony's chest to guard Tony's heart from being pierced by encroaching shrapnel. Without that device guarding Tony's heart, he will die.

While Tony is inventing the first Iron Man suit literally from spare parts, Yinsen attempts to stall their impatient captors in order to buy Tony more time. He takes a fatal bullet doing so. As he lay dying, Yinsen lets Tony know he's ready to go see his family in the afterlife.

"Thank you for saving me," says Tony.

Yinsen whispers back, "Don't waste your life."

That plea assumes that there's an objective purpose to life. But where does objective purpose come from? It can only come from God. Otherwise purpose would just be a subjective matter of opinion among creatures. Without a standard beyond the creation, there would be no way to tell if Tony was really wasting his life.

Purpose is also required to discover if something is good or bad. To see this, think about football for a minute. How do you know that your quarterback throwing a touchdown is better than your quarterback throwing an interception? Because you know the purpose of the game: to score more points than the opposing team! If there were no purpose to the game, no play could be considered good or bad.

Saving lives is just assumed to be a self-evident good purpose in most movies and literature. And for the most part, good and bad *are* self-evident because God has written His law on our hearts. That's why we don't often ask *why* something is good or bad.

But the *why* question is critical because it's a powerful argument for God's existence that is often misunderstood or mischaracterized by atheists. The moral argument for God doesn't claim atheists can't know or do good things. They clearly can. The moral argument for God just shows that there would *be* no objective good to know or do unless God exists.

As with objective purpose, objective good can only exist if God exists. Without God's nature as the fixed standard of good, morality would just be a matter of opinion, and we couldn't justify the truth that love is better than murder. Nor could we justify saying that the Avengers' purpose of saving innocent lives was better than Thanos's plan to kill half of the universe's population.

Yinsen's plea starts Tony on the long journey to becoming a true hero where he eventually sacrifices for others. That transformation takes a lot of time. In fact, across all of the MCU, Robert Downey Jr. playing Tony Stark has almost six full hours of screen time—more than any other actor in a star-studded MCU.

Iron Man ends with perhaps one of the most fitting lines for Tony Stark as a character—one that Downey improvised. He's supposed to get up at a press conference and deny any connection to Iron Man, keeping his anonymity intact *a la* Bruce Wayne or Clark Kent. Instead, he owns it, declaring to the world "I am Iron Man" and basking in the self-serving glory that comes with it.

Notice that for all his bravado and perceived self-sufficiency, it was Tony's own missile that nearly killed him. And Tony wouldn't be alive if it wasn't for Yinsen's skillful surgery—a surgery that literally guards Tony's heart from damage.

We have the same problems. We tend to buy into the same self-sufficiency delusion. And our own immoral actions are often the seeds of our own pain and suffering. That's why the Bible has this stark warning, especially appropriate for Tony Stark and all of us:

Above All Else, Guard Your Heart

Solomon, the wisest man in the Old Testament, pursued everything his heart desired. He tried to get self-sufficiency and happiness by acquiring everything Tony had—wine, wisdom, women, wealth, works of beauty. But they all left him empty and, in some cases, brought tremendous pain and suffering into his life. That's why Solomon implored readers of his proverbs to obey his warning: "Above all else, guard your heart, for everything you do flows from it" (Proverbs 4:23).

Above all else!

By "heart," Solomon doesn't mean the organ in your chest pumping blood but the ruling center of your life. What does it mean to guard your heart? You must guard what you dwell on, guard your emotions, and guard your desires because your heart will determine the direction and outcome of your life.

Your heart can change over time, or it can change in an instant. That's why impulse control and the ability to delay gratification are necessary for any success. If you're not disciplined, you can easily be lured off the right path by the temptations that cross your path each day. You must guard your heart by shunning evil and consciously directing yourself toward good. If you don't, your nature—which is bent toward evil and selfishness—will eventually lead you and others into destruction.

The rich and self-sufficient are most susceptible to letting their heart's guard down. When we're rich, we believe we are secure, and we often foolishly think we have no need for God or the moral guidelines He provides for our protection. If we have money, we tend to think we're bulletproof.

This led Jesus to warn, "It is easier for a camel to go through the eye of a needle than for someone who is rich to enter the kingdom of God" (Matthew 19:24). That's not because money is inherently bad. Money is good. The *love* of money is inherently bad, especially when we prioritize it over God and people. According to Jesus, the poor are blessed because they know they need God.

Life is not about getting the most stuff or experiencing the most pleasure. If it were, Americans would be the happiest people in the world. But we're not. We are among the world leaders in drug use, suicide, and divorce—all indicators of unhappiness.

Despite having all of the stuff he thinks will make him happy, Tony eventually realizes he's unhappy with his life and his life's work. Not only did his own missile nearly kill him, he's not as secure as he thought, and his work is being used for evil. Even still, he doesn't want to relinquish any power or control over his life.

The Power Problem

Tony rockets into *Iron Man 2* wanting things his way and taking all the glory for himself (hardly the attitude of a true hero). That's where he becomes even more the center of national attention than he was previously. The US Senate subpoenas Tony and tries to get him to turn over his Iron Man technology, a request he refuses on national TV.

"I've successfully privatized world peace!" Tony declares to the Senate committee. "My bond is with the people, and I will serve this great nation at the pleasure of myself," he says to TV cameras as he exits the Senate.

"If there's one thing I've proven, it's that you can count on me to pleasure myself!"

Again, these are the words of a playboy, not a self-sacrificing hero. That's one of the reasons the senators are concerned. Tony is only in it for himself. They know that such power in Tony's hands could result in disaster.

Actually, too much power in *anyone's* hands could be a threat to *everyone*, precisely because of our fallen human nature. We tend to be dangerous when there are no checks on our power. Without checks, disaster is just one unilateral decision away. That's why the Feds don't want to allow Tony to have complete power over his suits. He could become a rogue force that would threaten national security and world peace.

Lord Acton, a member of the British Parliament, famously summed up the power problem this way: "Power tends to corrupt, and absolute power corrupts absolutely."

James Madison, the father of the United States Constitution, applied that same truth about our fallen human nature to argue for a government with separated powers. He wrote, "If men were angels, no government would be necessary."

The truth is men are *not* angels, and without proper government, a civilized society would be impossible. We have a fallen nature that originated when Adam and Eve made the choice to disobey God. The rest of the Bible presents God's plan to rescue us from that terrible choice and the trillions of terrible choices we've personally made since then.

Ironically, Tony Stark knows the truth about human nature. In fact, he justifies his arms business by telling a judgmental journalist, "It's an imperfect world, but it's the only one we got. I guarantee you the day weapons are no longer needed to keep the peace, I'll start making bricks and beams for baby hospitals."

Peace in society, and in personal relationships, is hard to maintain because selfishness is easy. Love takes work. Even Paul, the world's greatest Christian apostle, admitted in his letter to the church in Rome that his sinful nature prevented him from doing what's right: "For I know that good itself does not dwell in me, that is, in my sinful nature. For I have the desire to do what is good, but I cannot carry it out. For I do not do the good I want to do, but the evil I do not want to do—this I keep on doing" (Romans 7:18-19).

Robert Downey Jr. believes roughly the same thing about his own human nature. Here's how he describes his reason for getting off drugs and the fact that even though he's sober, his nature is still fallen:

> I had to tell myself that I didn't have to enroll in the same
> program for the next forty years, with the same things dragging
> me down—the resentments, the unadulterated anger, the
> [expletive] rage. I allowed myself to let go of that [expletive],
> and it means that I'm no longer a miserable p——k. That's not
> to say that I'm in the clear yet. I might be shifting out of it,
> but I'm still the same guy.[4]

Our depraved nature can make us slaves to drugs, illicit sex, or any other sin. As Solomon warned, we can become "trapped by evil desires"

(Proverbs 11:6). That's why we must, above all else, guard our hearts, because everything we do flows from the condition of our hearts.

The transformation of our hearts so that we become servants like Christ often takes a lifetime of slow progress to achieve. Theologians call this process sanctification. It wouldn't make for a good movie (or a series of movies) if Tony Stark immediately became a saint. There would be no drama, and it certainly wouldn't seem realistic. Although there are exceptions in real life, sanctification is usually an up-and-down process that takes time and divine help. Guarding your heart, according to Paul, involves the long-term process—"the renewing of your mind" (Romans 12:2)—which in turn changes your desires and behaviors.

As Tony's mind is renewed, he comes to realize that he can't just live for himself. Living for yourself—or "living your truth," as they call it these days—isn't the path to happiness. It may seem right in the beginning, and certainly living for yourself brings some temporary benefits, but it's empty in the end. As counterintuitive as this sounds, you have to deny yourself and "take up [your] cross" as Jesus put it (Luke 9:23). The way to be first is to be last. The way to be exalted is to give up your privileges and serve. Those who truly find themselves put God and others first.

Tony is living for himself at the start of the MCU, but he's dead inside. It's not until the end of *The Avengers* (see below) that Tony finds "the hero gig" to be very fulfilling. That's when he realizes there's more to life than just having a bunch of stuff or doing things that only benefit himself. He needs an identity. He needs a purpose. He needs to serve.

The "hero gig" doesn't come naturally to us either. It's much easier to put ourselves first rather than our friends, neighbors, and—more often than we care to admit—even our closest loved ones. But that's not the path to contentment. We tend to be diverted off that path by three temptations:

Sex, Money, and Power

Our friend J. Warner Wallace of ColdCaseChristianity.com is a homicide detective in southern California who specializes in cold cases. He's been on *Dateline* more than any other detective in the country because he's solved murders that are decades old. Jim says power is only one of the three major temptations we all face.

Whenever he investigates a murder (or any crime), he knows there are only three possible motivations behind the crime. He doesn't have to look into a thousand reasons why a guy was murdered, only three. The guy is dead because the killer was motivated by sex, money, or power—or some combination of the three.

Those are the same three reasons we all decide to sin. Sex, money, and power are good things, but sometimes we take shortcuts to get them. The fact that those are good things is exactly why we will risk losing our families, fortunes, and even our freedom to get them. Rarely does anyone do evil for evil's sake. We do evil to get good things.

This is why John, an eyewitness and follower of Jesus, wrote this warning:

> Do not love the world or anything in the world. If anyone loves
> the world, love for the Father is not in them. For everything
> in the world—the lust of the flesh [sex], the lust of the eyes
> [money], and the pride of life [power]—comes not from the
> Father but from the world. The world and its desires pass away,
> but whoever does the will of God lives forever.
>
> I JOHN 2:15-17

Those of us who think we are immune to temptation are actually the most vulnerable. Solomon, the man who had everything, wrote, "Hell and Destruction are never full; so the eyes of man are never satisfied" (Proverbs 27:20, NKJV). This proverb nails the really illogical aspect of our fallen natures. Even when we have all those good things—a wonderful spouse and plenty of money and power—we are never satisfied. We are somehow still tempted to try to get more. Unchecked, that attitude leads to a place where no one is ever satisfied: hell.

Tony seemingly has it all, but he's still not content. "I build neat stuff, got a great girl, occasionally save the world. So why can't I sleep?"

Because those who put their identity in sex, money, or power (or anything else temporal) will feel despondent when they discover those things don't ultimately satisfy. They may provide temporary pleasure but not lasting happiness. Recognizing there's a big difference between pleasure and happiness is one key to guarding your heart. It will help you avoid trading long-term happiness for short-term pleasure.

Augustine famously observed in his *Confessions* that our hearts are restless until we find our rest in God. Nothing in this world will fill the God-sized hole in our hearts. But we keep trying to find something.

Tony, quoting an anonymous wise man, said that "we create our own demons." He's right. And it can even happen when we love good things more than ultimate things. Sex, money, and power are good things, but they can become demons when we prioritize them over people or God.

That's exactly Tony's problem according to *Iron Man 3* producer and president of Marvel Studios, Kevin Feige. "The love triangle in this movie is really between Tony, Pepper, and the suits," Feige revealed. "Tony, Pepper and his obsession with those suits, and the obsession with technology."[5]

In *Civil War*, Tony admits this conflict caused him and Pepper to break up for a time:

STEVE ROGERS: Is Pepper here? I didn't see her.

TONY STARK: We're kinda . . . Well, not kinda . . .

STEVE ROGERS: Pregnant?

TONY STARK: No. Definitely not. We're taking a break. It's nobody's fault.

STEVE ROGERS: I'm so sorry, Tony. I didn't know.

TONY STARK: A few years ago, I almost lost her, so I trashed all my suits. Then, we had to mop up HYDRA . . . and then Ultron. My fault. And then, and then, and then, I never stopped. Because the truth is, I don't wanna stop. I don't wanna lose her. I thought maybe the Accords could split the difference. In her defense, I'm a handful.

Many of us can relate. How often are we putting our career, money, or technology over the people we say we love? Will our next job, pay raise, or smartphone upgrade really fill the void in our hearts and make us happy?

Robert Downey Jr. personally made the same discovery. After recovering from drug addiction, Downey realized it's foolish to set our hearts and identity on temporal things. He said, "I've had all the stuff before. The big spread and the cars and the dough and all that. It is nice to have. But it's nicer to be free from the attachment to identifying with it."[6]

His character, Tony Stark, eventually realizes that identifying with temporal things isn't enough. You've got to put your identity and hope in something eternal. "No amount of money ever bought a second of time," Tony says. Sex, money, and power are merely pointers to something far greater.

The MCU only makes passing references to God and puts all value in human relationships (like most movies). But there's a great danger when we do that in our personal lives. If you put a person in place of God in your life—if you rely on a person for your identity or to "complete you" and fulfill all your needs—you will crush that person with impossible expectations and wind up bitterly disappointed yourself.

We must put our identity and hope in the One who made us and died for us. Any other identity we take as primary—even identities grounded in good things such as other people—won't last or satisfy. It only makes sense that our ultimate commitment should be to the ultimate One—the Eternal One. We were created to know and enjoy Him forever. Knowing God through Christ is our purpose (John 17:3). He is the one thing we can never lose.

God wants you to know Him because, according to God:

You Are My Greatest Creation

Tony certainly has daddy issues. He's in disbelief when Nick Fury tells him that his dad thought he was the only one who could finish his work.

"[My dad] wasn't my biggest fan," he responds. "He was cold, he was calculating, he never told me he loved me; he never even told me he liked me . . . You're talking about a man whose happiest day of his life was shipping me off to boarding school."

Yet the film of Howard Stark that Nick left behind becomes a turning point in Tony's development. In it, Howard says this about his son: "Tony, you are my greatest creation."

That could be said by every parent, including yours. Human beings have never created anything close to the amazing creature that you are. And of all the thousands of creatures on earth, there are none made in the image of God as we are, which means only humans are God's representatives. No other creatures are tasked to carry out God's will on earth as we are. Nothing could be more affirming to human identity than to have the Creator of all things tell us that we are His creations who can be adopted into His family and then assist Him in building His Kingdom. (A friend of ours has four young daughters. Every night when he puts them to bed, he asks, "Are you a princess?" "Yes!" each replies. "Why?" asks dad. "Because the King of the universe has adopted me into His family!")

Despite the catharsis Tony experiences when he learns his father loved him, there are still some unresolved issues between the two—namely that Tony never got to say goodbye to his father. He even invents a way to recreate memories, B.A.R.F. (Binary Augmented Retro-Framing—gotta love the acronyms Tony invents!) that allows him to relive his final, painful interaction with his dad before his dad's death.

In *Endgame,* Tony is finally able to get some closure by solving time travel (in an evening) and then going back in time to actually interact with his father. In this short interaction, Tony realizes that his father would do anything for him and that his dad regretted his own selfish orientation.

"The greater good has rarely outweighed my own self-interest," Howard laments. Would Tony look back and regret his own legacy?

That question pings on Tony's conscience throughout the MCU (and, as we have seen, presupposes an objective standard of morality and purpose that can only exist if God exists). But the immediate result is that Tony is reborn by the discovery of his late father's affirmation and confidence in him. It propels him on the path to becoming the hero he's meant to be.

For those who have been slowed by a bad relationship with their dad, Tony's daddy issues make him especially relatable. It can be difficult to imagine a loving heavenly Father when you don't have a loving earthly father. Perhaps that's why most of the leading atheists over the past 250 years had either a bad relationship or no relationship at all with their fathers.[7] Perhaps that's also why Jesus warned those who mistreat the young, "It would be better for them to be thrown into the sea with a millstone tied around their neck than to cause one of these little ones to stumble" (Luke 17:2).

Yet once you know and accept the unconditional love of your heavenly Father, there is nothing that can shake you from Him. The apostle Paul, who suffered severe hardship and eventual martyrdom, wrote these words in what may be the climax of the entire Bible: "For I am convinced that neither death nor life, neither angels nor demons, neither the present nor the future, nor any powers, neither height nor depth, nor anything else in all creation, will be able to separate us from the love of God that is in Christ Jesus our Lord" (Romans 8:38-39). Believers in Christ can attack life with confidence knowing that their ultimate destiny is secure.

With the affirmation of his father, Tony is now determined to make his own legacy better than his dad's. That leaves him to answer this question:

Does the Suit Make the Man, or Does the Man Make the Suit?

Tony uses his dad's work to discover a new element that will guard his heart from destruction and enable him eventually to save the world. Yet his dad also says this on the film left behind by Nick Fury: "Everything is achievable through technology: better living, robust health, and for the first time in history, the possibility of world peace."

Ironically, that's exactly what Tony Stark begins to realize is *not* the case, both personally and globally. Personally, he's got all the technology a man could want—much of it he's created himself—but he's still miserable. Globally, technology is exactly what is causing power struggles that may hinder world peace. Technology in the wrong hands can destroy us, which is one reason why the US government in *Iron Man 2* wants to get control of Tony's Iron Man suits.

Science and technology have made us more comfortable and connected, and have helped us live longer. But they can also pose a danger. That's because science and technology are amoral. Science can tell us how to make a bomb, but science can't tell us whether or not we ought to use it. Morality is not something you find in a test tube.

It's the people using science who concern us. They are the ones who infuse science with morality or immorality. Will they use science for good or evil?

We never have to worry about what Jesus will do with His power because He is morally perfect and doesn't have a fallen nature. But the rest of us are bent toward evil. That's why our greatest problems will always be moral rather than technological.

As rocket scientist Werner von Braun put it, "While science seeks control over the forces of nature around us, religion controls the forces of nature within us."

Tony's real struggle is always with himself. Can he tame the forces within him to make good use of the suit? This is most evident in *Iron Man 3*, where he battles post-traumatic stress disorder (PTSD). His struggle revolves around the question of identity: does the man make the suit, or does the suit make the man?

"If you're nothing without this suit, then you shouldn't have it," he tells a young and inexperienced Peter Parker in *Spider-Man: Homecoming*. Parker had gone rogue and wasn't being a team player. The kid thought he was self-made, had all the answers, and could suddenly do it all. He recklessly put lives in danger. So Tony takes away the Spider-Man suit until Parker learns a lesson in humility.

We can have that same problem. Give us a little success and we tend to get cocky. We forget about God and others because we wrongly think we're self-made people. A self-made man makes the mistake of worshiping his creator.

Tony slowly realizes he's not a self-made man (after all, he inherited his wealth!). His personal struggles of doubt, stress, and confusion in *Iron Man 3* lay that bare. After nearly getting killed as his house is destroyed, his suit automatically flies him to Tennessee where he is forced to be still, regroup, and refocus.

In another parallel to Tony Stark in real life, Robert Downey Jr. found that being forced to be still is a gift from God. He wrote this to his sister: "It is my newfound experience that in order to get things done,

I must be still. When that is afforded by an imposed restriction (illness, weather, incarceration, generally being grounded), I now believe it is God's way of giving you some true freedom to 'catch up' on what you need to accomplish . . . inwardly."

We should take Robert's advice. You can't know or grow in God if you're constantly distracted. Without deliberate time for stillness, study, and prayer, we'll never achieve our mission of becoming more like Jesus.

In the end, Tony discovers it's not the suit that makes the man but the man that makes the suit. But how does a flawed man improve enough to make the suit?

Iron Sharpens Iron

Iron Man gets better not just by battling his enemies but also his friends. Take his conflicts with Steve Rogers for example. Tony and Steve are two strong-headed men with very different philosophies on life.

Early in their relationship, Steve thinks that Tony is nothing without his armor and only fights for personal gain. He believes Tony's motives aren't always pure and that eventually he won't be able to invent his way out of a problem.

Not to be outdone, Tony quickly points out that everything that makes Steve special "came out of a bottle." Tony thinks Steve is a rigid boy scout who can't think for himself.

It turns out both men are right about the other and ultimately help each other become better. Tony helps Steve see he needs to slow down a little and enjoy relationships in life, and Steve's criticisms propel Tony toward selflessness.

The same is true in our own lives. If you never had an obstacle—if everything went your way every time—you wouldn't grow but would become the equivalent of a self-centered, spoiled celebrity. Without challenges from friends and foes alike, we might not experience the friction that forges improvement. "As iron sharpens iron, so one person sharpens another," wrote Solomon (Proverbs 27:17).

We see this sharpening process throughout the MCU. Tony mostly fights for himself in the first two *Iron Man* movies. But in *The Avengers*, Tony gives us a glimpse of his progression when he flies a nuclear missile meant for New York City into a wormhole to destroy the invading alien Chitauri army, not knowing whether or not the effort will kill him.

While the good guys win this battle, it sets up an inevitable showdown with ultimate evil—our first sighting of Thanos happens during a post-credits scene. Despite the victory against the mischievous Loki and the Chitauri, we're not done yet.

After the near miss with the invading Chitauri, Tony believes the world needs a better defense system: Ultron. He attempts to combine his artificial intelligence, JARVIS, with the artificial intelligence inside Loki's scepter to create a new program that will be in charge of Tony's global defense initiative. He does this unilaterally with little input or support from the other Avengers, other than Bruce Banner.

He fails spectacularly. The AI Ultron goes rogue and takes his mission of world peace so seriously that it intends to kill all of mankind in order to accomplish it.

Before the Avengers can stop him, Ultron manages to destroy almost the entire country of Sokovia. The Avengers eventually triumph, but Tony has a crisis of conscience that leads into the next film. In his attempt to shield the world from harm, his ego was almost the source of the world's destruction.

Fortunately, Tony grows through this mistake. He becomes humbler and more open to the input of others. In fact, Tony is now so open to input that he agrees to put checks on his ego and reverses his previous stance: he will now turn over parts of his technology and subject the Avengers to government control. Ironically, Steve, normally the poster boy for trusting the government, begins to distrust such external control, which results in the aptly named next movie in the series, *Civil War*.

Despite the internal conflict between the Avengers in *Civil War*, we see that Tony continues to grow as a leader by becoming a mentor to Peter Parker. Tony sees Peter as a son. There's a lot of himself in Peter—the talent, the intellect, and the willingness to be a hero. Peter just needs someone to mentor him. Tony knows it's necessary for him to take on the mentoring task, just like Christians are to mentor or disciple new believers.

Notice that Tony doesn't say, "Peter, now that you believe you're a superhero, my work here is done." Sadly, that's what many Christians do. They get someone to repent and believe in Jesus, but they don't disciple that person. They don't do anything to support or guide that person as he or she ventures out into real life as an ambassador for Christ.

Tony realizes he must teach Peter skills, character, and wisdom to mold him into a true superhero. As we saw above with Tony taking away Peter's suit for a brief time, accountability is a big part of that process. Christians must do the same by helping people transform into the image of Christ for their good and the good of the Kingdom. Any movement, if it is going to survive and thrive, can't just make converts; it must make disciples.

Meanwhile, the friction between Tony and Steve grows to the point that they come to blows and nearly kill each other in Siberia. But they know they need each other:

STEVE ROGERS: If I see a situation pointed south . . . I can't ignore it. Sometimes I wish I could.

TONY STARK: No, you don't.

STEVE ROGERS: No, I don't. Sometimes . . .

TONY STARK: Sometimes I wanna punch you in your perfect teeth. But I don't wanna see you gone. We need you, Cap.

That friction will cost them in *Avengers: Infinity War* when a divided Steve and Tony lead separate teams and are defeated by Thanos. The disunity even results in Avenger deaths, including that of Spider-Man.

The lack of unity around shared principles weakens any team, and the Avengers will have to unify to have a chance in the rematch with Thanos. Not only that, but every individual on the team must be at their absolute best to win. Will Tony be at his best?

As Steve feared, eventually there will be a problem that Tony can't outsmart. Thanos appears to be that problem. Fortunately, by this point, Tony has been sharpened enough to realize what's going to be required of him. He doesn't want to die, but he might have to in order to save others.

And there's a new complication. Tony is now married to Pepper, and they have a daughter together. So when he's given the opportunity in *Endgame* to go back in time to try again, we're left to wonder if he wants to risk his life or mess with time in such a way that it could affect their existence. As Tony points out, "Sometimes when you mess with time, it messes back."

Yet Pepper knows that Tony has been transformed through his intense struggles. Iron has sharpened Iron Man, and Tony won't be able to rest until he's tried to make everything right.

"I lost the kid [Peter Parker]," Tony tells Steve. He has to try to get him back. To do that, he'll have to go back in time and get the Infinity Stones.

Tony is now ready to use his technology not for his own personal benefit but to save the world. Meanwhile, Thanos and his allies—the equivalent of Satan and his demons—reach the climactic battle, intent on using technology for evil.

Endgame

When we arrive at the final battle in *Endgame*, we see the fully sanctified version of Tony Stark. The self-absorbed billionaire we first met is gone.

Standing before us is a man who wants desperately to protect his family and is willing to risk all so that others may live. Over several movies, he's been transformed into a hero who won't sit on the sidelines, even if it means sacrificing his life.

However, it doesn't look like Tony or any of the Avengers will have the opportunity to sacrifice in order to prevail. In the final battle, Thanos swats the Avengers away like flies. All hope appears to be lost when Thanos recovers the Gauntlet with all of the Infinity Stones, giving him nearly unlimited power to destroy the Avengers. Except this time, Thanos isn't content with killing half the life in the universe. He intends to start over.

"I will shred this universe down to its last atom and then, with the stones you've collected for me, create a new one," he declares. Thanos merely needs to snap his fingers to make his victory complete.

Prompted by Dr. Strange that this is the one chance in fourteen million that the Avengers might win, Tony lunges and grabs Thanos's hand. Thanos tosses him away and repeats the line he used earlier in the movie, "I am . . . inevitable." He snaps his fingers. Only then does he realize that the stones are no longer on his gauntlet. Tony, having designed the gauntlet Thanos is wearing, just used his nanotechnology to transfer the stones to his own suit.

Having all six Infinity Stones on his own gauntlet, Tony chooses to respond with the now-famous line that ended the first Iron Man movie, "And I . . . am Iron Man." With that, he snaps his fingers, and Thanos and his army turn into ash.

The Avengers win, and the kid is back. But Tony has less than a minute to live. Fading away, he can't speak. Peter Parker puts his hand behind Tony's head, "We won, Mr. Stark." But he then crumbles in tears when Tony can't respond. "I'm sorry, Tony."

Pepper nudges him aside. She puts her hand over Tony's illuminated heart, looks into his eyes, and whispers, "We're going to be okay. You can rest now."

Tony's light goes out.

He's gone.

The most charismatic and beloved superhero in the entire MCU is dead.

He just did something Steve said he would never do: he jumped on a grenade to save others.

Jesus made a similar decision. While He didn't have to undergo moral growth like Tony, Jesus saw that sacrifice is necessary to save the world. Tony carried the weight of the world on his shoulders, and Jesus carried the weight of our sins on His. Tony voluntarily gave his life to defeat Thanos—the physical embodiment of death—and Jesus voluntarily gave His life to defeat Satan and death itself.

Who Is Iron Man?

Tony ends *Iron Man 3* with this monologue: "If I were to wrap this up tight with a bow or whatever, I guess I'd say my armor, it was never a distraction or a hobby, it was a cocoon. And now, I'm a changed man. You can take away my house, all my tricks and toys. One thing you can't take away . . . I am Iron Man."

Tony found his identity. Iron Man isn't a suit of armor; it's the change Tony made in going from selfish to selfless. Similarly, *Christian* isn't just a label. It's someone who is being changed into the character of Christ.

The word *Christian* only appears three times in the New Testament. Meanwhile, the word *disciple* appears nearly *three hundred* times. Yes, we are saved by faith alone. Our identity is not achieved; it is *received* as a gift and can never be taken away. But while we are saved by faith alone, our faith is not alone. After we accept God's grace, we are sanctified by His Word (John 17:17) and prepared by God to do good works—works of service and sacrifice to build God's Kingdom rather than our own (Ephesians 2:8-10).

The *Endgame* Tony Stark is a fantasy version of what you are intended to be. If you are a Christian, you are . . . Iron Man.

For Personal Reflection or Family/Small Group Discussion

1. What is the most attractive/unattractive characteristic of Tony Stark to you? Why?

2. Tony Stark is a lot more like most of us than Steve Rogers is. Tony is much more susceptible to the temptations of sex, money, and power than Steve. How are you most like the early Tony Stark?

3. Tony allows failure and suffering to transform him from a selfish playboy into someone who sacrifices himself for others. What failures and suffering have you had to overcome, and how have they transformed you?

4. How do you "guard your heart" (Proverbs 4:23) to ensure that you don't make emotional decisions that will sabotage your future?

5. Tony really struggles with identity. Is he defined by his occupation (being Iron Man) or something else? Who or what defines you? What is the only stable and eternal identity?

3

HARRY POTTER

The last enemy that shall be destroyed is death

INSCRIPTION ON THE HEADSTONE OF
LILY AND JAMES POTTER'S GRAVE

*But Christ has indeed been raised from the dead, the firstfruits of those who have
fallen asleep. For since death came through a man, the resurrection of the dead
comes also through a man. . . . The last enemy to be destroyed is death.*

I CORINTHIANS 15:20-21, 26

ARGUABLY, there has not been a single fictional character in popular
modern literature and film that has had more in common with the life,
death, and resurrection of Jesus Christ than Harry Potter.

What? The story in a series of books that some Christians boycotted?

Yes. Harry's story mirrors the life, death, and resurrection of Jesus
even more than Gandalf from *The Lord of the Rings* or Aslan from *The
Chronicles of Narnia*. Harry Potter is the "savior" of J. K. Rowling's
Wizarding World. And he emulates many of the same character traits
that Jesus possesses, just not to the same level of perfection.

"There is a lot of Christian imagery in the books. That's undeniable,"
admitted Ms. Rowling. "But I never wanted to talk too openly about
it because I thought it might show people who just wanted the story
where we were going."[1]

In fact, according to Rowling, the entire Harry Potter series is summed
up by two Bible verses found on tombstones in the story: "The last enemy

that shall be destroyed is death" (1 Corinthians 15:26, KJV), and "Where your treasure is, there will your heart be also" (Matthew 6:21, KJV).

"They're very British books, so on a very practical note Harry was going to find biblical quotations on tombstones," Rowling explained. "I think those two particular quotations [Harry] finds on the tombstones at Godric's Hollow, they sum up—they almost epitomize the whole series."[2]

The quote from 1 Corinthians is engraved into the tombstone of Harry's parents, and Matthew's quotation of Jesus is on that of Albus Dumbledore's relatives. We'll see why they epitomize the series as we go.

To some Christians, there is something uncomfortable in comparing a Hollywood hero to Christ, especially those involved in unbiblical behavior like Harry Potter. But to a certain extent, that's true of other Hollywood heroes. Harry is a wizard, but so is Gandalf. Tony Stark is a playboy. Batman is a vigilante. Luke Skywalker levitates spaceships. And every villain in these stories is, by definition, engaged in some kind of unbiblical behavior. In fact, that's the nature of all stories that deal with evil (including those in the Bible). Since Hollywood heroes have almost universal appeal, particularly to young people, we might want to overcome any discomfort to show them how the characters and stories they love point to Jesus.[3]

To be clear, we are absolutely not saying that Jesus and Harry are the same—only that Harry has more in common with Jesus than do most other characters in film. This chapter will highlight four of those commonalities:

- Prophecy
- Morality
- Death
- Resurrection

This isn't an exhaustive list. Since Harry Potter is the subject of seven books (totaling over a million words) and eight movies (running an aggregate of nearly twenty hours), you'll understand we have to leave a lot out. But this list covers the most important themes.

The first theme begins before the beginning. The stories of Jesus and Harry start with prophecies made before they were born.

Prophecy: What Harry and Jesus Have in Common

In the opening scene of *Harry Potter and the Sorcerer's Stone*, Albus Dumbledore, a man we later find out is the headmaster of the magical school called Hogwarts, appears on a dark street with a device that can cause all the lights on the block to go out. He crosses a tabby cat that suddenly transforms into a witch called Professor Minerva McGonagall.

As the two walk on, a huge bearded man descends out of the sky on a motorcycle; he is carrying an infant. The man is a half-giant named Hagrid. He has just carried Harry away from the treachery of the evil Lord Voldemort, the most powerful dark wizard of all time. Harry's parents were killed by Voldemort, but Harry, despite being an infant, survived and somehow injured or maybe even killed Voldemort.

Dumbledore makes arrangements with Harry's aunt and uncle to care for Harry, and they are clearly unhappy with the situation. We are also left with the distinct impression that Dumbledore is leaving Harry with his non-magical aunt and uncle for reasons other than their being his next of kin. While this encounter is not fully spelled out in the movie, the book gives us this exchange between McGonagall and Dumbledore:

> "That's not all. They're saying he [Voldemort] tried to kill
> the Potters' son, Harry. But—he couldn't. He couldn't kill
> that little boy. No one knows why, or how, but they're saying
> that when he couldn't kill Harry Potter, Voldemort's power
> somehow broke—and that's why he's gone."
> Dumbledore nodded glumly.

"It's—it's true?" faltered Professor McGonagall. "After all he's done . . . all the people he's killed . . . he couldn't kill a little boy? It's just astounding . . . of all the things to stop him . . . but how in the name of heaven did Harry survive?"

"We can only guess," said Dumbledore. "We may never know."

We find out later that Dumbledore has more insight into why Harry survived than he reveals. Placing the baby with his aunt and uncle was part of Dumbledore's plan. It would magically protect Harry until he was old enough to fulfill his messianic role that was foretold before he was born. The audience is not privy to this revelation until the fifth book/movie, *Harry Potter and the Order of the Phoenix*. Much of the plot surrounding Harry's life is dedicated to reaching the climax, the moment when Harry learns the truth that Dumbledore has known from the beginning: Harry—and Harry alone—has the power to save the world from the evil Lord Voldemort.

The prophecy identifying the Savior who will defeat Voldemort is told by seer and Hogwarts professor Sybill Trelawney. She declares:

The one with the power to vanquish the Dark Lord
approaches. . . . Born to those who have thrice defied him,
born as the seventh month dies. . . . And the Dark Lord will
mark him as his equal, but he will have power the Dark Lord
knows not. . . . **And either must die at the hand of the other
for neither can live while the other survives.** . . . The one
with the power to vanquish the Dark Lord will be born as the
seventh month dies. . . .

This prophecy applies to Harry, who was born at the end of July (on J. K. Rowling's birthday) and whose parents defied Voldemort three times. Voldemort hears the first part of this prophecy at the height of his power and attempts to murder Harry shortly after his birth. He kills both of Harry's parents, but the curse meant to kill Harry rebounds on Voldemort and nearly kills him instead. This leaves Harry with the curious lightning-shaped scar marking him as Voldemort's equal and making him famous. Harry is clearly a messianic figure. His purpose is to defeat Voldemort, who is the embodiment of evil, death, and destruction.

Just as Voldemort hears about the prophecy of Harry, King Herod hears about the prophecy of Jesus. Like Voldemort, Herod seeks to nip his problem in the bud by attempting to kill his newborn rival. He does so by ordering all the boys in Bethlehem age two and younger be put to death (Matthew 2:16). But like Harry, Jesus survives the attack by being carried out of the area. While Harry is carried to Little Whinging (near London) by Hagrid, Jesus is carried to Egypt by his parents.

Jesus begins his ministry as an adult being baptized by His cousin, John the Baptist, who recognizes that Jesus is "the Lamb of God, who takes away the sin of the world!" (John 1:29). Harry also has a forerunner—someone who recognizes that Harry is the savior.

"Dumbledore is John the Baptist to Harry's Christ," J. K. Rowling revealed in an interview. Dumbledore recognizes that Harry is the one. This becomes explicit in *Harry Potter and the Half-Blood Prince*, where Dumbledore says to Harry, "Your blood is worth more than mine."

In the Bible, the prophecies of a coming Savior in the Old Testament are more numerous and specific than those in the Harry Potter story. God predicted that this Redeemer would be born from the seed of a woman (Genesis 3:15)—from the tribe of Judah (Genesis 49:10), and from the line of David (Jeremiah 23:5). Although a man, this Redeemer would also be God (Isaiah 9:6). He would be born in the city of Bethlehem (Micah 5:2) and would physically visit the temple in Jerusalem (Malachi 3:1). Seven hundred years in advance, the prophet Isaiah gave a detailed description of what this Suffering Servant would endure to take our sins upon Himself (Isaiah 52:13–53:12). After He suffered, He would rise from the dead (Isaiah 53:10). And all of this would take place 483 years after the decree to restore and rebuild Jerusalem (Daniel 9:25), which works out to AD 33.[4]

Putting all these prophetic pieces together makes it hard to deny the divine inspiration of the Old Testament. The Messiah is supernaturally predicted hundreds of years before His arrival by different authors who lived at different times. And only Jesus of Nazareth fulfills all of the predictions.

The predictions about the missions of Harry and Jesus are also essentially the same: salvation. And not just salvation for their own people—wizards and Jews respectively—but for everyone. In Harry's story, salvation would come from defeating Voldemort, which would achieve world peace. This is true for both wizards and muggles (non-magical or "normal" people), as both are affected by Voldemort's evil ways.

The same is true of Jesus. His purpose for coming into the world is to bring salvation, not just for the Jews but for the Gentiles as well (Luke 2:32; Galatians 3:28). This salvation will ultimately result in world peace in the form of a new heaven and earth (Revelation 21). Until that time, those who die in Christ will be absent from the body but present with the Lord (2 Corinthians 5:8).

Achieving salvation in their respective worlds will require both Jesus and Harry to behave morally. That's the next parallel we'll investigate.

The Mirror That Reflects Morality

J. K. Rowling doesn't personally believe in the magic depicted in her story. It's just that in her fantasy Harry Potter world, magic provides powerless children with power they have nowhere else. Magic lifts the imagination, but magic isn't the center of the story—human nature is.

"Harry enters this [magical] world, and he thinks it will be an escape, but it's not," Rowling says. "Human nature is human nature, whether or not you can use a wand."[5]

Her point is that the characters have to grow personally in order to achieve their mission of overcoming evil. "That was an emotional journey that had very little to do with magic," she claims.[6]

In this sense, the fantasy world of magic just provides the weapons by which the characters battle evil, one another, and their fallen nature. What has made the story compelling for millions is not so much hocus pocus curses (there are literally hundreds of *unsuccessful* books and films containing fantasy magic) but the fact that Rowling creates compelling characters who must battle their own fears, faults, and inadequacies to overcome evil with good.

In other words, Rowling's story is really a tale about developing the moral fiber necessary to defeat evil. Thus, the moral development of Harry Potter is central to the series.

One of our earliest introductions to Harry's moral development involves the Mirror of Erised in *Harry Potter and the Sorcerer's Stone*. "Erised" is the word *desire* spelled backward. This gives it a clever symbolism not only because of what it is used for but also because it is a mirror.

The same is true for the text that is inscribed around the mirror. This is nearly impossible to see in the movie, but the book spells it out: "*Erised stra ehru oyt ube cafru oyt on wohsi*." Read backward and with the proper spacing, it says "I show not your face but your heart's desire."

Before proceeding with the mirror, we need to know what the Sorcerer's Stone is (it's called the "Philosopher's Stone" in the original UK version). In Harry's world, it is a single red stone created by a sorcerer. Its two most important attributes are that it can be used to transform any metal into pure gold and that it can be used to create an Elixir of Life, which allows whoever drinks it periodically to live forever. The creator and owner of the stone, Nicholas Flamel, has been alive for over six hundred years. Naturally, most of the conflict in the book centers on getting control of the stone. Harry's ability to protect the stone revolves around the lesson he learns from the mirror.

How does he discover this mirror? Students at Hogwarts School of Witchcraft and Wizardry, like those at most boarding schools, spend time with family and loved ones over the Christmas holiday. Since Harry's parents are dead and he has a less-than-loving place to go home to, he remains behind at the cavernous school along with a few other students. Among Harry's gifts that year is an invisibility cloak along with an anonymous note explaining the gift, "Your father left this in my possession before he died. Use it well." As you can no doubt imagine, eleven-year-old Harry enjoys roaming the school wearing this invisibility cloak so he can venture undetected into the places no students are supposed to go.

In his secret explorations, he uncovers a mirror that reflects back his parents in the mirror alongside him—something that as an orphan he has never experienced. Overjoyed and with great excitement, he invites his best friend, Ron Weasley (also left behind this holiday), to join him the next night.

Harry sees his parents again, but when Ron looks into the mirror, he sees himself as an older, much more popular version of himself. Confused, the two realize that the mirror causes them to see different things, but they don't get much further than that. Ron isn't too keen on going back, but Harry, drawn by the parents he has never met, keeps returning to the mirror.

On the third night, Harry is confronted by Professor Dumbledore. Rather than reprimanding Harry for roaming the corridors during the night, Dumbledore instead tells him more about the mirror:

> "Can you think what the Mirror of Erised shows us all?" Harry shook his head.
>
> "Let me explain. The happiest man on earth would be able to use the Mirror of Erised like a normal mirror, that is, he would look into it and see himself exactly as he is. Does that help?"
>
> Harry thought. Then he said slowly, "It shows us what we want . . . whatever we want. . . ."

"Yes and no," said Dumbledore quietly.

"It shows us nothing more or less than the deepest, most desperate desire of our hearts. You, who have never known your family, see them standing around you. Ronald Weasley, who has always been overshadowed by his brothers, sees himself standing alone, the best of all of them. However, this mirror will give us neither knowledge or truth. Men have wasted away before it, entranced by what they have seen, or been driven mad, not knowing if what it shows is real or even possible.

"The Mirror will be moved to a new home tomorrow, Harry, and I ask you not to go looking for it again. If you ever do run across it, you will now be prepared. It does not do to dwell on dreams and forget to live, remember that. Now, why don't you put that admirable cloak back on and get off to bed."[7]

This reveals something important about Harry's character. While Ron sees his desire in the mirror (his own fame), Harry sees his family. Rather than desiring what motivates most people—sex, money, and power (fame)—Harry simply craves the family that was taken from him.

Near the end of *Sorcerer's Stone*, Harry again encounters the mirror. Knowing that someone is about to attempt to steal the stone (they suspect Snape), Harry, Ron, and their friend Hermione Granger sneak their way through the protective enchantments guarding the stone (including Fluffy, the monster dog!). After passing all but the last enchantment, Harry finds that Lord Voldemort has returned, albeit as a shadow of his former self. Not having a body of his own, he is forced to share one with his servant.

Surprisingly, the servant is not Professor Snape, as they had suspected, but rather Professor Quirrell, who also happens to be Harry's Defense Against the Dark Arts teacher. It's more than a little ironic that the same teacher charged with protecting Harry from the dark arts also happens to have Lord Voldemort literally growing out of the back of his head, hidden underneath a turban. Does this remind you of a similar incident in Jesus' inner circle? Judas was supposed to protect Jesus and the disciples from money trouble. Instead, Satan *entered* Judas to betray Jesus (Luke 22:3; John 13:27).

Having managed to get past the rest of Dumbledore's protective enchantments, Quirrell stands in front of his last challenge, the Mirror of Erised. The stone will be his if he can get past the mirror.

Just then, Harry enters.

Harry knows exactly what the mirror is, but Professor Quirrell does not.

"I see the Stone . . . I'm presenting it to my master . . . but where is it?" Confused, he consults Voldemort, who tells him to put Harry in front of the mirror, suspecting that Harry is the key to unlocking the puzzle.

Professor Dumbledore, unbeknownst to any of them, had hidden the stone inside the mirror in such a way that only one who had a truly selfless reason for wanting to find the stone could get it. Harry, of course, fits this description. He's not likely to succumb to the temptations of sex, money, or power and misuse the stone. He would just keep it safe.

Once in front of the mirror, Harry is surprised to feel the stone drop into his pocket.

At this point, Voldemort confronts Harry for the first time since his defeat when Harry was a baby. But Voldemort remains unable to touch Harry and is forced to flee. This is due to a powerful magical enchantment created when Harry's mother died to save him:

HARRY: But why couldn't Quirrell touch me?

DUMBLEDORE: Your mother died to save you. If there is one
    thing Voldemort cannot understand, it is love. He didn't
    realize that love, as powerful as your mother's for you,
    leaves its own mark. Not a scar, no visible sign . . . to have

been loved so deeply, even though the person who loved us is gone, will give us some protection forever. It is in your very skin. Quirrell, full of hatred, greed, and ambition, sharing his soul with Voldemort, could not touch you for this reason. It was agony to touch a person marked by something so good.

Sacrificing yourself to save someone else is the highest form of love as Jesus Himself said and then demonstrated when He agreed to go to the cross (John 15:13). Harry's mother sacrificed herself to save Harry, and Christ sacrificed Himself to save us.

While we have all sorts of problems in this fallen world (as the Scriptures promise), the sacrifice of Jesus guarantees that our eternal future is secure. The apostle Paul couldn't be more emphatic about the security that God's love provides us when he declares that nothing "will be able to separate us from the love of God that is in Christ Jesus our Lord" (Romans 8:39).

When life gets difficult, that truth is easy to forget. That's one reason Christians need to keep meeting together—to remind, to encourage, and to strengthen one another with the help of the Holy Spirit.

As we mentioned above, there is a similar kind of strengthening in the fantasy world of Harry Potter. It is one of Dumbledore's primary reasons for making Harry visit his aunt and uncle every summer. By allowing Harry into their home even grudgingly, his aunt and uncle extend the enchantment created by Harry's mother's sacrifice, which protects him from Voldemort while in a home inhabited by his family members.

This strengthening cements moral traits about Harry that we see over and over again. While never portrayed as morally perfect, Harry is consistently described as having a pure heart and the moral fiber to resist temptation. Rather than *perfect*, he's better described with a word often used in Scripture of characters such as Noah, Abraham, and Job:

righteous. It is Harry's righteousness more than his magical prowess that allows him to eventually overcome the ultimate evil in Lord Voldemort.

Jesus, of course, lived a morally perfect life, which was prophesied seven hundred years in advance by Isaiah: "He was assigned a grave with the wicked, and with the rich in his death, though he had done no violence, nor was any deceit in his mouth" (Isaiah 53:9). Christ's perfection in life forms the foundation for our salvation.

Harry can provide salvation in his world because he has the only kind of character the mirror will accept—the ability to resist using his power, or that of the mirror, for personal gain. This moral strength is evident in Harry throughout the entire series. As Dumbledore put it, "It is our choices, Harry, that show what we truly are, far more than our abilities."

Despite having incredible magical powers, Harry doesn't really use them for personal gain. He has a heart to help others rather than himself.

This same moral trait is often overlooked in Jesus and the apostles. Notice they never even try to use their divine power for personal gain. Miracles were always used to promote God's Kingdom, not their own.

This is quite astonishing when you think about it. If you had the power to perform miracles, wouldn't you at least try to use it to enrich yourself and advance your personal agenda? *I need a new house, a new car, and an expensive vacation. Then I'll get back to you, Lord.* You've got to have strong moral fiber to resist that temptation!

Sadly, many so-called Christian teachers today erroneously teach that God's power is in your hands to enrich or benefit yourself. They distort the teachings of Jesus and His apostles not to benefit others but themselves. If today's false teachers could stand in front of the Mirror of Erised, their ungodly character would be exposed. Their "name it and claim it" prosperity teachings were never taught or intended by Jesus or any of the apostles through whom God performed miracles. We're not here to build our kingdoms but His Kingdom.

The truth is that difficulty and persecution are promised to followers of Jesus. And unless Jesus comes back during our lifetime, we will all experience physical death.

Death is something we can't fix ourselves. Only Jesus can. Ironically, His death is actually the key to securing life for us. It turns out that the death of Harry Potter has a similar effect on the people in his world.

Death: Christ the Sacrificial Lamb versus Harry the Pig for Slaughter

The same prophecy about Harry's birth foretells the ending of the series as well: eventually either Harry or Voldemort will kill the other. The plot twist, of course, is how it happens. Harry learns that, paradoxically, he must let himself die in order for Voldemort to be defeated.

Harry discovers this through the memory of his former Potions teacher and nemesis, Severus Snape. For most of the series, Harry believes Snape to be a double agent—someone who claims to be on his side but who is secretly spying for Lord Voldemort. This seems to be confirmed at the end of the sixth book, *Harry Potter and the Half-Blood Prince*, when Snape kills Professor Dumbledore on Lord Voldemort's orders.

Lord Voldemort later kills Snape because he thinks that by killing Snape he can master the Elder Wand—a wand so powerful that its user cannot be beaten in magical combat. Unknown to Voldemort, Harry witnesses Snape's murder. With Snape's dying breath, he gives Harry a memory. Confused about why his longtime foe would do such a thing, Harry heads to the headmaster's office, where he is able to study the memories with a magical instrument called a Pensieve.

As Harry experiences Snape's memories, he learns a few vital pieces of information. The first is probably the biggest plot twist of the series: Snape was actually one of the good guys! He was a double agent, but for Harry's side. Snape's memory shows that he was in love with Harry's mother, and once she became a target of Voldemort as a result of the prophecy about Harry, Snape turned into Professor Dumbledore's most trusted spy.

Snape also reveals that Dumbledore was slowly dying and knew his death was imminent. It was Dumbledore's wish that Snape, rather than one of Voldemort's other followers, kill him. This would help prove Snape's loyalty to Voldemort and prevent Draco Malfoy (Harry's rival at Hogwarts) from being forced to do it against his will.

Finally, Harry learns he must die if Voldemort is to be defeated and that Voldemort must be the one who kills him. And, shockingly, this had been Dumbledore's plan all along!

The explanation behind this twist is complicated. In his quest for eternal life, Voldemort split his soul into vessels called Horcruxes, magical devices that would shelter pieces of his soul, which would prevent him from dying even if his physical body were to be destroyed. A Horcrux could be created only while killing someone else, since the magic required to do it was dark and powerful.

As he continued to kill people during his rise to power, Voldemort split his soul seven times, and the Horcruxes were hidden away for safekeeping. This is how Voldemort survived when he attempted to kill Harry the first time.

This much was known to Harry, who spends most of *The Half-Blood Prince* and *The Deathly Hallows* searching for Voldemort's Horcruxes. But Dumbledore reveals to Snape his theory that the curse that was meant to kill Harry as an infant had an unintended consequence. After Voldemort's own curse rebounded on him, part of his soul latched onto the infant Harry, creating a final Horcrux. This explains Harry's unusual connection to Voldemort, such as his ability to talk to snakes the way Voldemort can and the occasional glimpses he receives of the Dark Lord's mind.

HARRY: So if all of his Horcruxes are destroyed, Voldemort could be killed?

DUMBLEDORE: Yes, I think so. Without his Horcruxes, Voldemort will be a mortal man with a maimed and diminished soul.

Thus, in order for Voldemort to be defeated, Harry must die so the Horcrux that is a part of him can be destroyed. Dumbledore has known this from the beginning and has been grooming Harry for this very moment.

Snape is incredulous, "I have spied for you and lied for you, put myself in mortal danger for you. Everything was supposed to be to keep Lily Potter's son safe. Now you tell me you have been raising him like a pig for slaughter!"

The imagery is strikingly similar to Jesus as the sacrificial Lamb. Harry realizes that he has been groomed simply to die at the proper moment to defeat evil in his world. Like Jesus, he makes the decision to sacrifice himself. He then walks alone out to the Forbidden Forest to meet Voldemort, who has no idea that Harry's death is one of the keys to ending his own immortality.

In fact, both Voldemort and Satan have no idea that the death of their rivals will backfire on them. God kept hidden the fact that Jesus' death would actually defeat Satan and secure the forgiveness of the human race, which Satan had led astray. The apostle Paul wrote that God's plan—the atoning death and resurrection of Jesus—was a "mystery that has been hidden" so that "none of the rulers of this age understood it, for if they had, they would not have crucified the Lord of glory" (1 Corinthians 2:7-8).

But how was the mystery hidden? Wasn't it prophesied?

Yes, but as we saw just a few pages ago, the prophecies of the coming Messiah are spread all over the Old Testament, from Genesis to Malachi. You can't go to one place and read the complete plan. That's why Satan couldn't piece it all together—it was a "mystery that has been hidden"— until the events of the New Testament took place. If it was telegraphed too clearly beforehand, the forces of evil wouldn't have carried out God's plan of sacrifice and crucified Jesus.[8]

The same is true for Voldemort. When Voldemort casts the killing curse to end Harry Potter, he doesn't realize he's helping to end himself. If he had, he would not have gone through with it.

There's a curse in the Old Testament as well: "Anyone hung on a tree is under God's curse" (Deuteronomy 21:23, CSB). Jesus was hung on a tree and was under God's curse—the judgment of our sins.

Both Harry and Jesus are subject to a curse that kills them. But their deaths also defeat the source of evil in their respective worlds.

In the end, we see that this fantasy story and the true story are eerily similar. As Voldemort spread his evil ways to creatures in his world, Satan has done the same in the real world. Harry must defeat Voldemort to save his world, and Jesus must defeat Satan to save the real world. Satan spread sin to the human race, and Jesus took that sin upon Himself. When Jesus died, the ultimate effects of sin died with Him. Then Jesus gave us a foretaste of our future when He rose from the dead.

Resurrection: What a Scarred Forehead and Pierced Hands Show Us

Have you ever thought about what was going through the minds of Jesus' followers after His crucifixion on what we now know as Good Friday? What would you have felt and thought if you were one of His followers on Saturday? You've just spent three years with this man. You've watched Him do miracles, heal the sick, feed crowds of people, and do things you can barely comprehend. You thought He was the Messiah. But then He was beaten and crucified and laid in a tomb. Something incredibly dramatic must have happened afterward to turn them and the entire world around.

While the Saturday reaction of downcast apostles is only briefly alluded to in Scripture, we see a much more visceral reaction from

Harry's friends after his death. Voldemort parades Harry's corpse around briefly for all of his allies to see. Their champion, The Boy Who Lived, has been killed just like everyone else who has opposed the Dark Lord. Their screaming devastation is palpable.

Fortunately for them, their period of mourning was much shorter than three days. In the afterlife, Harry realizes that Voldemort's killing curse has failed to end his life a second time (though it destroyed the part of Voldemort that was in Harry), and he has a brief dream-like encounter at King's Cross station with Dumbledore. Harry has a decision to make. He can either continue "on" to the afterlife or return and finish the fight. Obviously, he chooses the latter. But in their conversation, Dumbledore reveals the true nature of Harry's role in the wizarding world:

> You are the true master of death, because the true master does not seek to run away from Death. He accepts that he must die, and understands that there are far, far worse things in the living world than dying.

Paul affirms the same idea implied by Dumbledore—that life is better on the other side—in his letter to the Philippians:

> For to me, to live is Christ and to die is gain. If I am to go on living in the body, this will mean fruitful labor for me. Yet what shall I choose? I do not know! I am torn between the two: I desire to depart and be with Christ, which is better by far; but it is more necessary for you that I remain in the body. Convinced of this, I know that I will remain, and I will continue with all of you for your progress and joy in the faith, so that through my being with you again your boasting in Christ Jesus will abound on account of me.
>
> PHILIPPIANS 1:21-26

As Harry's "dead" body is being paraded around by Voldemort, a battle between Voldemort's followers and the remainder of Harry's allies at Hogwarts begins. It is notable that now, after years of letting Harry be the hero, those whom Harry had befriended and encouraged through the years come to realize the full extent of their own powers and willingly take on the evil villains. Even the normally quiet and bullied Neville Longbottom joins the action and manages to destroy Voldemort's last Horcrux, his pet snake, Nagini.

Harry, now returned from death unbeknownst to everyone else, uses the distraction to don his invisibility cloak and disappear into the mayhem. Voldemort's team suffers major losses at the hands of those now emboldened in their powers and with Harry aiding his friends from beneath the cloak. A crescendo is reached when Ron's mother, Molly, defeats Voldemort's lieutenant, Bellatrix Lestrange. Voldemort—who is not quite dead yet—is left to comprehend life without her. Harry uses this moment to reveal himself, and their final confrontation begins.

Harry begins by pointing out that the same magical charm his mother used to protect him from Voldemort as an infant—a willing sacrifice made in love—now protects all of the people he died to save: "I've done what my mother did. Haven't you noticed how none of the spells you put on them are binding? You can't torture them. You can't touch them."

Harry, sure that he has won, offers Voldemort a final chance to surrender and show some remorse for the pain and destruction he has caused. Not yet feeling beaten, Voldemort is defiant and mocking:

"Is it love again?" said Voldemort, his snake's face jeering. "Dumbledore's favorite solution, love, which he claimed conquered death, though love did not stop him falling from the tower and breaking like an old waxwork? Love, which did not prevent me stamping out your Mudblood mother like a cockroach, Potter—and nobody seems to love you enough to run forward this time and take my curse. So what will stop you dying now when I strike?"

But unbeknownst to Voldemort, Harry is the true master of the Elder Wand. Not only that, but Snape had been working against Voldemort the whole time, undermining him and giving Harry the time he needed to destroy the Horcruxes one by one. Armed with this knowledge, Harry knows he cannot lose. Voldemort's time is at an end. In one final exchange of spells, Harry emerges victorious, the master of death.

If you were to write a dialogue of Jesus explaining to Satan how He has beaten death, it would probably look something like the final encounter between Harry and Voldemort. In the books, there is no long and drawn-out magical battle like we see in the movies, but rather a war of words and ideas followed by a quick, triumphant conclusion. When Jesus rebuffs Satan's temptations in the desert, he does so by quoting the Word of God, not by exerting force. He makes declarations and later defeats death by rising from the dead, which proves His divine authority and His claims to be God.

Jesus declares, "The reason my Father loves me is that I lay down my life—only to take it up again. No one takes it from me, but I lay it down of my own accord. I have authority to lay it down and authority to take it up again. This command I received from my Father" (John 10:17-18).

Now that death has been defeated, both Harry and Jesus give proof of it in the aftermath of their victory. In Harry's case, the epilogue fast-forwards to a scene nineteen years after the defeat of Voldemort. The last line of the last book tells us all that we need to know. The lightning-shaped scar that has come to define his existence since his childhood troubles him no more: "The scar had not pained Harry for nineteen years. All was well."

In the real world, Jesus rises from the dead and appears alive on at least twelve occasions. He reveals Himself to individuals, to skeptics (such as Thomas, Paul, and James), and to groups, one of which included at least five hundred people. His resurrection could have been easily disproven by His enemies (primarily the Romans and temple Jews) by merely parading His dead body around the city. But they couldn't do that. They even admitted His tomb was empty by concocting the unbelievable story that His disciples had stolen His body.

In other words, according to the Jews, the early followers of Jesus all decided to abandon many of their sacred Jewish practices and then invent the resurrection story in order to get themselves beaten, tortured, and murdered. But it takes more faith to believe *that* than to believe Jesus actually rose from the dead!

His resurrection could have been easily disproven, but it wasn't. And how could Jesus of Nazareth—a three-year itinerant preacher from an obscure part of the Roman Empire—become the most influential human being in history if He didn't rise from the dead?

If Jesus rose from the dead, then the essentials of Christianity are true. For if Jesus rose from the dead, then He is God, and whatever God teaches is true. (We've covered the evidence for this in detail elsewhere.[9])

Jesus not only won by dying on the cross, He nailed our punishment to the cross and publicly shamed the evil forces that opposed Him. Paul writes that God "forgave us all our sins, having canceled the charge of our legal indebtedness, which stood against us and condemned us; he has taken it away, nailing it to the cross. And having disarmed the powers and authorities, he made a public spectacle of them, triumphing over them by the cross" (Colossians 2:13-15).

Just as the forces of evil were publicly shamed at the cross, so will all unbelievers be shamed at the final judgment. Their sins will be made known because they have rejected the only payment for their sins.

When Harry finally defeats Voldemort, the embodiment of evil in his fantasy world, he redeems the rest of his world. The same happens in the real world through Jesus, who declared, "The Son of Man did not come to be served, but to serve, and to give His life as a ransom for many" (Mark 10:45).

Jesus pays a ransom to buy back those He loves (that includes you) from the consequences of evil brought on by our own bad choices. This is "redemption," which is the one-word summary of the entire Bible. Paradise lost in Genesis is paradise regained in Revelation through the redemption that Christ achieved.

But Jesus' resurrection wasn't His only miracle with a message. Jesus demonstrated that He is the Redeemer and Savior of the world by performing miracles that address our deepest problems. He didn't do magic tricks like sawing a woman in half or making a building disappear. He didn't do any of the dark magic depicted in the Harry Potter series. No, the miracles of Jesus send a distinct message—that He is the Savior who can fix all the things wrong with the world. His miracles were deliberately done to correct the four elemental problems we have in this life: sin, nature, sickness, and death.

Since Jesus rose from the dead and did those miracles during His first coming, we can trust that in His second coming, "'He will wipe every tear from their eyes. There will be no more death or mourning or crying or pain, for the old order of things has passed away'" (Revelation 21:4).

The Ultimate Triumph Depends on Love

In his final confrontation with Harry at the end of *Sorcerer's Stone*, Voldemort makes a claim that describes a dangerous belief many in our culture are starting to adopt: "There is no good or evil, only power!"

That's a dangerous belief because, number one, it's false; and number two, it leaves us with no other choice than to oppress those with whom we disagree. For if we cannot recognize that there is an objective standard of goodness we are obligated to follow, then we cannot settle our differences by argument and reason. ("Ah, I now see that your position is morally correct, so I defer to it.")

Instead, by rejecting objective moral goodness, those who get the most power could justify violently oppressing their opponents. Power is substituted for reason and morality. Why use reason if there is no moral standard to reason toward? The rejection of real morality is why the totalitarian impulse of the "cancel culture" is scaring people into silence and making our public discourse less open, less safe, and less true.

There's a better way—a way that the entire Harry Potter series advocates.

Before Harry's final confrontation with Voldemort, Dumbledore warns Harry, "It will take uncommon skill and power to kill a wizard like Voldemort, even without his Horcruxes."

"But I haven't got uncommon skill and power," said Harry, before he could stop himself.

"Yes, you have," said Dumbledore firmly. "You have a power that Voldemort has never had. You can—"

"I know!" said Harry impatiently. "I can love!"

Love is the key to the entire series. Not the anything-goes kind of "love" our culture insists on. That's not actually love at all. The Harry Potter series promotes the kind of love that seeks the good of the other person, which means it's the kind of love that stands against evil—even evil that loved ones want to do to themselves or others. The question is, do we love people enough that we will risk ourselves to protect them; maybe even sacrifice ourselves for them?

When Oprah Winfrey asked J. K. Rowling, "What do you know for sure?" Ms. Rowling harkened back to 9/11, when people were crying to their loved ones on their cell phones as they literally jumped to their deaths from the towers of the burning World Trade Center.

She said, "I definitely know that love is the most powerful thing of all. I remember thinking that . . . I'm about to make myself cry . . . but I remember thinking that when 9/11 happened because those last phone calls were all about [love]—the last thing knowingly that I'm going to say is 'I love you.' What's more powerful than that? Beyond fear, beyond death."

When the news about 9/11 broke, Ms. Rowling got an email from her editor, Arthur Levine. He wrote in the subject line: "And they say we shouldn't teach our children about evil."

Yes, the Harry Potter series certainly explores material that the Bible condemns as evil (as virtually all stories do). Some might want to shield their children from stories that traffic in such things. But others might use the compelling storyline as an occasion to educate children about such matters and even to open the door to Christ to those who would otherwise be uninterested. With the almost universal appeal of Harry Potter, knowing something about the story can open up opportunities to evangelize and get young believers more interested in the adventure of Christianity.

You can share the commonalities between Jesus and Harry—their prophetic births, righteous lives, sacrificial deaths, and physical resurrections from the dead—with people who won't attend a church or a Bible study. If you asked them to imagine what they would see if they looked into the Mirror of Erised, they might just realize they desire the loving and sacrificial God that Harry was patterned after.

For Personal Reflection or Family/Small Group Discussion

1. What is the most attractive/unattractive characteristic of Harry Potter to you? Why?

2. If you stood in front of the Mirror of Erised, what would you see?

3. What did you think and how did you feel when Harry was killed? When he was raised? How does your reaction help you better comprehend the death and resurrection of Christ?

4. What commonalities between the stories of Harry and Jesus do you think are worth discussing with non-Christian fans of Harry Potter?

5. What arguments do you find persuasive for and against Christians watching movies like the *Harry Potter* series?

4

STAR WARS

I put the Force into the movies in order to try to awaken
a certain kind of spirituality in young people—more a belief in
God than a belief in any particular religious system.

GEORGE LUCAS

DO YOU REMEMBER THE FIRST TIME you saw a *Star Wars* movie?

I (Zach) was eleven when *The Phantom Menace* was released. It was the first movie I was excited about seeing in theaters. It was also the first movie I can recall seeing people dress up in costume for. When people are dressing up, it's not just a series of movies, it's a cultural phenomenon with staying power.

The series spans generations. My dad (Frank) was fifteen when the original movie hit the big screen on Memorial Day in 1977. People were dressing up that summer as well. The movie made almost seventy (!) times its production budget, much of it on the backs of repeat moviegoers.

The Turek household has always loved *Star Wars*. Some of my fondest childhood memories are of us watching the original trilogy as a family. My dad loves to quote Darth Vader—"I find your lack of faith disturbing!" (which is perfect for a house raised on apologetics). When my dad officiated the wedding of my brother Spencer, he had the quartet play "The Imperial Death March" during the ceremony. (No, it wasn't when the bride was coming down the aisle!)

The original *Star Wars* was a new kind of movie with groundbreaking special effects, spectacular set design, intriguing characters, powerful music, and an inspiring mix of futuristic technology with old-school mythology. The fight between good and evil wasn't new, but the experience of the fight was.

Star Wars helped to usher in a new age of filmmaking, one that pushed the boundaries of technology many believed was still too limited to believably portray science fiction on the big screen. Writer and director George Lucas developed special effects that made it not just believable but spectacular. He breathed new life into an industry that had seen little change since the 1950s. The effects were so innovative that Lucas started a company called Industrial Light & Magic, which has subsequently produced special effects for almost three hundred movies over the last forty-five years, including many of the films we discuss in this book.

The original movie is now the world's fourth-highest-grossing film (adjusted for inflation) of all time, only behind *Gone with the Wind*, *Avatar*, and *Titanic*. It won seven Oscars in 1978, and in 2004 the American Film Institute declared the film to have the best movie score of all time (composed and conducted by the prolific John Williams, who also wrote the scores for the *Indiana Jones* films, *Jaws*, *Close Encounters of the Third Kind*, *E. T. the Extra-Terrestrial*, *Superman*, the first three *Harry Potter* films, and many others).

In recent years, *Star Wars* has also expanded into TV shows, such as the animated series *The Clone Wars* and *Rebels*, as well as the more recent Disney+ show *The Mandalorian*, which was written and produced by Jon Favreau, the director of the first two *Iron Man* movies and the hit Christmas movie *Elf*.

The series has had staying power even without new films. Under the radar for many moviegoers are more than one hundred *Star Wars* novels in what is now known as the Star Wars Expanded Universe. Those books were foundational in building my lifelong love of reading and good storytelling. And don't forget the toys. In 2011, a year in which no *Star Wars* movie was released and six years after the most recent film up to that time, *Star Wars* toys brought in an estimated $3 billion in gross revenue.

All told, the *Star Wars* franchise has taken in close to $70 billion in revenue from all sources (box office, DVDs, books, toys, retail sales, etc.), giving it more total revenue than both the Marvel Cinematic Universe and the Harry Potter universe combined!

A Galaxy Far, Far Away

Imagine that you're in the Millennium Falcon on one side of our Milky Way galaxy trying to outrun an Imperial warship. Chewbacca is in the copilot's seat when Han Solo jumps up and tells you to get in his seat.

"Let's see what you can do, kid!"

He orders you to punch the Falcon to lightspeed. As you slam the throttles forward, the ship shakes, and light streams into a blur in your windshield.

You're gone.

You're now streaking through space at 186,000 miles *per second.*

How long does it take you to get to the other side of the galaxy? A few minutes? A few hours? A few days, maybe?

No, it takes you 100,000 *years* at the speed of light!

What?

Yes, this galaxy is enormous! But it's nothing compared to the entire universe.

Researchers at the University of Hawaii used something all around them—sand—to help us comprehend the vastness of the universe. They estimated that the number of stars in the universe is about equivalent to the number of grains of sand on all the beaches on earth *times 100,000.*

Marinate on that for a minute: This universe has as many stars as grains of sand on 100,000 earths!

What are the distances between those stars? In our galaxy, the average distance between stars is about thirty trillion miles. At space shuttle orbit speed of about 18,000 miles per hour (*that's five miles per second*), it would take nearly 200,000 years to travel between two stars in our galaxy. If you're in the Millennium Falcon traveling at lightspeed, it will take you about four years to travel between just two of the billions of stars in our galaxy.

And what about galaxies far, far away? How many of them exist? Billions of them!

We mention this because the Bible repeatedly tells us that the heavens will help us discover what God is like. Three thousand years ago, David wrote, "The heavens declare the glory of God" (Psalm 19:1). In about 700 BC, the prophet Isaiah wrote that God gave him a way to understand what He is like. God said:

"To whom will you compare me?
 Or who is my equal?" says the Holy One.
Lift up your eyes and look to the heavens:
 Who created all these?
He who brings out the starry host one by one
 and calls forth each of them by name.
Because of his great power and mighty strength,
 not one of them is missing.
ISAIAH 40:25-26

When we "look to the heavens," what do we see? Stars in a virtually infinite expanse. The infinite expanse of the heavens yells at us what God is like! He created, named, and sustains each of the trillions and trillions of stars.

This is the scientific principle of understanding a cause by its effects.

In other words, we know God by His effects. We see a creation (the effect), and we know there must be a Creator (the Cause). We see design in the universe (the effect), and we know there must be a Designer (the Cause). We sense a moral law obligating us to behave a certain way (the effect), and we know there must be a Moral Lawgiver (the Cause).

The universe in which we live, and in which *Star Wars* takes place, is an effect of God. If the effect has as many stars as grains of sand on 100,000 earths separated by trillions of miles, what must the Cause be like?

Obviously, the Cause must be enormously powerful to create such a vast and wonderful effect out of nothing. The Cause must also be spaceless, timeless, and immaterial, because space-time and matter had a beginning, as even atheists now admit. Therefore, the Cause of creation can't be a natural cause, because nature didn't exist. The Cause must transcend nature; it must be something supernatural.

Finally, the Cause must be personal and intelligent in order to make a choice to create such a vast and precisely fine-tuned universe out of nothing. Without a personal Someone to make a choice to create this universe, nothing would exist today.

Therefore, from the effect we call the universe, we can conclude that a spaceless, timeless, immaterial, powerful, personal, intelligent Being exists who brought this vast and wonderful universe into existence. This is called the Cosmological Argument for the existence of God.

From this argument alone, we don't know if this is the Christian God. But once we do some research and discover that Jesus of Nazareth actually rose from the dead to prove He was God, then we realize that the Being who rose from the dead is the same Being whose divine nature created the universe out of nothing, just as the Bible declares (Colossians 1:16). The only question for each of us is, "Will I accept this evidence and conclusion?"

The reason we want you to consider these attributes of the true God is because they will help us understand how the god of *Star Wars* differs in comparison.

The Religion of the Force

The *Star Wars* series comprises eleven wonderful movies (some more wonderful than others) that, by design, are infused with overtly religious issues. George Lucas said, "I put the Force into the movies in order to try to awaken a certain kind of spirituality in young people—more a belief in God than a belief in any particular religious system."

He admits that he wants to get young people to at least think about the big questions in life: "Is there a God? What does God look like? What does God sound like? What does God feel like? How do we relate to God? Just getting young people to think at that level is what I've been trying to do in the films."

Not bad for Hollywood! But what kind of answers do the movies provide to viewers, and how do they compare to Christianity?

Lucas claims he's not trying to direct viewers to definite answers. "What eventual manifestation that takes place in terms of how they describe their God, what form their faith takes, is not the point of the movie."[1]

Of course, it was unavoidable that his movie would depict a specific kind of worldview with its own view of god. The Force isn't a Christian view of God. The god of *Star Wars* is closest to the god of pantheism—it is omnipresent and binds the universe together, but the Force makes no moral demands on its users.

Moral demands are, of course, part of Christianity, which often uses the same light-versus-darkness language found in *Star Wars*. God calls us to be in the light, as He is (1 John 1:7). Those who are in sin are depicted as being in darkness, while those who have accepted Christ as their Savior are in the light of the Lord. In his letter to the Ephesians, Paul writes:

For you were once darkness, but now you are light in the Lord. Live as children of light (for the fruit of the light consists in all goodness, righteousness and truth) and find out what pleases the Lord. Have nothing to do with the fruitless deeds of darkness, but rather expose them.

EPHESIANS 5:8-11

This idea of affiliating oneself with the light separates Christianity from any type of Force-based religion in a big way. The Force itself is quite clearly neutral—equally accessible to both sides and not preferring one over the other. Since the Force is not personal, it *can't* command anyone to do good with its power.

In this way, pantheism is a lot like atheism. Whether you call nature "the Force" or simply matter and energy, you have no grounds for objective morality. Impersonal nature has no authority or capacity to tell you or anyone what to do.

Yet there is morality throughout the *Star Wars* series. Although the Force is technically neutral, George Lucas admits *Star Wars* is a "morality play." In fact, virtually all good stories, including all superhero movies, are morality plays. There are always good guys and bad guys. Evil always needs to be defeated, which presupposes that there is an objective standard of good we *ought* to follow. An objective standard of good that all humans are obligated to follow can only exist if a personal God exists.

Since the Star Wars universe doesn't have a personal God, how is morality justified in the movies? It isn't. But that's okay. They're movies; not everything has to be justified or make sense. The Force, like Harry Potter's magic, isn't meant to be grounded in reality. It's science fiction. Just like we don't see people flying on broomsticks, we don't see people wielding lightsabers or moving spaceships around with their minds.

While Lucas claims the Force is morally neutral, the audience isn't. Because God has written the Moral Law on our hearts, we intuitively and immediately know that the Jedi are the heroes of the story and that the light side is morally better than the dark side.

The repeated goal of "balance" in the Force is another difference between the Force of *Star Wars* and the God of Christianity. "The film is ultimately about the dark side and the light side," said George Lucas. "Those sides are designed around compassion and greed—we all have those two sides of us—and we have to make sure that those two sides of us are in balance."

This is really an odd statement to make.[2] Do we really want a "balance" between compassion and greed or between other forms of good and evil? Can you imagine your grandma telling you that as long as you do just as many nice things to the little boy next door, you can do all the bad things to him you want? Christians (and all people) should be fighting to eradicate evil completely, not balance it with good.

Furthermore, contrary to the Force of *Star Wars*, God and Satan are not "in balance" as if they are equal and opposite forces. As we saw in the introduction, God is the one sovereign power, and all other creatures derive their power from Him. Just as evil cannot exist without good, Satan cannot exist without God. Neither can the angels and demons. Neither can we.

C. S. Lewis put it well, "Christianity agrees with Dualism that this universe is at war. But it does not think this is a war between independent powers. It thinks it is a civil war, a rebellion, and that we are living in a part of the universe occupied by the rebel."[3]

The Christian concept of faith is also different from the religion of the Force. In *Star Wars*, faith means not trusting your senses but your feelings. It's why in *A New Hope* Obi-Wan prompted Luke to turn off his targeting computer and trust his feelings.

Christianity is exactly the opposite. Faith is trusting in what you have good reasons to believe is true, and the primary way you get those reasons is by using your senses. Once you've discovered those reasons, you don't trust your feelings when they contradict the facts. Feelings are fickle and subject to changing emotions. Feelings change, but facts don't.

In *Star Wars*, the more faith you have, the more power you have.

That's why Yoda can lift the spaceship out of the mud on Dagobah while Luke cannot. But that's not the way the real world works.

Imagine you and your friend get on a flight to Hawaii. If you totally trust the pilots but your friend is scared to death (your faith is strong but your friend's is weak), does that mean you'll get there but your friend will crash? Of course not. Once your friend is on the plane, the strength of your friend's faith isn't the issue. The skill of the pilots is. It's the same in Christianity. It's not the amount of faith that has power—the faith of a mustard seed is enough. Instead, *power lies in whom you put your faith in*. Jesus, not humanity, is the source of our power.

Despite these differences, there are some parallels between major plot points in *Star Wars* and Christianity. For example, the hero of the prequel trilogy, Anakin Skywalker, is prophesied to be "The Chosen One" and appears to have been conceived by the Force itself. His mother claims that he had no father, thus mirroring the prophetic coming of Jesus and His virgin conception.

But the more significant parallels we will cover are the recurring Christian themes of sacrifice and redemption in the *Star Wars* series. Lucas knows these themes are essential to good storytelling. Of course, for redemption to take place, someone has to be fallen. Darth Vader is the most obvious candidate for redemption (and we'll get to him). But the more fun candidate is a charismatic, egotistical, rule-bending skeptic on the "good" side called Han Solo.

From Skeptic to Believer

Han Solo starts out as a committed skeptic about the Force. He tells true believer Luke Skywalker, "Kid, I've flown from one side of this galaxy to the other, and I've seen a lot of strange stuff, but I've never seen anything to make me believe that there's one all-powerful Force controlling everything. There's no mystical energy field that controls my destiny. It's all a lot of simple tricks and nonsense."

He also asserts, "Hokey religions and ancient weapons are no match for a good blaster at your side."

Harrison Ford admits his character appeals to the naysayers watching. "There's somebody there representing you saying, 'What, really? Are you sure? I'm not so sure,'" he said. "And that's what gives you the liberty of being in the church before you really are asked to believe."[4]

As a skeptic with an ego, Han is only halfway on the team. He tells Princess Leia, "Look, I ain't in this for your revolution, and I'm not in it for you, Princess. I expect to be well paid. I'm in it for the money."

Luke responds, "Take care of yourself, Han. I guess that's what you're best at, isn't it?"

Yes, Han is in it for himself. He plays by his own rules, takes no crap from anyone, and even informs the uptight princess that she likes him "because [he's] a scoundrel."[5]

A scoundrel? Yes, that's what makes him interesting and fun! We can predict what the upright and dedicated Luke will do, but not Han. He's too unpredictable because he's committed only to himself, not to the team or the mission. (*Solo* is the perfect name for him.)

After a small victory, Han tells Luke, "Great, kid. Don't get cocky." Ironic, because Han is the cockiest character in the entire series! He utters lines like:

"Look, Your Worshipfulness, let's get one thing straight. I take orders from just one person: me."

"Afraid I was gonna leave without giving you a goodbye kiss?"

"I think you just can't bear to let a gorgeous guy like me out of your sight."

"Sorry, sweetheart, I haven't got time for anything else."

"Well, Princess, it looks like you managed to keep me here a while longer."

"You know, sometimes I amaze even myself."

"I'm not really interested in your opinion, 3PO."

"Don't everybody thank me at once."

"Never tell me the odds!"

In many ways, Han Solo is Tony Stark to Luke's Captain America.

But there are differences. One big difference between Han and Tony Stark is that Han is in debt—so much debt that he nearly gets himself killed by the slimy organized crime reptile, Jabba the Hutt (who is way bigger than a hut).

"Han, my boy, you disappoint me. Why haven't you paid me?"

Han promises to eventually pay up, but he's in too deep. He'll never be able to repay Jabba, so Jabba makes Han a frozen wall ornament. Han is now paralyzed in debt, literally.

Will Han survive? Is there any way he can be rescued and turned into a completely committed good guy? Yes, and it takes a committed good guy to do it.

Luke will stop at nothing to free his friend Han, spending several months planning and organizing the rescue mission with Leia, Chewbacca, and Lando Calrissian. In the end, Luke not only frees Han but also sets him free forever by destroying the one who held him in chains (actually carbonite). This redemption motivates Han to eventually become a true believer and fully devoted member of the team.

In *The Force Awakens*, he says, "I used to wonder about that—thought it was a bunch of mumbo jumbo: a magical power in the battle between good and evil, the dark side—the crazy thing is—it's true. The Force, the Jedi. All of it. It's all true."

Almost like the apostle Paul's, Han's transformation is so complete that his role is flipped in the new trilogy from that of skeptical scoundrel to loving parent to his son, Ben Solo (Kylo Ren), and mentor to Rey.

Just as Luke saved Darth Vader in *Return of the Jedi*, Han tries to redeem his son, Kylo Ren, at the end of *The Force Awakens*. Sadly, while Kylo Ren eventually renounces the dark side, Han's offer to help his son is met with Kylo running him through with a lightsaber. Han is left with a final caress of his son's face before falling to his death.

There are a few parallels to Christianity in what happens with Luke and Han, whether intentional by Lucas or not. First, it's true that we are all paralyzed in massive debt because of our own bad behavior. If you or I were to add up all of our sins throughout our lifetime—sins of omission and commission—we would be crushed under the weight of our staggering debt. Like Han, we can only be liberated by a Savior.

Second, once we are liberated, we should be motivated out of gratitude to our Savior to become part of Christ's team to do good works and recruit others to the team.

And third, while there is certainly enough evidence that unbelievers can examine to know Christianity is true, some truths only become real once you've become a Christian. Just like you won't fully experience the Force until you believe, you won't fully experience the Holy Spirit until you accept Christ. Once you've yielded to the Holy Spirit, then He will begin to transform your life.

There are even some truths God actually hides from those who deem themselves too smart for Christianity. Jesus said, "I praise you, Father, Lord of heaven and earth, because you have hidden these things from the wise and learned, and revealed them to little children" (Matthew 11:25).

What? Wouldn't it make sense to give skeptics *more* evidence? Not if they *refuse* to believe, regardless of the evidence they already have.

Holding truths back from those bent on unbelief is actually an act of mercy, because those with more knowledge will be held more accountable. As Jesus warned, "To whom much is given, from him much will be required" (Luke 12:48, NKJV).

Enticed and Dragged Away

How did you feel the first time you saw Darth Vader on the screen? Probably exactly how Lucas wanted you to feel. This guy is evil.

But Darth Vader didn't start out that way. He started out as Anakin Skywalker, hero of the prequel trilogy. His fall from grace in science fiction is not much different from our Fall here in the real world.

In *Star Wars*, we see characters who affiliate with the dark side of the Force become corrupted over time. Like a gateway drug, committing small sins makes it easier to commit big ones. This is something that we've all probably seen. People who break bad can usually remember the first instance of bad behavior that started their slide down the slippery slope, but by the hundredth time, the behavior has become so natural that they don't even think about it. And they are on to behaving even more badly.

Conversely, you have probably met people with good habits who seem relatively unfazed by scenarios that might cause others to stumble. It's hard to bribe a teetotaler with a fifth of Jack Daniels, but a drug addict might kill someone for just a few grams of heroin.

Small sins have a tendency to draw you into big sins, and you usually don't notice where they are taking you. As C. S. Lewis put it, "The safest road to hell is the gradual one—the gentle slope, soft underfoot, without sudden turnings, without milestones, without signposts."[6]

But why do we start down this gentle slope to begin with?

The apostle James—who was the pastor of the church in Jerusalem and was martyred for his faith in AD 62—had some inspired insights about this. He wrote, "Each person is tempted when they are dragged away by their own evil desire and enticed. Then, after desire has conceived, it gives birth to sin; and sin, when it is full-grown, gives birth to death" (James 1:14-15).

Enticed means "to catch by use of bait." In other words, sin involves some level of deception. When we sin, we are deceived; we're like an animal caught in a trap or a fish being dragged away by a hook.

This process of being enticed and dragged away into greater and greater sins could be summed up by Yoda's warning, "Once you start down the dark path, forever will it dominate your destiny." Darth Vader admitted as much when he tried to entice Luke with his famous line, "If you only knew the power of the dark side."

In *Star Wars*, you can clearly tell who has been enticed and dragged away. A character's moral fall is typically shown through physical deformities and injuries. Users of the dark side often have significantly altered facial features and eyes (Emperor Palpatine), or physical deformities like the loss of limbs and mechanical parts (Darth Vader), signifying their loss of humanity. Users of the light side are generally depicted as being whole and unscarred. As Lucas put it:

> Darth Vader was a—a composite man. I mean, he was . . .
> half-machine, half-man. And that's where he lost a lot of his
> humanity is that he—you know, he has mechanical legs. You
> know—and he has mechanical arms possibly and he's hooked
> up to a breathing machine. So there's not much, actually,
> human left in him.[7]

In the real world, we also see physical effects of sin, but not always so quickly. Sin brought sickness and death into the world, and it has also separated us from God. Only a divine Redeemer—someone who is sinless and can conquer death—can make the world new and bring us back into God's family.

Dragged Away to a Depraved Mind

So how does Anakin get dragged away and trapped by his own desires to eventually become Darth Vader? Anakin starts out a slave who is set free and gets to live out his dream of becoming a Jedi. But he has a lust for power and a weakness related to fear. We see him live out the great Jedi Master Yoda's warning, "Fear is the path to the dark side. Fear leads to anger. Anger leads to hate. Hate leads to suffering."
The prequel trilogy shows us this fall.

When Anakin is first brought before the Jedi Council as a young boy in *The Phantom Menace*, Master Yoda—the oldest and most respected Jedi Master—remarks that he senses great fear in him. While there is nothing wrong with being afraid, Anakin is never able to overcome his fear. Throughout the prequel trilogy, his actions are almost always driven by the emotion of fear rather than by reason.

At one point, Anakin reveals, "You're asking me to be rational. That is something that I know I cannot do. Believe me, I wish I could just wish away my feelings, but I can't."[8] Anakin's inability to be rational and control his feelings will ultimately contribute to his downfall.

In *Attack of the Clones*, we see Anakin's fear lead to anger. He is afraid for his mother and, later, for his soon-to-be wife, Padme. When Anakin loses his mother, he butchers an entire village of Sand People in a fit of murderous rage. "Not just the men," he declares, "but the women and the children too." Later, when Padme is almost killed on Geonosis, a furious Anakin loses his arm when he foolishly rushes to engage Count Dooku, a far more skilled opponent, in single combat.

But anger isn't at the end of the spectrum of wrongdoing. When most people get angry, they do so in response to an event. In other words, anger is a secondary emotion that usually isn't premeditated. When Anakin committed a horrible crime against the Sand People, he did not walk into the village intending to kill everyone. He was triggered by his mother's death and believed they were responsible for it. This is why we legally distinguish between first-degree murder (premeditated) and second-degree murder (not premeditated/a crime of "passion"). Anakin's crime of passion is a terrible one, but he still has further to fall.

In *Revenge of the Sith*, we see Anakin's anger become hate. He has become resentful of the Jedi Order, which does not seem to respect his accomplishments, and he fears they would exile him if they knew he was married. He sees a vision of the future in which his wife, Padme, appears to die in childbirth.

Already feeling powerless, he is told by Master Yoda that he needs to give up his worldly attachments. Instead, he turns to Chancellor Palpatine, who reveals himself to be a Sith Lord and promises to help Anakin save his wife. We can see here how far Anakin has fallen. Palpatine reveals himself to be exactly the enemy the Jedi have been hunting for the entire prequel trilogy, but Anakin doesn't seem to care because Palpatine has what he wants.

The actor who plays Anakin, Hayden Christensen, actually used the word "lured" in describing that scene. He said, "Palpatine lured Anakin into a very impressionable state." George Lucas went so far as to say, "This is where Anakin actually succumbs to the influences of the devil."[9]

Indeed, Anakin is being dragged away by the enemy because of his worldly desires. In biblical terms, they are idols that will lead to suffering in his life and in the lives of those around him.

Refusing to give up his worldly desires, Anakin completes his fall by willingly slaughtering all of the children in the Jedi Temple—a premeditated act born out of hatred for the Order that he feels has betrayed him. His actions cause Padme to abandon him in horror, and she later dies in childbirth of a broken heart. Hence, Anakin's nightmarish dream comes true, but tragically, his actions were the driving force behind it.

Obi-Wan battles Anakin and then scolds him as Anakin slides into a burning lake of fire, "You were the chosen one! It was said that you would destroy the Sith, not join them. You were to bring balance to the Force, not leave it in darkness."

Disgraced, disfigured, and now near death from his many injuries, Anakin becomes subject to the now Emperor Palpatine. The Emperor seals Anakin's fate by encasing him in a suit of armor that makes it possible for his body to function, though with ongoing pain. The transformation from Anakin Skywalker to Darth Vader is now complete.

As we have seen, Darth Vader's physical appearance displays the effects of his immoral choices. But don't miss the fact that the same is true of his mind. His mind becomes increasingly more depraved because of those same choices.

Obi-Wan had warned him, "Be mindful of your thoughts, Anakin. They'll betray you."

This is exactly what the Bible also warns us about. In the first chapter of his amazing letter to the Roman church (Rome was the largest city in the world at the time), Paul describes what happens to our minds when we "suppress the truth" about God in order to pursue worldly desires. Our "thinking [becomes] futile and [our] foolish hearts [are] darkened." If we persist, "God [gives us] over to a depraved mind, so that [we] do what ought not to be done" (Romans 1:18, 21, 28). When our slide into depravity is complete, we not only do evil, we actually cheer on others who are doing evil as well. Is there any better description of our culture today than this from a two-thousand-year-old letter?[10]

Once someone has a depraved mind, they may still know, at least intellectually, that their murderous deeds are evil, but they will justify those deeds because they are for the "right" cause. The ends justify the means. As George Lucas put it, "Nobody who is evil thinks of themselves as evil. They think they are doing good, even though they are not" (see Proverbs 16:2; 21:2).

Hitler dehumanized and murdered the Jews because he thought he was doing good by creating a super race. Ironically, Anakin resorted to mass murder in his good quest to defeat death. Jesus defeated death by suffering evil, not doing it.

Paul realized that depraved minds affect people of every generation.

That's why he urged the Romans (and us) to "not conform to the pattern of this world, but be transformed by the renewing of your mind" (Romans 12:2). Unless we actively resist the darkness of our culture by renewing our minds with God's truth and love, we risk futile thinking, depraved minds, and all sorts of evil. As Darth Vader himself warned, "You underestimate the power of the dark side. If you will not fight, then you will meet your destiny."

The Redeemer Strikes Back

Anakin's fall to the dark side was tragic, especially since he had the capacity to choose a better path. He was not predestined to fall to the dark side. While prophecy and destiny are key topics in *Star Wars*, we are also led to believe characters make their own moral choices. In *Star Wars*, like real life, our choices determine our destiny. Anakin was supposed to be "The Chosen One" to bring balance to the Force. Unfortunately, Anakin's choices brought his own nightmare.

But that nightmare doesn't have to last forever. Redemption is another powerful and prevalent theme in *Star Wars*, reminding us that no one is beyond saving—even someone as horrible as Darth Vader. This is particularly true when someone loves Vader enough to never give up on him.

Luke never gives up. As Anakin's son, Luke in many ways functions as his counterpoint—how Anakin could have turned out had he made better choices. Luke has similar gifts as his father, but Luke makes much better choices to end up on the light side. Anakin's actions in the prequel trilogy lead to the fall of the Jedi, while Luke's actions in the original trilogy lead to their triumph over the Sith.

Like his father, Luke starts his journey in *A New Hope* on the desert planet of Tatooine, where he quickly encounters an aged Obi-Wan Kenobi, who introduces him to the Force and the Jedi. Luke quickly proves himself to be fearless. He assists in the rescue of Princess Leia from the clutches of Darth Vader and subsequently destroys the Death Star by following Obi-Wan's advice and trusting the Force instead of his targeting computer.

In *The Empire Strikes Back*, Luke escapes with the rest of the Rebel Alliance from the ice planet Hoth and begins his training as a Jedi on Dagobah under Master Yoda's tutelage. Similar to his father's experiences, Luke has a vision that his friends are in danger on Cloud City. He wants to go off immediately and assist them, but Master Yoda warns against it. Yoda knows Luke's training isn't done and sees the potential for him to follow his father's footsteps. Like the rest of us, Luke could ruin his life and those of his loved ones if he gives in to temptation or acts on emotional impulse.

But here again Luke shows he is different from his father. In the prequels, Anakin seems like he is in a constant state of panic. He is consumed with fear, first for his mother and later for his wife. That fear causes him to make foolish and immoral decisions. Luke, on the other hand, controls his fear and makes more rational decisions. He knows the danger of going to help his friends, but he controls his fear and goes anyway. While in Cloud City, Luke's arm is severed (another parallel to his father's life), but he also learns that Darth Vader is his father.

Return of the Jedi sees Luke assume his rightful place as a Jedi (they're really not trying to trick anyone with the title, are they?). After rescuing Han from Jabba the Hutt, Luke heads back to Dagobah. There, Yoda and Obi-Wan confirm the truth that Vader is Luke's father and tell Luke he must confront him again in order to finish his training.

Notice that Luke isn't told to defeat Vader, as we might expect, only that he has to confront him. Luke assists Han and Leia in landing the Rebel Alliance strike force on the forest moon of Endor and then voluntarily turns himself over to the Empire. Again, Luke shows his fearlessness. He is willing to walk into the lions' den and does so with a purpose, for now he understands his goal: the redemption of Darth Vader.

But Vader is not so easily swayed. Luke senses the conflict in him, "Search your feelings, Father. You can't do this. I feel the conflict within you. Let go of your hate."

Vader rebuffs Luke's overtures, declaring, "It is too late for me, Son. The Emperor will show you the true nature of the Force. He is your master now."

Now we reach the climactic moment of Luke's journey. Will he resist the temptation to fall to the dark side, or will he follow in his father's footsteps? Vader brings Luke before the Emperor on the second Death Star, and the Emperor attempts to goad Luke into attacking him. Luke refuses, but the Emperor finally plays his trump card: he has lured the Rebel Alliance into a trap on Endor, and the Death Star is fully operational.

Frustrated and enraged, Luke finally attacks but ends up in another lightsaber duel with Vader. Realizing his mistake, Luke backs off, but Vader senses his secret—that Leia is his sister. When Vader vows to turn her to the dark side in Luke's place, Luke finally snaps. They duel again, and this time Luke cuts off his father's prosthetic arm.

Sensing that he is close to the point of no return, Luke comes back to his senses. He resists succumbing to fear, remains calm even when provoked to anger, and refuses to strike his father down.

Luke tosses his lightsaber to the side, declaring, "I am a Jedi, like my father before me." His love for his father shines through, even though Vader has done nothing to deserve it. He prioritizes love for his father over hatred. In this way, Luke is the counterpoint to Darth Vader.

Meanwhile, the Emperor becomes so annoyed with Luke for rejecting his offer to join the dark side that he zaps Luke with Force lightning. Luke cries out to his father for help. Finally, overcome with his son's plight, Vader redeems himself. He grabs the Emperor and tosses his master down the Death Star's reactor shaft, mortally wounding himself in the process.

After years of the Emperor dragging Anakin away from the light and into the dark, it is now fitting that Luke begins to drag his father back into the light toward an escaping spacecraft. But it's too late.

Near death, Vader, who is actually now Anakin Skywalker again, wants Luke to remove his mask so he can see his son.

ANAKIN: Just for once, let me look on you with my own eyes.

[*Luke takes off his mask and head covering.*]

ANAKIN: Now go, my son. Leave me.

LUKE: No, you're coming with me. I will not leave you here. I've got to save you!

ANAKIN: You already have, Luke. You were right. You were right about me. Tell your sister you were right . . .

LUKE: Father, I won't leave you!

The now-redeemed Anakin Skywalker dies in his son's arms.

In the end, the prophecy came true: Anakin actually fulfilled his role as "The Chosen One" by destroying the Sith, including the Emperor and himself.

Can Bad People Go to Heaven?

How can Vader be forgiven? He's the lowest of the low. He killed people indiscriminately and even helped to destroy an entire planet on a whim. So how, after one good act—even one that saves the galaxy—can Vader be redeemed? He dies contentedly in his son's arms, but surely he can't be going to whatever heaven is in *Star Wars*, can he?

The answer to our question is yes. Anakin's redemption continues into the afterlife. As Luke put it, "No one's ever really gone." At the celebration on Endor at the end of *Return of the Jedi*, Luke sees the Force ghosts of Yoda, Anakin, and Obi-Wan watching over him. (This is eerily similar to Jesus appearing with Moses and Elijah transfigured.)

In this scene, Anakin is depicted as being back to his "true" self before his fall. In fact, after the prequels were released, Lucas was so committed to this idea that he went back and altered this scene in *Return of the Jedi*. He digitally replaced the actor who portrayed Anakin in the original scene with Hayden Christensen (the actor who played Anakin in the prequel trilogy) to reinforce the idea of Anakin's redemption. In the *Star Wars* universe, Anakin is redeemed in every sense of the word despite his many misdeeds all because he made a choice to (in the end) side with good over evil.

As Christians, we also know that redemption is just one choice away. The difference is that we aren't saving ourselves as Vader did. As sinners, we can't possibly save ourselves.

Perhaps you're thinking, "Why not? I'm a pretty good person. I've done more good than bad, so God will accept me into heaven."

There are a couple problems with this popular sentiment. First, it contradicts the Bible, which claims no one is really good. John, friend of Jesus and eyewitness of His life and resurrection, wrote:

> If we claim to be without sin, we deceive ourselves and the truth is not in us. If we confess our sins, he is faithful and just and will forgive us our sins and purify us from all unrighteousness. If we claim we have not sinned, we make him out to be a liar and his word is not in us.
>
> My dear children, I write this to you so that you will not sin. But if anybody does sin, we have an advocate with the Father— Jesus Christ, the Righteous One. He is the atoning sacrifice for our sins, and not only for ours but also for the sins of the whole world.
>
> I JOHN 1:8–2:2

Notice here that everyone has sinned and that all who claim otherwise are deceiving themselves. Paul affirms, "There is no one righteous, not even one" (Romans 3:10), and Jesus declares, "There is only One who is good," referring to God (Matthew 19:17). That excludes all of us humans from the category of "good"!

No one is really good by God's perfect standard. While some sins are worse than others, we are all guilty of sin.

The fact that none of us is really good helps answer a question that skeptics routinely ask: "If God exists, how come there is so much evil in the world? Why doesn't He just eradicate it?" The answer is that He might just start with *me and you*. We think God should stop Darth Vader and the evil people in our society, but we never think God should stop us. Yet we do evil every day. If God said He was going to eradicate all evil at midnight tonight, would you still be alive at 12:01? We wouldn't.

The second problem with the claim that you can make it to heaven on your good works is that such reasoning wouldn't even hold up in a court of law. It contradicts our most basic concept of justice. Since when do good deeds cancel bad deeds? Does the fact that you've helped the poor somehow mean you've never been guilty of lying? Does philanthropy wipe away a sex offender's guilt? Are murderers declared not guilty if they do great things or their good deeds outnumber their murders? If our own imperfect sense of justice demands that evil must be punished *regardless of how much good the evildoer has done*, what about God's perfect justice?

An infinitely just God cannot allow sin to go unpunished. Otherwise, He wouldn't be *infinitely* just. Jesus claimed that His mission was "to give his life as a ransom for many" (Mark 10:45). The sacrifice of Christ is the only way an infinitely just God can remain just while justifying sinners (Romans 3:26). That's why Jesus is the only way to heaven. We all need Him because He is the only one who can redeem us out of our eternal problem—the problem of death and punishment.

Since we are all guilty of wrongdoing and no amount of good works can change that fact, then our good works can't save us from the punishment we deserve. Instead, we receive forgiveness and righteousness by grace through faith, apart from our works. As Paul declared, "For it is by grace you have been saved, through faith—and this is not from yourselves, it is the gift of God—not by works, so that no one can boast" (Ephesians 2:8-9).

So can bad people go heaven? Yes. In fact, *only bad people go to heaven.*

Do Not Be Afraid: God Can't Alter the Deal

When Darth Vader went back on his word to Lando and Princess Leia in *The Empire Strikes Back*, he declared, "I am altering the deal. Pray I don't alter it any further." (I tried this line on my wife recently. It didn't work. Not recommended!)

This is the essence of Vader. He can't be trusted because he does whatever he wants to get whatever he wants. He lies and has no concern for others. As Jesus declared, Satan is a "murderer" and a "liar" (John 8:44). He disguises himself as an "angel of light" (2 Corinthians 11:14), deceiving humanity by making sin look attractive and good.

But as we'll see more in the Batman chapter, real evil relies on objective good to exist, and objective good relies on God to exist. Therefore, since we all know evil exists, God must exist. This is the same God who created and sustains you and this massive universe with as many stars as grains of sand on 100,000 earths!

This infinitely good God cannot do evil by going back on His Word. He cannot "alter the deal" as Darth Vader did. That means we can trust His promises, even in the face of fear.

Here's what God promises to His people in both the Old Testament and the New Testament: "Be strong and courageous. Do not be afraid or terrified because of them, for the LORD your God goes with you; he will never leave you nor forsake you" (Deuteronomy 31:6; see also Hebrews 13:5).

Jesus said, "Do not be afraid of those who kill the body but cannot kill the soul. Rather, be afraid of the One who can destroy both soul and body in hell" (Matthew 10:28).

If you've repented of your dark ways and accepted the Redeemer—the true Lord and Ruler of the universe—your eternity is secure, and you can say with confidence, "You can't win, Satan. If you strike me down, I will become more powerful than you can possibly imagine."

For Personal Reflection or Family/Small Group Discussion

1. What is the most attractive/unattractive characteristic of Han Solo to you? Why?

2. How do the *Star Wars* concept of faith and the Christian concept of faith differ? How do the Force and the God of the Bible differ?

3. Anakin was enticed and dragged away to the dark side by his own desires. In what areas of your life are you vulnerable to being enticed and dragged away?

4. Can a bad person, such as Darth Vader, go to heaven? Why or why not?

5. One of the key themes in *Star Wars* is redemption. In Christianity, redemption is a gift. But those who are redeemed rarely accept redemption without help from others. They have people who help them along the way and believe in them (like Luke not giving up on Darth Vader). What are some examples from the Bible in which one person helps another person accept the redemption provided by Christ? Who led you to Christ? Are you leading anyone?

THE LORD OF THE RINGS

Gandalf, I thought you were dead. But then I thought I was dead.
Is everything sad going to come untrue?
SAMWISE GAMGEE, *The Return of the King*

IMAGINE THAT YOU HAVE TO SEND someone on a rugged mission to save the world. What kind of qualities would you want that person to have? It would probably be someone with the qualities of the heroes we've discussed elsewhere in this book. It wouldn't be a three-foot-tall man who lived in a meadow, drank beer, and ate seven meals a day.

But that's who J. R. R. Tolkien picked.

Now, imagine you are that three-foot-tall man. The authorities tell you you'll need to walk barefoot from your hometown to an entirely different country and chuck a ring into a volcano. No one will offer to give you a map, and you won't know how to get there without help.

Since you are so small, you won't be able to physically defend yourself against any of the dangers you will encounter on your quest. Along the way, the government of the other country is going to send teams of assassins to try to kill you. The wildlife will try to kill you as well.

That ring you need to chuck into the volcano is also the most desired object in the world, which means that everyone you meet may try to kill you and take it from you if they know you are carrying it.

Sounds like something that might be a bit out of your league, doesn't it? Yet that's exactly what the hobbit Frodo Baggins is asked to do.

Frodo is as unlikely of a hero as you will find in all of literature. Hobbits are not only tiny in stature but also love a quiet, peaceful life. They are not a warlike people and prefer to keep to themselves. Above all, they share a love of food, drink, and the land. They are the meek that inherit the earth, the merciful who receive mercy, the pure in heart, and the peacemakers (Matthew 5:3-12)—not exactly a list of traits the world would build a hero around.

But somehow, by the end of the story, the entire Fellowship of men, elves, and dwarves will have placed all of their hope in two hobbits, Frodo and Sam. Thematically, this fits within the structure Tolkien has set up. Victory over evil can be achieved, but not by strength of arms.

Before we see how Tolkien does this, we need a little background on J. R. R. Tolkien and the masterpiece he's created.

Who and What Are Behind *The Lord of the Rings*?

John Ronald Reuel Tolkien (1892–1973) was a World War I veteran and a professor of Literature in Oxford, England, and he is best known as the author of *The Lord of the Rings*. He wrote the book between 1937 and 1949. But due to the high cost of paper after World War II, the book was divided into three volumes and published between 1954 and 1955.

Since then, more than 150 million books have been sold, and the movies have grossed about three *billion* dollars. The series has been so successful that Tolkien is widely considered to be the father of the modern fantasy genre and is credited with creating one of the most extensive fantasy series of all time. *The Lord of the Rings* is seen by many as a precursor to popular modern fantasy works that include such titles as *Game of Thrones* and *The Wheel of Time*.

The series chronicles the adventures of a fellowship of heroes as they try to destroy the One Ring, which was created by the main antagonist, Sauron, in his effort to subjugate all life on Middle-earth. The Ring represents the destructive power of sin, especially the lust for power (although Tolkien left this conclusion to the reader).

The Ring grants its wearer invisibility—something we'd especially like to have when we misbehave. Since we don't want the world to see us for what we are in the dark, the power of invisibility sticks out as something we would want if we were evil. The Ring also increases the wearer's power but corrupts their desires (something sin tends to do in real life). Creatures are mesmerized by and drawn to the Ring, but almost no one can handle its power once they have it (which trades on our inability to handle absolute power responsibly).

The Lord of the Rings focuses on three primary character arcs in the struggle to defeat Sauron and destroy the Ring: Gandalf as the main strategist of the forces of good against the forces of Sauron; Aragorn as a ranger from the North who eventually assumes his rightful mantle as the king of Gondor; and Frodo as the unlikely bearer of the Ring, who ultimately bears the hope of all living things. (We'll get to these heroes shortly.)

Tolkien put immense thought and detail into his work. He not only created the complex story that spans millennia but also the unique calendars and many languages for the characters in the story!

What motivated Tolkien to embark on such a vast work?

We said in the introduction the majority of films were not written with Christianity overtly in mind, but there are exceptions. *The Lord of the Rings* is the biggest exception. In fact, one Tolkien expert put it this way: "If you like *The Lord of the Rings*, you should like Christianity."[1]

Tolkien was a devout Catholic and was quite open about how his beliefs influenced his work. He admitted that *"The Lord of the Rings* is of course a fundamentally religious and Catholic work; unconsciously so at first but consciously in the revision."*

It's no surprise, then, that Tolkien considered the fundamental theme of *The Lord of the Rings* to be death and immortality: "I do not think that even Power and Domination is the real center of my story. . . . The real theme for me is about something much more permanent and difficult: Death and Immortality."[2]

Death and immortality are central to Christianity. But Tolkien intended Christianity to come through only symbolically rather than directly. He was writing myth, not a sermon.

"I have cut out practically all references to anything like 'religion,' to cults and practices in the imaginary world," he said, "for the religious element is absorbed into the story and the symbolism."[3]

Part of the reason Tolkien eliminated all overt references to Christianity is because he disliked strict allegories of Christianity, such as *The Pilgrim's Progress*. Yet he never revealed definitively how he would characterize the literary style that connects *The Lord of the Rings* to Christianity. Scholars continue to argue over that question.

Professor Michael Jahosky thinks the best characterization is parable. That is, *The Lord of the Rings* is a parable about the king coming to Middle-earth akin to Jesus' parables about how He is the King coming to our earth. After reflecting on the work of N. T. Wright, Alister McGrath, Peter Kreeft, and others, Jahosky writes, "Suddenly, I realized that Tolkien's mythology was a story about what Jesus' stories are about: The good news of the return of the king."[4]

The Return of the King is, of course, the title of the third volume (and movie) in the series. And while there is not a complete one-to-one correlation between King Aragorn and King Jesus, as there would be in an allegory, Aragorn does represent Jesus symbolically in more ways than other characters (as we will see). After all, he is literally the returning king.

The True Myth

While parable is arguably the best way to describe how *The Lord of the Rings* relates to Christianity, there is certainly no argument about the series being a mythical story. But the meaning of the word *myth* needs some clarification here. We normally think of myth as the stuff of legend—"fairy stories" that probably never happened yet often teach us something important about the real world. But Tolkien believed Christianity was the true myth: the fairy story that actually occurred in history, and he helped convince his good friend C. S. Lewis of that belief too.

Why use myth over any other genre? C. S. Lewis answers the question in his review of *The Fellowship of the Ring*: "The value of the myth is that it takes all the things we know and restores to them the rich significance which had been hidden by 'the veil of familiarity.'"[5]

Likewise, Tolkien advised that "we need, in any case, to clean our windows; so that the things seen clearly may be freed from the drab blur of triteness or familiarity—from possessiveness."[6]

People in the West may have heard the Christian story so much that its familiarity breeds a kind of apathy. So rather than speaking academically about the historicity of the New Testament or allegorically about Christ's rising from the dead, Tolkien aims to make us *feel* that Christianity should be true; that a returning King would be good news.

He does this by creating a vast, enchanted universe full of adventure, with mythical creatures, cunning villains, epic heroes, and enough plot twists to draw us into a morally depraved world that seems just as bad as our own. Tolkien's storytelling also makes us feel the importance of virtues such as courage, self-control, wisdom, justice, faith, hope, and love and even countercultural Christian values such as the power of weakness, the willingness to suffer, and the offer of mercy. That's what Jesus does through parables. Stories are often the best way to teach virtues and theology.

The enchanted world of Middle-earth also helps us break out of the stunted materialistic worldview that holds sway in our culture—not the "He who has the most toys wins" kind of materialism, but the kind that reduces all of us to mere molecules in motion and everything that happens solely to physical causes.

Materialism asserts that nothing but matter and energy exist, which means the entire spiritual realm, including God and objective morality, can't exist either. Most atheists assert materialism is true because they have no coherent way of explaining how immaterial reality can exist without God.

Unfortunately for them, materialism undercuts itself. For if true, the rationality necessary for us to find truth—including the assumed truth that only matter and energy exist—can't be trusted because our thoughts are merely the product of blind physics rather than reason.

No one revealed the bankruptcy of this atheistic worldview better than C. S. Lewis, who wrote:

Suppose there was no intelligence behind the universe, no creative mind. In that case nobody designed my brain for the purpose of thinking. It is merely that when the atoms inside my skull happen for physical or chemical reasons to arrange themselves in a certain way, this gives me, as a by-product, the sensation I call thought. But if so, how can I trust my own thinking to be true? It's like upsetting a milk-jug and hoping that the way the splash arranges itself will give you a map of London. But if I can't trust my own thinking, of course I can't trust the arguments leading to atheism, and therefore have no reason to be an atheist, or anything else. Unless I believe in God, I can't believe in thought: so I can never use thought to disbelieve in God.[7]

As usual, Lewis is spot on. Unless we were designed to have a mind with free will that can transcend mere physics—something atheism denies—then reason shouldn't work. Yet here we are, thinking away. In other words, since we obviously *can* trust our thinking, we should not trust any worldview that makes real thinking impossible by their, literally, unreasonable assumptions. Atheistic materialism does just that.

In the blind predetermined world of materialism, meaning and morality don't exist either. For if human beings are nothing but molecular machines—mere moist robots—driven completely by the laws of physics, then not only are your thoughts untrustworthy, but you have no responsibility for your behavior (physics made you do it!). And your life and the lives of your loved ones ultimately amount to nothing.

Do you *really* believe the people you love the most are nothing but bags of chemicals? Do you *really* believe murder is not objectively morally different from love? Do you *really* believe there is no such thing as good or bad, saint or sinner, rationality or irrationality, love or justice? You have to believe those things to be a consistent materialist, and you have to take them on blind faith, since materialism makes thinking unreliable.

Tolkien and Lewis both understood that materialism is far too restrictive a worldview to explain the dignity of human beings and the virtues that we all know exist and that we all long for. Today, our impulse for justice and utopia is just as strong as theirs. We all know this world is fallen, as the headlines and protests attest, and we all long for the world to be set right. Tolkien's world amps up the reality of injustice and virtue to get us to better recognize them in our own world. In this sense, *The Lord of the Rings* is not an escape from our world but an awakening to our world as it really is.

Now, let's see how Tolkien does all this through three heroes central to the story: Gandalf, Aragorn, and Frodo.

Gandalf: A Messenger of God

The wizard Gandalf is one of the few characters who plays a major role in both *The Hobbit* and *The Lord of the Rings*. Gandalf is of a race of beings called the Maiar (Istari in Elvish) that outwardly resemble men but are much greater in wisdom and power. There are five Maiar in total who were sent to Middle-earth to contend with Sauron, and three appear in *The Lord of the Rings*—Saruman the White, Radagast the Brown, and Gandalf the Grey.[8]

At first glance, Gandalf appears to be on a Christlike story arc, similar to Aslan in *The Chronicles of Narnia*. He is the first to identify the true nature of the Ring when he correctly guesses that it is the same Ring that Aragorn's ancestor Isildur took after cutting it from Sauron's hand thousands of years earlier. Gandalf is the one who gathers the Fellowship together, sets their course, and chooses their path. He "dies" fighting the Balrog in Moria, and the Fellowship is distraught at his passing, not unlike Jesus' followers after His crucifixion. Gandalf later "resurrects," receives new powers, and is reborn as Gandalf the White. He continues the fight against Sauron until Sauron is defeated. How much closer to Christ can you get?

Well, the answer is actually a lot closer. There is no one hero in *The Lord of the Rings* who represents all of the characteristics of Jesus. Tolkien spreads them out among many. While Gandalf's resurrection story mirrors that of Christ, Tolkien, in his writings, likens Gandalf to an angel:

> He was an incarnate "angel" . . . sent to Middle-earth, as the great crisis of Sauron loomed on the horizon. By "incarnate" I mean they were embodied in physical bodies capable of pain, and weariness, and of afflicting the spirit with physical fear, and of being "killed". . . . Why they should take such a form is . . . precisely to limit and hinder their exhibition of "power" on the physical plane, and so that they should do what they were primarily sent for: train, advise, instruct, arouse the hearts and minds of those threatened by Sauron to a resistance with their own strengths, and not just to do the job for them.[9]

In the Bible, an angel is a messenger of God. That's what Gandalf is. He's not the savior of the world; he's the one moving behind the scenes, guiding and nurturing the people who will be the saviors. They will defeat the Satan figure, Sauron, not him.

While Gandalf is fearsome in battle, he never faces Sauron or even his chief lieutenant, the Witch-king, in single combat. In fact, he even acknowledges that he would likely not triumph in a contest of arms, telling Aragorn, "I am Gandalf, Gandalf the White, but Black is mightier still." Later, after their triumphant victory at the Battle of the Pelennor Fields, he doubles down on this assertion:

> Against the Power that has now arisen there is no victory.
> . . . Hardly has our strength sufficed to beat off the first great assault. The next will be greater. This war then is without final hope, as Denethor perceived. Victory cannot be achieved by arms. . . . I still hope for victory, but not by arms.

Gandalf's mission is to guide and teach more than it is to fight. It's the relationships he develops with Frodo, Aragorn, and others that help them jointly defeat Sauron.

Gandalf is similar to angels in other ways. There is a hierarchy among the Maiar, just as there is a hierarchy of angels in the Bible. (Michael, for example, is described as an "archangel" in Jude 9, implying that he has authority over other angels.) The Maiar are initially presided over by Saruman, whom Gandalf describes as "the chief of my order and the head of the Council." After Gandalf's return from the "dead" and Saruman's betrayal, Gandalf takes Saruman's place.

Unlike almost every other major character, Gandalf is given no genealogy by Tolkien, implying that, like angels, he has no parents and no children, nor does he have any romantic interests. It is also clear he serves a higher power. Upon his resurrection, he comments, "Naked I was sent back—for a brief time, until my task is done." He echoes this in his comments to Denethor, the steward of Gondor, saying,

The rule of no realm is mine, neither of Gondor or any other, great or small. But all worthy things that are in peril as the world now stands, those are my care. . . . For I also am a steward. Did you not know?

Gandalf's most significant contributions as an angelic advisor and teacher are to Frodo, who trusts Gandalf implicitly to guide him in a world in which he is out of place. If Frodo fails, the world is over.

It is Gandalf who recognizes that the hobbits are the world's only hope. The best fighters, like Aragorn, Legolas, Gimli, and Boromir, are relegated to the sidelines because the power of the Ring is toxic, even to the most noble among them. Only the least among them—hobbits—Gandalf concludes, have any hope of resisting the Ring's temptations long enough to get the job done.

This contrast is by design. In their book *Finding God in The Lord of the Rings*, Kurt Bruner and Jim Ware note part of the appeal of Frodo is that he acts in contrast to his culture. We expect knights to be courageous—it's part of their job. But we truly admire and aspire to be like ordinary people who do extraordinary things, and Frodo, by any reasonable standard, is ordinary. *Rocky* doesn't become one of the best sports movies of all time if he is a champion in his prime, winning fights he's supposed to win. Instead, we root for underdogs and are enthralled with ordinary people who are willing to sacrifice everything in order to accomplish something great.

Perhaps Gandalf's most important counsel across *The Hobbit* and *The Lord of the Rings* is to show pity on the creature Gollum, the previous owner of the Ring. Gollum serves as our warning about the dangers of the Ring's power and, ultimately, the power of sin. This is described briefly by Galadriel in the opening credits of *The Fellowship of the Ring*: "The Ring gave to Gollum unnatural long life. For five hundred years it poisoned his mind."

The scenery is even more dramatic in *The Return of the King*, where we see Smeagol kill his cousin Deagol over the Ring. We then watch it slowly consume him to the point where he shuns the outside world to live alone in the Misty Mountains for hundreds of years, adopting a new name, Gollum, and forgetting his previous life. Notice that Gollum possesses an object that grants him untold power as well as the ability to become invisible and yet he still chooses to live in isolation. The Ring granted him unnatural long life, but as Gandalf notes, "He hated it and loved it, as he hated and loved himself."

Once Gollum loses the Ring and Bilbo finds it in *The Hobbit*, he finally departs from his home under the mountain to regain his "Precious." That brings Gollum to Frodo. But before we get to Frodo, let's take a look at the coming king.

Aragorn: The Concealed and Revealed King

The Bible teaches that one day the world will be set right. In fact, heaven and earth will become one. This will occur after the return of King Jesus, who will rejoin the immaterial souls of the redeemed with their resurrected bodies. He will wipe every tear from their eyes and then live forever with them in a remade heaven and earth, free of sin, pain, sickness, and death. All things will be remade new, except those who want to continue in their rebellion and stay in their sin. God will grant them their wish to stay separated from Him. But their evil will be defeated, quarantined in a place called hell.

The Lord of the Rings makes similar promises. The king will return to set things right, defeat evil, and restore peace. That's why the title of Frodo and Bilbo's journal about their adventures is titled "The Downfall of the Lord of the Rings and the Return of the King." Sauron (the Lord of the Rings) will be defeated when the King (Aragorn) returns.

But neither Jesus nor Aragorn meet the expectations of the people when they first arrive. They don't look or act like kings, at least not the kings their people were expecting!

Aragorn seems miscast as a king, especially early on in the story. We are introduced to him in *The Fellowship of the Ring* as the hobbits flee the Shire and are pursued by Sauron's Ringwraiths (also known as the Nazgul)—ancient kings of men who have fallen under Sauron's sway. Aragorn starts the story going by the name of Strider. He helps save the hobbits from the Ringwraiths in the town of Bree, though the hobbits are initially mistrustful of him. He appears to be rough around the edges and not at all kingly.

When he accompanies them into the wilderness as they journey to Rivendell, we see the following conversation between Frodo and his fellow hobbit, Merry:

> **MERRY:** [*whispered aside*] How do we know this Strider is a friend of Gandalf?

> **FRODO:** I think a servant of the enemy would look fairer and feel fouler.

> **MERRY:** He's foul enough.

> **FRODO:** We have no choice but to trust him.

Not exactly how you'd dream up your ideal king now, is it?

When Jesus arrives in Jerusalem, the reviews from His people are even worse. He looks and acts nothing like the King the Jewish establishment expected. They wanted and expected a political king who would overthrow the Romans in the land, not the sin in their hearts. The sacrificial King wasn't anticipated or desired. (Only by looking back in the Scriptures does the prophesied plan become clear.) The conquering King is coming, but that's not until Jesus returns.

The main point of the incarnation is not that Jesus is God—although that's certainly necessary and true. The main point of the incarnation is that the King is coming to earth to set things right and to rule. This will be fully accomplished when He comes again.

In addition to their less-than-welcoming reception, both Jesus and Aragorn are slow to reveal their true identity and for similar reasons. Both need time to complete their missions. Revealing their identity too early or too overtly could be counterproductive. If you want people to follow you freely and without coercion, you may want to win them over by the strength of your character rather than overwhelming them with the obvious power of a king.

Like Jesus, Aragorn continues to quietly prove his worth, knowing that it is not yet time to overtly reveal himself. Boromir, a warrior of great renown in this story, is originally skeptical of him because his father, Denethor, serves as the steward of Gondor who awaits the return of the king. Yet he eventually begins to respect Aragorn, saying shortly before his death, "I would have followed you, my brother . . . my captain, my king."

As we mentioned earlier, the parallels between Jesus and Aragorn are not exact because *The Lord of the Rings* is a parable of the biblical story, not a strict allegory. So unlike Jesus, Aragorn needs to quell his own doubts about his worthiness. He is haunted by the tale of his forefather, Isildur, who thousands of years prior had cut the Ring from Sauron's hand. But instead of destroying it, he'd claimed it for his own. When Isildur was killed, the Ring was lost, eventually being found by Gollum and then Bilbo. The story was so well known across the land that many referred to the Ring as "Isildur's Bane."

Aragorn even fears that he will fall into the same trap as Isildur. He says as much to his future queen, Arwen, in Rivendell:

ARWEN: Why do you fear the past? You are Isildur's heir, not Isildur himself. You are not bound to his fate.

ARAGORN: The same blood flows in my veins . . . the same weakness . . .

ARWEN: Your time will come. You will face the same evil. And
you will defeat it. . . . The shadow does not hold sway yet
. . . not over you and not over me.

She is later proved correct. While Boromir falls under the Ring's
sway and tries to take it from Frodo, Aragorn, like Jesus, resists the
temptation and stays true to the mission, telling Frodo before they part
ways, "I would have gone with you to the end . . . into the very fires of
Mordor."

One thing that isn't in doubt is Aragorn's combat prowess. He defeats
several of the Nazgul at once on Weathertop Hill and slices through
the opposition in several other battles, culminating in his leading the
defense of Helm's Deep in *The Two Towers*. But he still refuses to openly
embrace his rightful title as the king of Gondor, preferring to remain
anonymous as a ranger from the North. He even allows Gandalf to lead
the Fellowship until Gandalf falls to the Balrog in Moria. When Gandalf
"resurrects," Aragorn again defers to him.

Jesus defeats His enemy, Satan, twice: first overcoming his temptations in the desert by quoting the Scriptures; and second, by sacrificing
Himself to free us from the penalty of our sins. While Tolkien acknowledges that Aragorn is a valiant warrior, it isn't really the focus of what
makes him a worthy king. Instead, Tolkien seems more concerned about
four things that make him a true king and savior: (1) his ability to resist
the temptation of the Ring (sin); (2) his ability to lead and influence
even those who are skeptical about him (like Boromir); (3) his willingness to sacrifice his life for his people; and (4) his ability to heal. These
are all qualities of Jesus.

We first see Aragorn's ability to heal at Weathertop. When Frodo
is stabbed by the Witch-king (the leader of the Nazgul), it is Aragorn
who manages to keep him alive until he can receive further care from
Elrond in Rivendell. But a more drastic example is after the Battle of
the Pelennor Fields. In the battle, Merry and Eowyn are nearly killed

by the Witch-king the day after Boromir's brother, Faramir, was badly wounded. After the battle, Aragorn goes to the Houses of Healing and is able to revive each of them from the brink of death. Tolkien actually spends an entire chapter on this in *The Return of the King*, writing that:

> At the doors of the Houses many were already gathered to see Aragorn, and they followed after him; and when at last he had supped, men came and prayed that he would heal their kinsmen or their friends whose lives were in peril through hurt or wound, or who lay under the Black Shadow. And Aragorn arose and went out, and he sent for the sons of Elrond, and together they laboured far into the night. And word went through the City: 'The King is come again indeed.' And they named him Elfstone, because of the green stone that he wore, and so the name which it was foretold at his birth that he should bear was chosen for him by his own people.

Note the similarity to Jesus in Matthew 15:29-31:

> Jesus left there and went along the Sea of Galilee. Then he went up on a mountainside and sat down. Great crowds came to him, bringing the lame, the blind, the crippled, the mute and many others, and laid them at his feet; and he healed them. The people were amazed when they saw the mute speaking, the crippled made well, the lame walking and the blind seeing. And they praised the God of Israel.

Aragorn not only heals his people but, like a noble king, is also willing to sacrifice himself for them. If his people and the world are going to be saved, Aragorn must take action that will likely cost him his life. He wants to march out the remnants of the armies of Rohan and

Gondor in order to force Sauron's much superior forces to empty Mordor and engage in battle. It's a last, desperate hope—not for victory by strength in battle but as a way of getting safe passage for Frodo and Sam through Mordor, which would otherwise be crawling with Orcs.

Gimli sums up this plan to divert Sauron perfectly: "Certainty of death. Small chance of success. What are we waiting for?"

With his small remaining army now assembled for battle, just seconds away from almost certain death, Aragorn charges back and forth on horseback in front of his men, yelling these words:

> Hold your ground—hold your ground! Sons of Gondor—of Rohan . . . my brothers! I see in your eyes the same fear that would take the heart of me. The day may come when the courage of Men fails; when we forsake our friends and break all bonds of fellowship; but it is not this day—an hour of wolves and shattered shields, when the Age of Man comes crashing down—but it is not this day!!! This day we fight! By all that you hold dear on this good earth—I bid you stand, Men of the West!

This is Aragorn's final act to prove his mettle—inspiring his men to stand and fight in the face of impossible odds with the hope that two small hobbits will have the chance to fulfill their quest. Will their desperate gamble pay off? Everything now depends on Frodo.

Frodo: The Power of Weakness

While Frodo exhibits some heroic attributes, most of his qualities seem to work against hero status. In addition to the fact that he's only three feet tall, he is passive. He doesn't seek out adventure, riches, or power. You get the distinct impression that he'd rather be at home in the Shire with his friends than trying to save the world. He also isn't the smartest or the bravest, even among the hobbits.

Yet the tiny Frodo somehow endures hunger, thirst, heat, cold, physical injury, and countless other challenges without complaint. Over the course of his journey, he is stabbed with a poisoned knife on Weathertop; nearly freezes to death trying to climb a mountain as Saruman sends snowstorms against the Fellowship; is almost impaled by a spear in Moria; is nearly killed by Boromir, a member of the Fellowship who tries to take the Ring from him; has to fight off several murder attempts by the Ring-coveting Gollum; is stung and nearly mummified by the giant spider, Shelob; and has to traverse the barren wasteland of Mordor with little food and almost no water.

The entire time all these trials challenge him, Frodo has to carry around the Ring, which seems to grow physically heavier the closer he gets to his goal. It weighs down his spirit so much that he can't even remember the taste of food by the time they get to Mount Doom.

How does he accomplish all of this? His weaknesses lead to a strength we call humility, which brings Frodo to ask for help. Frodo thus solves most of his challenges by asking for help, by following his intuition, and by sheer force of will rather than through superpowers or combat prowess. As Tolkien is said to have put it, "It is not the strength of the body, but the strength of the spirit."

Frodo asks for help many times from Gandalf, Galadriel, and his fellow hobbit and traveling partner, Sam Gamgee, who is the most loyal and helpful of them all, despite being rebuffed by Frodo more than once.

FRODO: Go back, Sam! I'm going to Mordor alone.

SAM: Of course you are, and I'm coming with you!

Sam is loyal, no matter the obstacle. The real problem is Gollum, who is deceptively acting as a "guide" for Frodo through Mordor. He attempts to drive a wedge between Sam and Frodo so that he can get back his "Precious"—the Ring. Gollum frames Sam (whom he calls "the fat hobbit who hates Gollum"), which entices Frodo to make a nearly fatal mistake. He tells Sam to go home while on the very doorstep of Mordor!

No longer under the watchful eye of Sam, Gollum can now lead Frodo into a trap and steal the Ring. Thankfully, it's not long before Sam shakes off the rejection and returns to save Frodo from three of the most disgusting opponents you could imagine: the conniving, double-crossing Gollum; a giant venomous spider ten times his size; and several murderous, slime-spewing Orcs whose breath alone could wilt a warrior. Sam stands up to them all and frees Frodo!

As Gimli put it, "Faithless is he that says farewell when the road darkens." The road becomes nearly pitch black, but faithful Sam will not be deterred.

Because of Sam, they are now able to press on toward Mount Doom and the completion of their quest. Sauron doesn't see them coming. Like most tyrants, he assumes his foes will do what he would do in their position—use the power of the Ring to conquer in battle.

Frodo has access to the Ring and yet chooses not to use it. Like Jesus, who had access to infinite power, he walks freely to his doom to save the world. Death is conquered with meekness and humility, not strength and power.

Since the powers of darkness do not understand that evil can be defeated by sacrifice rather than power, Sauron assumes Aragorn has the Ring and empties Mordor to meet him in battle outside the Black Gate. This allows Frodo and Sam to cross unscathed through Mordor.

Several times in his letters, Tolkien insists that Sam is "the chief hero" of *The Lord of the Rings*. That's never more obvious than when Frodo collapses carrying the Ring up Mount Doom.

Speaking of the Ring and then Frodo, Sam declares, "I can't carry it for you, but I can carry you!" He then fireman-carries Frodo through, well, fire! (Can you imagine a better friend than Sam?)

Sam here provides a beautiful picture of the suffering servant predicted by the prophet Isaiah and fulfilled in Jesus, who not only died for us but also bears our burdens. While Christ rarely takes our burdens completely from us (if He did, we wouldn't grow), Jesus does carry us through difficulty.

He urges us, "Come to me, all you who are weary and burdened, and I will give you rest. Take my yoke upon you and learn from me, for I am gentle and humble in heart, and you will find rest for your souls. For my yoke is easy and my burden is light" (Matthew 11:28-30; see also Psalm 68:19-20). Peter echoes Christ's words when he tells us to "Cast all your anxiety on him because he cares for you" (1 Peter 5:7).

Like Frodo, we need to admit we are weak and ask for help. Like Sam, we need to serve and help the weak whenever we can.

Thanks to Sam, Frodo is now standing inside Mount Doom and over the volcano. All he needs to do to complete their insanely difficult mission of saving the world is to simply drop the Ring into the lava. But suddenly he refuses to do it!

> Then Frodo stirred and spoke with a clear voice, indeed with a voice clearer and more powerful than Sam had ever heard him use, and it rose above the throb and turmoil of Mount Doom, ringing in the roof and walls.
>
> "I have come," he said. "But I do not choose now to do what I came to do. I will not do this deed. The Ring is mine!"

Gollum suddenly reappears and begins to fight with Frodo to recover the Ring. This shouldn't be happening. Gollum's behavior should have led to his demise several times by now. Why has he been spared? To see why, we have to go way back to when Gandalf urged Frodo to have pity and show mercy to Gollum as Bilbo already had. Here is the conversation they had in the Mines of Moria, all the way back in *The Fellowship of the Ring*:

"It was Pity that stayed [Bilbo's] hand. Pity, and Mercy: not to strike without need. . . ."

"I am sorry," said Frodo. "But I am frightened; and I do not feel any pity for Gollum."

"You have not seen him," Gandalf broke in.

"No, and I don't want to," said Frodo. "I can't understand you. Do you mean to say that you, and the Elves, have let him live on after all those horrible deeds? Now at any rate he is as bad as an Orc, and just an enemy. He deserves death."

"Deserves it! I daresay he does. Many that live deserve death. And some that die deserve life. Can you give it to them? Then do not be too eager to deal out death in judgement. For even the very wise cannot see all ends. I have not much hope that Gollum can be cured before he dies, but there is a chance of it. And he is bound up with the fate of the Ring. My heart tells me that he has some part to play yet, for good or ill, before the end; and when that comes, the pity of Bilbo may rule the fate of many—yours not least."[10]

Gandalf, a messenger from God, knew that Gollum needed to be spared because his evil deeds would somehow play a part in the fate of the universe. He was right.

During the fight for the Ring, Gollum bites off Frodo's finger and is reunited with his Precious at last. But as he celebrates his triumph, he stumbles and falls into the lava, destroying himself and his idol, the Ring. The words of Jesus couldn't be more aptly applied: "Whoever finds their life will lose it, and whoever loses their life for my sake will find it" (Matthew 10:39).

As the Ring dissolves, Mordor is destroyed along with Sauron and his evil allies. Somehow, totally unseen by the plans of men, the quest is achieved. It's as if a mysterious force had been working behind the scenes all along.

There was. We call it Providence—God working behind the scenes. Frodo made a valiant effort, but there's no room for pride. He cannot claim that it was on his power alone that the task was completed. As noted Tolkien scholar Stratford Caldecoot says, "It is not Frodo who saves Middle Earth at all, nor Gollum. It can only be God himself, working through the love and freedom of his creatures. The scene is a triumph of Providence over Evil but also a triumph of Mercy."[11]

The idea that there is a higher power working for good is seen periodically throughout *The Lord of the Rings*, though rarely is it so apparent. Tolkien writes:

> I have purposely kept all allusions to the highest matters down
> to mere hints, perceptible only by the most attentive. . . .
> So God and the angelic gods . . . only peep through in such
> places as Gandalf's conversation with Frodo: "behind that
> there was something else at work, beyond any design of the
> Ring-maker's."[12]

It made no sense to pity Gollum and show him mercy repeatedly, but that's because we are stuck in time and can't see the ripple effect of all the interacting choices and forces that bring forth the final results. As Gandalf put it, "For even the very wise cannot see all the ends."

This insight certainly helps us make sense of what appears to us to be purposeless evil in our own lives. Things might not make sense at the moment, but there is an unseen realm that only God can see completely. He brings good from evil. Paul assures us, saying, "We know that all things work together for good to those who love God, to those who are the called according to His purpose" (Romans 8:28, NKJV). Notice he doesn't say all things *are* good, but that they *work together for good*. Nor does he say that we *see* God causing all things to work together for good. It says that we *know* God is doing that.

Sauron, Gollum, or people in your own life might do evil (as we all do), but good will ultimately triumph if you align yourself with Jesus. God can use our evil, and even the evil of lifelong atheists, to ripple forward for good!

Once freed of the Ring's influence, Frodo remembers what Gandalf said:

> Do you remember Gandalf's words: Even Gollum may have something yet to do? But for him, Sam, I could not have destroyed the Ring. The Quest would have been in vain, even at the bitter end. So let us forgive him! For the Quest is achieved, and now all is over. I am glad you are here with me. Here at the end of all things, Sam.

Given the similar circumstances, Frodo could say to Gollum what Joseph said to his brothers who sold him into slavery years before: "You meant evil against me, but God meant it for good in order to bring about this present result, to keep many people alive" (Genesis 50:20, NASB).

The defeat of evil and the salvation of the world required the trio of heroes to each do their part. Gandalf had to arrange the pieces on the chessboard in such a way that the team would be successful. Frodo had to bear the brunt of the hardship and take the Ring into Mordor. And Aragorn had to inspire his men to make salvation possible. Their tasks are similar to those of the triune Godhead: The Father plans salvation; the Son accomplishes salvation; and the Holy Spirit inspires salvation among the people.

Weak Heroes of the Bible

It is in his use of the weak, perhaps more than anywhere else, that we see Tolkien's true Christian colors. Just a brief look at a few of the biggest heroes in the Bible will demonstrate this point. These are unlikely "heroes" because they are all either physically, emotionally, or morally weak.

- *Abraham*: Like Frodo, he doesn't even know where he is going. When he gets there, he doesn't wait on God's promise but takes matters into his own hands (another woman). He also lies (twice!) to protect himself, putting his wife in danger each time. Nevertheless, God blesses the entire world through Abraham.

- *Joseph*: The spoiled youngest son of Jacob is sold into slavery and then put into jail in Egypt on false charges. Yet he rises to a very high position in Egypt and saves his family and other countrymen from famine. God uses the evil done to someone weak to bring about good.

- *Moses*: He's a stutterer and murderer who's afraid to accept God's call on his life. When he finally does, he wanders around the desert for forty years and morally fails to the point where God doesn't permit him to enter the Promised Land. But Moses liberates Israel from slavery to Egypt, which foreshadows Christ, who liberates the world from slavery to sin.

- *David*: He's a shepherd boy and the most unlikely of Jesse's sons to be anointed king. Soon after he is anointed by Samuel, he has to run for his life from the current king, Saul, who wants him dead. After David becomes king, he sabotages his reign by committing adultery with Bathsheba and then murdering her husband to cover up his sin. His moral failures weaken his reign so much that he has to flee from his own son who wants his crown. Yet through David's line, the Messiah comes!

- *Matthew*: He's a hated tax collector for the Romans, which means his own people consider him a traitor of Israel. Yet he writes a biography of Jesus (a Gospel) to the very Jews who consider him a traitor!

- *Peter*: He's an impulsive hothead and an ordinary fisherman. He's not a man of high social status or power. But Peter becomes the leader of the apostles and writes two letters in the New Testament.

- *Mark*: He's a traveling companion of Paul until he can't take it anymore and cuts the trip short. Paul is so annoyed that Mark has abandoned him that he won't take Mark on the next trip. Yet Mark matures and writes a Gospel that most scholars say is based on the experiences of Peter.

- *Mary Magdalene*: She's a formerly demon-possessed woman and one of the first witnesses of the Resurrection. Women were not considered reliable witnesses in that culture (and certainly not women who had been demon-possessed!), but that doesn't stop God from making her an eyewitness to the most important event in human history.

- *John*: He's just a teenager during the ministry of Jesus, yet he writes the most unique of all the Gospels and four other letters of the New Testament, including the book of Revelation.

- *Paul*: He's a man of prominence, but not the kind of prominence you might expect—he's an outspoken enemy and persecutor of Christians. He goes from a position of strength as a Pharisee to a position of weakness as a Christian. He writes nearly half of the books of the New Testament.

- *Most of all, Jesus*: He goes from most to least when He leaves heaven for earth and takes on the weakness of a human being, first as an infant and eventually as a sacrificial Lamb. As Paul observed, Jesus gave up the privileges of being God on earth and "humbled himself by becoming obedient to death—even death on a cross!" (Philippians 2:8).

God even used a weak nation to get all of this done. As Moses wrote about the people who would become Israel, "The Lord did not set his affection on you and choose you because you were more numerous than other peoples, for you were the fewest of all peoples" (Deuteronomy 7:7).

If God can use weak people in the Bible, why can't He use me and you? He can, and He does. God uses the weak to get His will accomplished. Ultimately, it is through weakness that Christ saves the world. And it is through weakness that Middle-earth is saved. As Lady Galadriel put it, "Even the smallest person can change the course of history."

Paul learned to rely on God through weakness and thus admitted what may seem like a paradox to the world but not to the Christian: "When I am weak, then I am strong" (2 Corinthians 12:10). Weakness becomes power when it forces you to rely on God. We must admit our weakness if we are going to be saved because we cannot save ourselves.

The King Returns

The time for the coronation has come. The king has returned. We finally see the transformation from Strider, the ranger of the North, into the king of Gondor. Although Aragorn has been the king all along, he isn't officially coronated as king until he's proven himself worthy of the title by defeating Sauron. Salvation comes first, then the coronation. Just like in the Bible.

The coronation Tolkien gives Aragorn is fitting, much like what we might imagine will be given to the true King, Jesus, when He returns:

> Then Frodo came forward and took the crown from Faramir and bore it to Gandalf; and Aragorn knelt, and Gandalf set the White Crown upon his head, and said: "Now come the days of the King, and may they be blessed while the thrones of the Valar endure!" But when Aragorn arose all that beheld him gazed in silence, for it seemed to them that he was revealed to them now for the first time. Tall as the sea-kings of old, he stood above all that were near; ancient of days he seemed and yet in the flower of manhood; and wisdom sat upon his brow, and strength and healing were in his hands, and a light was about him.[13]

Now that evil has been defeated and salvation accomplished, we also see Aragorn take Arwen as his bride. She symbolizes the church.

When King Jesus returns, He will "marry" His people, the church, and live with them forever after securing salvation and defeating evil (Revelation 21:2-4). What was lost in the beginning of the Bible is restored at the end—God's creation and God's people are made new as depicted in the wedding scene at the end of the Bible.

You're invited to that wedding. In fact, the five-word summary of Christianity is this: *God wants to marry you.* Are you going to accept the invitation? If you do, everything sad will one day come untrue.

For Personal Reflection or Family/Small Group Discussion

1. What is the most attractive/unattractive characteristic of Frodo to you? Why?

2. If Aragorn were *your* king, would you follow him? Why or why not?

3. How does God use the weak and ordinary to accomplish His will? Why are you stronger in your relationship with God when you are weak?

4. What is Sam's greatest characteristic? To whom are you a Sam?

5. The end of the chapter sums up Christianity this way: God wants to marry you. Do you agree or disagree? Why?

6

BATMAN

*Maybe it's time we stop trying to outsmart
the truth and let it have its day.*

ALFRED, *The Dark Knight Rises*

CHOOSE ANY VILLAIN FROM any story you want and turn them loose: Thanos, the Joker, Lord Voldemort, Darth Vader, Loki, take your pick. If you only get to pick one hero to stop them, who would it be and why?

It might seem easy to pick someone really powerful like Superman or the Incredible Hulk. But even god-like characters often have obvious weaknesses, like kryptonite or a bad temper. Smarter ones like Iron Man can have their emotions manipulated or their families targeted. You might want to pick Captain America to lead a team of heroes, but without his team he's pretty vulnerable. So, who should you pick?

In our opinion the clear answer is Batman—especially director Christopher Nolan's version of the character played by Christian Bale in *The Dark Knight* trilogy. Despite the fact that he is one of the few characters we talk about in this book without superpowers, Batman is the only superhero who has mastered his body, his will, his emotions, *and* his mind.

Put him up against a villain like Thanos, who is more powerful, and Batman can outsmart him. Put him up against the Joker, who wants to test his resolve, and Batman will not be denied victory. Put him up against Loki, who will want to deceive and manipulate him, and he will use his cunning to out-trick the mischievous trickster himself. Batman is even ready to fight Superman in case the world's most powerful hero turns into a villain. As Commissioner Jim Gordon recognizes, Batman is a watchful protector who stands ready to combat any foe and come out on top.

Batman is so prepared that he has plans in place to defeat the entire Justice League should they go rogue. He even has plans in place *for his own defeat* should he go rogue!

But recent depictions of his character by director Zack Snyder have demonstrated that Batman has his flaws and limits. As we will see, Batman is actually fighting two endless wars: one against himself and one against a growing culture of crime. His rigid personal discipline allows him to fight his baser nature, though he can never truly conquer it. Even Batman will need to repent.

Mainstreaming Superhero Movies

BARRY ALLEN (THE FLASH): What's your superpower again?

BRUCE WAYNE: I'm rich.

Despite lacking a specific superpower, Batman is without a doubt one of the most compelling superheroes who has ever been created. Since his creation by Bob Kane and Bill Finger in 1939, Batman's popularity has increased to the point where he is probably the most widely known superhero in America today. His unique blend of skills and relatable background give him a cross-cultural appeal that is undeniable, con-sidering the number of films that continue to be released featuring the character. And one particular Batman movie helped mainstream the entire genre of superhero movies.

The 1989 movie called *Batman*, directed by Tim Burton, is often viewed as the progenitor for the superhero genre of movies that has exploded in popularity in the last thirty years. It paired a major studio with a large budget, a talented director, and A-list actors such as Michael Keaton (Batman) and Jack Nicholson (the Joker). Since then, Batman has been played by several other famous (some even Oscar-winning) actors, including Val Kilmer, George Clooney, Christian Bale, Ben Affleck, and Robert Pattinson (movie forthcoming). But the success of Burton's film proved the general public had a big appetite for more. Without *Batman*, there may have been none of the subsequent DC or Marvel superhero movies that have since dominated the box office.

Despite his immense popularity, Batman has also undergone some pretty extreme makeovers since his release. Batman was originally introduced as a ruthless vigilante who didn't care if he maimed or killed the criminals he was hunting. This was toned down in the post–World War II era and eventually led to the lighthearted and gimmicky version of Batman portrayed by Adam West in the 1960s *Batman* TV show. It championed the importance of seat belts and eating vegetables and featured a utility belt that somehow held large cans of shark repellant and a giant bulletproof shield that could be deployed at a moment's notice.

Batman seemed to be fading from the public eye in the 1970s and early 1980s. But Frank Miller's *The Dark Knight Returns* comic book series in 1986 brought Batman back to his darker roots and laid the foundation for what most of us would consider to be the modern interpretation of Batman. This is the version of the character that has made its way into the latest movies and TV shows, and it is the version we will explore in this chapter.

The Caped Crusader

"The Caped Crusader" might seem like a throwaway title, but it actually demonstrates that Batman is absolutely on a crusade against crime. The word *crusade* has a religious connotation that communicates a fervor reserved for only the most intense of causes. You will find few if any people as intense as Batman, and thus *crusade* is probably the best word to describe his all-encompassing war on crime.

Batman is on a crusade because it's personal, and things usually only become important to people when they become personal. The seeds of Batman are planted when a young Bruce Wayne attends an evening show with his wealthy parents, Dr. Thomas and Martha Wayne. After the show, Bruce's parents are murdered in front of him by a small-time criminal, Joe Chill, in a robbery gone wrong.

It's easy to gloss over this event for those familiar with the story, but this event has a profound impact on Bruce. A good description of how it changes him is found in *The Dark Knight Rises* by John Blake (played by Joseph Gordon-Levitt), who also experienced the death of his parents when he was a child. He says this:

> Not a lot of people know what it feels like to be angry, in your bones. I mean, they understand, foster parents, everybody understands, for a while. Then they want the angry little kid to do something he knows he can't do, move on. So after a while they stop understanding. They send the angry kid to a boy's home. I figured it out too late. You gotta learn to hide the anger, practice smiling in the mirror. It's like putting on a mask.

After the death of his parents, Bruce starts down the road to putting on a mask after he swears an oath to spend the rest of his life fighting crime. He embarks on an intense regimen of intellectual and physical training that involves spending time abroad as well as receiving a world-class education. Upon returning to Gotham as a young man, Bruce knows he can't fight crime as himself. He needs an alter ego. Drawing upon a frightening experience with bats in his youth, Bruce aims to inflict that same fear on criminals by adopting the persona of a bat. In *Batman Begins*, Bruce describes his reasoning behind this by saying:

> People need dramatic examples to shake them out of apathy, and I can't do that as Bruce Wayne. As a man, I'm flesh and blood. I can be ignored. I can be destroyed. But as a symbol, I can be incorruptible, I can be everlasting.

Here's our first departure from most comic book heroes. Bruce is not wearing a mask to hide himself or his family. He's doing it to inspire others. Part of the legend of Batman is that he could be anyone.

Bruce uses his vast fortune and newfound skills to arm himself with a wide array of gadgets and technology to assist in his crime-fighting efforts. He also adopts two main rules that govern his behavior:

1. Batman does not use firearms
2. Batman cannot take a life

Batman exists because Bruce acknowledges the law is limited in its ability to stop crime or set things right—Joe Chill getting locked up isn't going to bring his parents back from the dead. In fact, Batman is fully aware that, as a vigilante, he is a criminal himself. He doesn't just want to put a stop to crime; he wants to ensure that justice is served. He realizes that sometimes justice doesn't come from a court of law or the police.

Criminals who go free due to lack of evidence or who bribe their way out of serving their sentences are now met with a menacing figure who stalks them in the night and isn't beholden to the criminal justice system. Still, Batman imposes a great deal of self-restraint on himself. Along with the rules above, Batman always hands criminals over to the police once he catches them.

In other words, Batman understands that goodness does not come naturally to him—he has to fight to overcome his baser impulses. He knows how easy it is to be bad and how hard it is to be good. C. S. Lewis put it best in *Mere Christianity* when he wrote:

> No man knows how bad he is till he has tried very hard to be good. A silly idea is current that good people do not know what temptation means. This is an obvious lie. Only those who try to resist temptation know how strong it is. After all, you find out the strength of the German army by fighting against it, not by giving in. You find out the strength of a wind by trying to walk against it, not by lying down.

In order to be able to save others, Batman must first be strong enough to control his own behavior and resist the temptation to become like the criminals he hunts. He is so obsessed with stopping them that he may be tempted to adopt their tactics.

His obsession encompasses his whole life. Other superheroes have families and want to have some semblance of a normal life. Superman doesn't always want to be responsible for saving the world; he craves downtime with Lois Lane as Clark Kent. Peter Parker wants a life as a normal teenager apart from being Spider-Man. But the inverse is true of Batman. Bruce wants to be free of a "normal" life so that he can hunt criminals. The billionaire Bruce Wayne presented to the people of Gotham is a diversion that masks his true mission: a single-minded devotion to fighting crime.

This is brought out clearly by Selina Kyle (Catwoman) when she asks Bruce, "Who are you pretending to be?" Bruce says, "Bruce Wayne, eccentric billionaire."

In *Batman Begins*, he tells Rachel Dawes, "It's not who I am underneath, it's what I do that defines me." Dangerously, he gets all of his identity from his job.

Notice that Batman doesn't really have a go-to partner like Lois Lane whom he wants to spend his "happily ever after" with. Despite a wealth of opportunity, Bruce's relationships never really go anywhere. Until Gotham is saved, there can be no distractions.

His biggest problem is that the crusade never ends. Here's the repeating cycle that defines almost every Batman story: Batman ventures out to fight crime in Gotham. The villain hatches an evil scheme. Batman must either solve the crime or figure out how to overcome the villain or both. Batman captures the villain and locks him up, thus saving the city. The cycle repeats.

Note here one thing that separates Batman from other heroes: there does not seem to be any way to break this endless and futile cycle. Batman doesn't have just one villain to overcome; his enemy is crime. Because crime will never be truly eradicated from Gotham, there will always be a need for Batman. Retirement doesn't seem to be on the table for Bruce. There is no "happily ever after"; there is just the next night. Both he and his trusty butler, Alfred, are always working.

> **BRUCE WAYNE:** Still working? You're getting slow in your old age, Alfred.

> **ALFRED:** It comes to us all, Master Wayne. Even you've gotten too old to die young, though not for lack of trying.

Not only that, the problem continues to grow. Gotham City keeps getting worse. As we'll see, the frustration this causes leads to Batman getting worse.

Why All the Darkness?

Batman does not give off the "beacon of shining light" motif we often see from other superheroes. He doesn't give press conferences like Tony Stark or speeches to rally the troops like Captain America.

While he certainly wants to inspire the public, his entire persona, all the way down to the costume, is designed to strike fear in the hearts of criminals. What he does is hunt bad guys. Usually alone. And he's almost always hunting them at night. Ever notice that? With the exception of the final fight in *The Dark Knight Rises*, Batman doesn't spend any time in any of the films in daylight. This is intentional on his part.

Most serious crimes are committed at night. Batman is all too happy to meet his foes where they believe that they are safest. He uses the night against his foes—masking his movements and blending in with the darkness, taking what was their greatest strength and using it against them. The hunter becomes the hunted.

In his Gospel, John said, "This is the verdict: Light has come into the world, but people loved darkness instead of light because their deeds were evil. Everyone who does evil hates the light, and will not come into the light for fear that their deeds will be exposed" (John 3:19-20). Our natures are not only bent toward darkness—it's easy to be bad but hard to be good—but we commit most of our sins in the dark, where we think no one else can see them.

Darkness will not hide your sins from Jesus, and neither will it help you in Gotham if Batman has his way. Criminals come to realize that darkness is no longer a safe place to commit a crime in Gotham City. Batman menacingly looms over the city of Gotham like an avenging angel doing his utmost to prevent another tragedy like the one he experienced as a child. Criminals fear him.

In *Batman Begins*, Batman dangles a crooked detective, Arnold Flass, from a rooftop. As he is interrogating him about where some drugs were being sent, Flass tells Batman everything he knows, swearing to God that he is telling the truth. Batman roars back at him "Swear to me!" as if he should fear Batman more than God.

In the original *Batman*, he tells another criminal, "I'm not going to kill you. I want you to do me a favor. I want you to tell all your friends about me."

Just the thought of a *bat man* is scary. Batman's use of technology doesn't define him like it does for say, Iron Man. Take Tony Stark out of the Iron Man suit, and you have a smart, rich guy. Take Bruce Wayne out of the bat suit, and most criminals would still be terrified of him if they knew he was the man behind the mask. He exudes darkness, and he shadows himself in darkness in order to fight it.

Batman is not just fighting in the dark; he's also fighting a losing battle against the darkness of human nature. He knows he can't eradicate evil or turn Gotham into a utopia. He's merely trying to limit the darkness. That's all law enforcement can do. Most laws are designed to prevent people from doing evil. Very few try to compel people to do good.[1]

Given the selfish bent of human nature, the realization that utopia is not possible in this life is what makes the entire Batman series so realistic. As long as human beings exist in our fallen state, there will be no final happy ending here on earth. There will just be night after night of fighting the same problem. For utopia to be achieved, a transformation of human nature must take place, and that's not going to happen by merely locking up bad guys.

In his futile fight against darkness, Batman almost becomes lost in darkness himself. We see this in *Batman v Superman: Dawn of Justice*.

The Problem of Evil in *Batman v Superman*

Many were upset by this film because their heroes seemed to become corrupted. (After all, why would Batman be fighting Superman?) But this movie addresses more theologically rich questions about God, evil, and our culture than any other Batman film, and perhaps any other film we've cited in this book. As one reviewer put it, "It may be a good movie, a bad movie, or anything in between, but it is without question an important film today, and a quintessential product of the America we inhabit."[2]

To see why, let's start with Superman.

Superman is probably the superhero most obviously patterned after Christ. Superman's father (Jor-El) sends his only son to earth to save people from a rebellion, although he knows that humanity will almost certainly reject his son. He comes as an infant and stays disguised as Clark Kent until his appointed time to save the world (age thirty-three), at which time he helps people by using his otherworldly powers and abilities. He experiences suffering and death before rising from the dead to save the world (and there are several other parallels).[3]

So why are people against Superman? And why are Lex Luthor and Batman trying to kill him?

The answer lies in one of the most vexing questions of all time: If there is a good God, why is there evil? Why doesn't He stop it! The film states this question and explores it directly.

After we see flashbacks to the murder of Bruce's parents, Bruce is racing through Metropolis trying to save people from the explosions and falling buildings that are the collateral damage from Superman's battle with General Zod at the end of *Man of Steel*. Bruce comes across one of his employees, Wallace Keith, whose legs are pinned under a steel beam. After removing the beam, he races to save a young girl from falling debris.

Bruce looks angrily up at the flying Superman, the supposed cause of all this mayhem. The look on his face questions the goodness of Superman. He's supposed to be a savior? He's causing all of this damage and would have let this girl die. What kind of a god is he? Despite the fact that Superman is trying to save the world from General Zod, Bruce comes to see Superman as a threat to humanity.

BRUCE WAYNE: He has the power to wipe out the entire human race, and if we believe there's even a one-percent chance

that he is our enemy, we have to take it as an absolute
certainty . . . and we have to destroy him.

ALFRED: But he is not our enemy!

BRUCE WAYNE: Not today. Twenty years in Gotham, Alfred;
we've seen what promises are worth. How many good guys
are left? How many stayed that way?

It makes sense to be concerned about someone getting too much
power. They are likely to abuse that power and use it for evil. History
confirms that. Abraham Lincoln put it well: "Nearly all men can handle
adversity, but if you want to test a man's character, give him power." Lex
Luthor sounds the alarm about granting too much power when he says
to Senator June Finch, "Do you know the oldest lie in America, Senator?
It's that power can be innocent."

Although, curiously, few of us think that truth applies to us personally; we are not distrustful of ourselves when we get power. Lex Luthor is
not concerned that *he* has too much power. We all think we can handle
it—that we can use it innocently. It's all those *other* people we need to
watch out for.

Meanwhile, Wallace Keith, who not only lost his legs but his family
in the fallout, climbs up and spray-paints "False God" in big red letters
on the city's Superman statue. If anyone considers Superman a god,
you're now warned that he's not a good god.

Lex Luthor has the same negative assessment of Superman *and* God.
After throwing Lois Lane off the top of a building to attract Superman
to his location, Lex launches into a scathing putdown of Superman:

We've got problems up here—the problem of evil in the world
. . . the problem of YOU on top of everyone else; you above all;
because that's what God is!

Lex reveals he's upset that God didn't save him from his abusive father. This motivates his rebellion against God and Superman, who both put themselves over human beings. Next, Lex cites the classic problem stated by the Greek philosopher Epicurus (341–270 BC): "I figured out way back, if God is all powerful, He cannot be all good. And if He is all good, then He cannot be all powerful."

He then applies it to Superman as if he's the god of this world, "And neither can you! [The people of this world] need to see the fraud you are with their eyes—the blood on your hands!"

According to Lex and Wallace, Superman is a false god who needs to be exposed for the fraud that he is. Lex eventually gets Superman to bend to his will, which is a satisfying turn: God bends to him rather than the other way around. He also tells Senator June Finch that "devils don't come from beneath us, they come from the sky."

Notice that Lex and Wallace have disdain for God based on their personal experience with evil. A good God would have stopped my abusive dad; a good God would have protected me from injury and my family from death.

This is such a common expectation that the Bible writers raise the same complaints to God, especially in Job and the Psalms. The New Testament writers, and even Jesus Himself, address the problem of evil in different ways as well. We don't have space to address all of that here,[4] but we can point out here that evil does not disprove God—it actually shows that God *does* exist.

How so? Because evil can't exist without good, and good can't exist without an objective standard of good, which is God's nature. This began to make sense to the great Christian scholar Augustine (AD 354–430) when he realized that evil can't exist on its own. Evil only exists as a lack or a deficiency in a good thing.[5]

Evil is like cancer: if you take all of the cancer out of your body, you have a better body; if you take the body out of the cancer, you have nothing because cancer can't exist on its own—it needs something good (a body) in which to exist. Evil is like rust on a car: if you take all of the rust out of a car, you have a better car; if you take the car out of the rust, you have nothing. In other words, evil is a parasite in good. That's why we often describe evil as negations of good things. We say someone is *im*moral, *un*just, *un*fair, *dis*honest, etc.

We could put it another way: the shadows prove the sunshine. There can be sunshine without shadows, but there can't be shadows without sunshine. That is, there can be good without evil, but there can't be evil without good; and there can't be objective good without God. So evil may show there's a devil out there, but it can't disprove God. Evil actually boomerangs back to show that God is real.

Now we can certainly question *why* God allows certain evils, as the biblical authors and Lex Luthor do. But to answer that God is not good would defeat the objection itself. Without God there is no good, which means there would be no evil. If there is no evil, then what is Lex Luthor complaining about? The objection evaporates. Only by stealing the standard of good from God can anyone even know what evil is.

Notice that Lex Luthor complains that God did not stop his father from hurting him. But Lex does not complain that God hasn't stopped *him* from hurting Lois Lane, Martha Kent, Batman, or Superman. Lex expects God to stay out of *his* business when he is hurting others. He only wants God to stop people from hurting him.

We do the same thing. We ask God to stop *other* people from doing evil, but we rarely ask God to stop us.

What about God not being all-powerful? That claim doesn't square with the facts either. First, we have other grounds for believing God is all-powerful (like the fact that He created the universe out of nothing and fine-tuned the universe with unimaginable precision).

Second, being all-powerful doesn't mean that God can do contradictory things. For example, he can't force *free* creatures to never do evil because then they wouldn't be free. And if we are not free, then we wouldn't have the ability to love or be morally responsible. Good and evil wouldn't even exist in a robot world.

Third, the ripple effect we've seen in previous chapters shows us that we can't conclude God isn't powerful enough to stop evil. That's because we can't see how the trillions of interacting choices in this world ripple forward to impact time and eternity. God might have morally sufficient reasons for allowing evil to continue. It might bring forth good down the line, even though we can't see the ultimate outcome from our limited perspective.

The claim that evil exists because God isn't all-powerful or all-good ignores two other aspects of God's nature—the fact that God is all-knowing and all-wise. Since He knows how things are going to turn out eventually, He wisely allows events that don't make sense to us to take their course.

In fact, as we've already seen, God's character and power *guarantee* good will come from evil to those who love Him (Romans 8:28). That's why a former pastor at Notre Dame in Paris once said, "If God would concede me His omnipotence for twenty-four hours, you would see how many changes I would make in the world. But if He gave me His wisdom too, I would leave things as they are."[6]

Is There Any Meaning to Life?

What is the meaning of your life? A consistent atheist will tell you there is no meaning to life, that we're just molecular machines in motion and that our choices don't matter. Life is like a monopoly game—all of the pieces go back into the box when you're done.

But is that really all there is to our existence? Is Batman spending his entire life fighting crime not morally better than if he were, say, spending his entire life selling children into the sex industry? Are the heroic acts we admire in the movies and in real life not really heroic at all? Is it true they serve no ultimate purpose or good because there is no ultimate purpose or good?

The book of Ecclesiastes explores this subject in some detail as King Solomon reflects on his own experience trying to find meaning in life. He tried to find meaning by indulging in pleasures that included wine, women, and wealth. He tried to find meaning by pursuing great causes like acquiring wisdom, expanding his empire, and creating great buildings. Nothing ultimately satisfied. He wrote that even when we are blessed materially, we end up worrying about it all:

> What do people get for all the toil and anxious striving with
> which they labor under the sun? All their days their work is
> grief and pain; even at night their minds do not rest. This
> too is meaningless.
>
> ECCLESIASTES 2:22-23

Solomon discovered that unless God exists, life is meaningless because we're going to die and our existence will end. We toil and strive just to leave our accomplishments and their fruits to someone else who is also going to die. This is meaningless!

The Joker is the Batman villain who represents meaninglessness. For the Joker, life is absurd; there's no plan or purpose to it. In the famous scene in *The Dark Knight* where the Joker (played by the Oscar-winning Heath Ledger) accosts a recuperating Harvey Dent in the hospital, he remarks:

> Do I really look like a guy with a plan? You know what I am?
> I'm a dog chasing cars. I wouldn't know what to do with one
> if I caught it! You know, I just . . . DO things. The mob has
> plans, the cops have plans, Gordon's got plans. You know,
> they're schemers. Schemers trying to control their little worlds.
> I'm not a schemer. I try to show the schemers how pathetic
> their attempts to control things really are. . . . I'm an agent
> of chaos.

He then blows up the entire hospital.

When the Joker asks Batman, "Why so serious?" the implication is obvious. Since there's no meaning to life, there's no meaning to Batman's mission. In a world without God, there is no real moral difference between building a hospital and blowing one up. So why be so serious, Batman, about saving lives when saving lives doesn't really matter?

Meaninglessness is also a theme of *Batman v Superman*. For much of the film, Superman appears to be struggling with his identity and place in the world. What exactly is his job? Is he really doing any good?

Batman is also in a dark place. When Ben Affleck was asked what makes his Batman different from previous portrayals, he said that his Batman "is a little older, he's a little more world-weary. He's been around the block once or twice, so he's a little wiser, but he's definitely more cynical and a little darker and more jaded," adding that Batman has gotten "more exposed to the violence and the criminal element of that world over time."[7]

Batman's long struggle against evil wears him down so much that he loses his moral compass. He begins to turn cruel. He starts to sear criminals with a brand of his bat wings, abandons his two rules regarding firearms and killing, and steals kryptonite in order to kill Superman. It's becoming harder and harder to separate his behavior from that of the criminals he hunts. Even Alfred recognizes the change in Batman.

In response to a headline about Batman branding criminals, Bruce says, "We've always had critics. Nothing has changed." Alfred responds:

Oh, yes it has, sir. Everything's changed. Men fall from the sky. The gods hurl thunderbolts. Innocents die. That's how it starts, sir. The fever. The rage. The feeling of powerlessness that turns good men cruel.

Christians can experience the same problem as Batman: the culture is often changing them more than they are changing the culture.

Christians must avoid two temptations when responding to the cruelty of the culture: they must resist being cruel themselves by returning insult for insult, and they must resist denying Christ, which they may be tempted to do to avoid persecution. Sadly, too many are succumbing to these temptations. Some Christians are spending more time condemning non-believers to hell than they are trying to help save them. Others are now avoiding persecution by siding with the culture and disagreeing with Jesus on issues such as sex, marriage, the authority of the Bible, and His divinity.

Peter learned that denying Christ is never the way forward. Here is what he told us to do when facing persecution:

"Do not fear their threats; do not be frightened." But in your hearts revere Christ as Lord. Always be prepared to give an answer to everyone who asks you to give the reason for the hope that you have. But do this with gentleness and respect, keeping a clear conscience, so that those who speak maliciously against your good behavior in Christ may be ashamed of their slander. For it is better, if it is God's will, to suffer for doing good than for doing evil.

I PETER 3:14-17

Yes, respectfully give people reasons for why you believe Christianity is true. But if they persist in their evil, it is better for you to suffer evil than to do it.

Cruelty and meaninglessness have become dominant in our society as people try to free themselves from what they see as God's restrictive morality. They insist that everyone can now live their "own truth" regardless of what anyone says. You can't tell people what's really right or wrong because every person gets to make up their own morality.

This moral relativism is laid bare in the movie when Clark is arguing with his boss at the *Daily Planet* about exposing some of Batman's immoral tactics. Clark thinks writing stories about this is the morally right thing to do.

CLARK: The police won't help; the press has to do the right thing.

PERRY: You don't get to decide what the right thing is!

CLARK: When the *Planet* was founded, it stood for something, Perry.

PERRY: And so could you if it was 1938. But it's not 1938. . . . You drop this thing!

So, it's no longer right to cover a morally important story because you can no longer say what's morally right or wrong anymore? Apparently.

This philosophy of meaninglessness (called nihilism) denies all moral and religious claims. Left unchecked, it will take us into anarchy and chaos, but many in our culture don't seem to recognize it. We don't realize that the moral obligations God gives us are not designed to unnecessarily restrict us. Rather, like guardrails on a bridge, they are designed to protect us in this dangerous world.

But in nihilism, we haven't really gotten rid of all rules. We've just replaced God's rules with our own. The problem is, we don't seem to recognize the self-defeating and dangerous nature of our own invented moral absolutes and truth claims.

- "You don't get to decide what the right thing is!" is really someone deciding they know what the right thing is. Namely, it's *right* to say there is no right thing, and it's *wrong* to tell people they are wrong.

- Those who say "It's wrong to impose your morals on me" are actually imposing one of *their* morals on you (that one and others).

- Those who say you shouldn't try to convert people to your beliefs are really trying to convert you to *their* beliefs (that one and others).

- Many in our culture today actually claim *it's true* there is no truth.

- When they say all truth is relative, that's not a relative truth but an absolute one.

- When people say it's wrong to judge, you should ask them, "Then why are you judging me for judging?" Actually, we would all be dead if we didn't make judgments—judgments between good and evil, safety and danger, right and wrong. Everyone makes judgments. The only question is, "Are your judgments right and true?"

We are not as smart as we think when we use these self-defeating claims to justify our desire to be free of God's guardrails. These claims are not only false but also dangerous because they lead us to believe that truth and evil don't really exist, which makes us vulnerable to lies and complacent in the face of real evil. In fact, we are now at the point where people are demanding we celebrate evil, exactly what the Bible warns us about repeatedly.[8]

When you buy a new car, it comes with a manual. The manual tells you how to care for and operate the car, and it also warns you about dangerous things you shouldn't do—behaviors that can destroy you and/or the car. Do you get mad at Hyundai or Ford for telling you the truth about those dangerous behaviors? So why do we get mad at God for essentially doing the same thing through the Bible? Why don't we accept guidance from our Designer? An all-good and all-knowing God definitely knows where the guardrails should be better than we do.

It must be because we don't like God's guardrails. It's not because we are being reasonable. To quote Alfred, "Maybe it's time we stop trying to outsmart the truth and let it have its day."

Killing God

Lex Luthor is so mad at God that he wants to kill Him. As if he's Satan, Lex manipulates and tempts Batman and Superman into battle. After blackmailing Superman by holding his mom hostage, Lex decrees:

> And now, you will fly to him, and you will battle him. To the death. Black and blue. Fight night! The greatest gladiator match in the history of the world: God versus Man! Day versus Night! Son of Krypton versus Bat of Gotham!

Batman is ready to rumble when Superman arrives. Among other weapons, he has taken the kryptonite he's stolen and tipped a spear with it. They fight to the point where Batman ties off a weakened Superman by his leg and drags him through debris. As he's about to fling him around like a hammer, he growls this nihilistic message to the false "god":

> I bet your parents taught you that you mean something; that you're here for a reason. My parents taught me a different lesson dying in the gutter for no reason at all. They told me that the world only made sense if you forced it to.

That's the atheistic response to meaninglessness, called existentialism. Since, according to atheists, there is no God and therefore no objective meaning to our existence, we have to invent our own meaning. We have to force this world to make sense, even though life is really absurd.

For years Batman has been trying to force meaning into his life by saving people in Gotham. But why? For what? People are going to die anyway. If there's nothing after that, what's the point? Now he thinks he's going to save more meaningless people by killing Superman, the "god" he believes is a threat to humanity.

In his excellent video review of this movie, historian and theologian Paul Anleitner points out, "It's fitting that as Batman moves deeper and deeper into nihilistic despair, he actually moves closer and closer into symbolically killing God through attempting to kill Superman."[9]

Pinning Superman's neck under his foot, Batman raises his krypton-tipped spear. He's about to kill God when Superman chokes out, "Don't let them kill Martha. . . . Save Martha."

"Why did you say that name?!" barks Batman. "Why did you say that name?!"

With the help of a flashback to his mom's death and the sudden arrival of Lois Lane, Batman is awakened to the fact that Martha is the name of Superman's mom, who's being held hostage by Lex Luthor. Recall that Martha was also the name of Bruce's murdered mother.

Critics have made fun of this seemingly trivial connection. But there's a deeper meaning. Batman realizes that he and Superman share a common humanity. They were both born of a woman. Batman isn't really killing God but a human being representing God who is willing to suffer to save humanity. Likewise, when Jesus willingly went to the cross, it wasn't His divine nature that died but His human nature.

Director Zack Snyder confirmed this connection to Christianity is intended. When asked on Twitter by a fan about the significance of Batman using a krypton-tipped spear to kill Superman, Snyder tweeted back a famous painting of Christ on the cross being lanced in His side with a spear. (You may also notice that crosses appear in several battle scenes in this movie.)

Following the revelation of Superman's humanity, Batman signals his repentance from nihilism by joining forces with Superman to save Martha and defeat Lex Luthor. Batman has a Damascus Road conversion; he goes from trying to kill God to proclaiming the need for Him.

In response, Lex unleashes plan B to kill God: a monster named Doomsday whom he calls "the devil."

I cannot let you win. I gave the Bat a fighting chance, but he
was not strong enough. If man won't kill God, the devil will do
it! An ancient Kryptonian deformity; blood of my blood, born
to destroy you! . . . Your Doomsday.

Just as Doomsday is about to obliterate Batman, who is pinned in his
downed aircraft, Wonder Woman appears and deflects Doomsday's
incinerating beam.

SUPERMAN: Is she with you?

BATMAN: I thought she was with you.

(More on her in the next chapter!)

As the battle rages, Superman takes up the kryptonite spear meant
to kill him and thrusts it into this Doomsday devil, but not before
Doomsday pierces Superman with a spear of his own. Thus Superman,
like Jesus, essentially sacrifices himself to save all of mankind. Notice he
needed his divine power combined with his humanity in order to do
so—just a man (in this case, Batman) could not accomplish the task.

As both the devil and Superman fall dead, Superman's body falls into
the posture of Jesus on the cross. A famous painting of Christ being taken
down from the cross is then reenacted on screen, with Batman handing
down Superman's lifeless body to Wonder Woman. The death of mankind
has been defeated by the death of the perfect man who also has a divine
nature. Men are saved by grace because of the sacrifice of the God-man.

Appropriately, "Amazing Grace" is played during Superman's funeral
procession, and Isaiah 26:19 is read (in the extended version of the film):

But your dead will live, LORD;
    their bodies will rise—
let those who dwell in the dust

wake up and shout for joy—
your dew is like the dew of the morning;
the earth will give birth to her dead.

We see dust dance on Superman's coffin, providing a subtle prediction of his coming resurrection. Bruce then relates that Superman's sacrifice has motivated him to start the *Justice League* (where they will later resurrect their savior).

Lex's killing of Superman symbolizes man's attempt to kill God. We think killing God will result in our liberation—that God is the ultimate oppressor. But the exact opposite is true.

As the ardent atheist philosopher Friedrich Nietzsche (1844–1900) predicted, if we kill God, then we will kill man. By this he meant that if we kill *belief* in God, then moral atrocities will soon follow. In fact, Nietzsche wrote that the coming twentieth century would be the bloodiest century in history precisely because we were killing belief in God. He turned out to be prophetic. More than one hundred million innocent people were murdered, largely at the hands of atheistic dictators such as Stalin, Mao, and Pol Pot.[10]

In *The Dark Knight*, the Joker's nihilistic philosophy is similarly prophetic. He tells Batman what the people of Gotham will do when difficulty arises:

See, their morals, their "code" . . . it's a bad joke, dropped
at the first sign of trouble. They're only as good as the world
allows them to be. I'll show you. When the chips are down,
these, uh, these "civilized people," they'll eat each other. See,
I'm not a monster. I'm just ahead of the curve. . . . The only
sensible way to live in this world is without rules.

We see people in our society today eating each other alive through cancel culture. And, tragically, we've quietly killed more than sixty million people through abortion since 1973. When belief in God dies, people die.

In his confrontation with Batman while awaiting trial in prison, Lex Luthor gleefully warns Batman about the evil coming to civilization now that God is dead. "Look at us. This is how it all caves in. Civilization on the wane, manners out the window, but who would believe me. I . . . I . . . I'm insane. I'm not even fit to stand trial."

Ironically, the brilliant Nietzsche went insane during the last decade of his life. While physical causes have been suggested, including complications from untreated syphilis, some believe his mental decline may be at least partially the result of his obsession with his hopeless, nihilistic philosophical outlook.

Nietzsche seems to have been one of the few atheists in history who really felt all of the implications of denying God, which includes denying meaning, morality, and hope. Such utter despair can lead to madness. He once wrote, "All superior men who were irresistibly drawn to throw off the yoke of any kind of morality and to frame new laws had, if they were not actually mad, no alternative but to make themselves or pretend to be mad."[11]

Rebelling against God and His morality only leads to destruction. We may think deconstructing belief in God will benefit us, but what is constructed in His place is far worse—an elite group of powerful fallen humans imposing their own invented morality on the masses. Only the elite benefit by their rules. That's not liberation; that's tyranny. It's what we get when we abandon God.

No God, No Justice

We started this chapter talking about Batman's passion for justice. When Batman stops a robbery or, as in *The Dark Knight Rises*, inspires his city to follow his example, he is being a force for good and justice.

But how many other robberies happen all over the city that he can't prevent? How many criminals freely walk the streets in other cities? If Batman manages to lock up the Joker, it may prevent the Joker from committing more crimes, but it won't bring his victims back from the dead. Who is going to provide justice or restitution for them? Not even Batman can right all of those wrongs. If we really want there to be justice for the Joker and restitution for his victims, there has to be something *beyond* even what Batman grants. The same is true in our world. No government can ensure complete justice. Many horrible crimes are never revealed or solved. In fact, governments are often responsible for committing those horrible crimes! Just like there is a standard beyond Batman, there is a standard beyond us and our government. If man invents morality, then there would never be any justification for protesting or reforming your government. We couldn't even say the Nazis were wrong. After all, they were just obeying *their* government. As C. S. Lewis wrote:

> The moment you say that one set of moral ideas can be better than another, you are, in fact, measuring them both by a standard, saying that one of them conforms to that standard more nearly than the other. But the standard that measures two things is something different from either. You are, in fact, comparing them both with some Real Morality, admitting that there is such a thing as a real Right, independent of what people think, and that some people's ideas get nearer to that real Right than others. Or put it this way. If your moral ideas can be truer, and those of the Nazis less true, there must be something—some Real Morality—for them to be true about.[12]

God is that "Real Morality," and He is the only one who has the power and knowledge to ensure ultimate justice is done—even for those hidden crimes that are never discovered here on earth.

You know how much a flawed being like Batman wants justice. Now imagine how much more an infinitely just God wants it. Batman may keep watch over Gotham, but God is keeping watch over the entire universe. He will ultimately bring true justice to all of us. As the conclusion to Ecclesiastes put it:

Now all has been heard;
here is the conclusion of the matter:
Fear God and keep his commandments,
for this is the duty of all mankind.
For God will bring every deed into judgment,
including every hidden thing,
whether it is good or evil.

ECCLESIASTES 12:13-14

If you think about your life and every hidden thing you've done, do you really want justice from God? Justice is getting what you deserve. Mercy is not getting what you deserve. And grace is getting what you don't deserve. The only way to avoid the justice you deserve is to accept the grace He offers by trusting in the Savior. Even a crime fighter like Batman needs grace. We all do.

For Personal Reflection or Family/Small Group Discussion

1. What is the most attractive/unattractive characteristic of Batman to you? Why?

2. Batman is dramatically changed and consumed by the murder of his parents. Is there anything from your past that consumes you now? How are you using that event for good?

3. Lex Luthor thinks the existence of evil disproves God. Why is he wrong? How does evil actually provide evidence *for* God?

4. How does the ripple effect help us trust God when we can't see any good coming from certain evil events?

5. Batman is all about ensuring justice is done. Contemporary culture is consumed with talk of justice. Why does true justice not exist (nor will it ever be done) unless God exists?

7
WONDER WOMAN

I used to want to save the world. This beautiful place. But I knew so little then. It is a land of beauty and wonder, worth cherishing in every way. But the closer you get, the more you see the great darkness simmering within. And mankind? Mankind is another story altogether.

Wonder Woman (2017), OPENING SEQUENCE

IMAGINE YOU'RE VISITING A FOREIGN COUNTRY. You see people worshiping statues of their gods at altars in enormous ornate temples. You know they're not worshiping the Christian God. In fact, they appear to be polytheists.

Since they know you're a tourist, they begin to take an interest in you. Just outside their most impressive temple—the one that took decades to build and the one in which they say their gods dwell—a group of worshipers asks you to tell them about *your* religious beliefs.

What are you going to say?

"Turn from these idols, you wicked heathens! There's only ONE God! Repent from your idolatry! And there are no gods in that temple. What's the matter with you?"

After you get out of the hospital, do you think you will take a different approach the next time?

Now, imagine you're in Athens in AD 51. You know that the Greeks have a pantheon of gods, the greatest of which is Zeus. About five hundred years earlier, they built an enormous temple to the goddess of war, Athena (hence "Athens"), on the high point of the city.

You stand just below that Parthenon on the Areopagus, which means "Hill of Ares," the god of war. The people who are now asking you about your beliefs are not commoners but the elite intellectuals of the city. The Areopagus is not just a place but a kind of city court. This is the same city court that sentenced Socrates to die in 399 BC for "not believing in the gods of the state."

What are you going to say to these rather intolerant people?

"Hey, dudes. We're cool. Have a nice day!"

Actually, the apostle Paul was in that exact situation. The medical doctor Luke, who was in Athens with him, wrote in Acts 17 that Paul was "greatly distressed" at all of the idols in the city (Acts 17:16). Yet he kept his composure. He took neither the "turn-or-burn" approach nor the safe approach. He told them the truth, but he did so in a way that didn't add additional offense to the gospel message.

Paul said, "People of Athens! I see that in every way you are very religious. For as I walked around and looked carefully at your objects of worship, I even found an altar with this inscription: TO AN UNKNOWN GOD" (Acts 17:22-23).

So far so good. Paul is wisely highlighting common ground by complimenting them for their religious observance. They built the "unknown god" altar to ensure they didn't ignore a god they didn't know about. Many of them were fearful that disaster would befall them if they did so. Paul then turns their ignorance about the unknown god to his advantage:

> So you are ignorant of the very thing you worship—and this is what I am going to proclaim to you.
>
> The God who made the world and everything in it is the Lord of heaven and earth and does not live in temples built by human hands.
>
> ACTS 17:23-24

Hold on! That's gutsy. As he's standing below the temple that is the centerpiece of their city—the one they think contains their goddess Athena—Paul tells them that the "unknown god" is the real God and that He doesn't live in temples!

> And he is not served by human hands, as if he needed anything. Rather, he himself gives everyone life and breath and everything else. From one man he made all the nations, that they should inhabit the whole earth; and he marked out their appointed times in history and the boundaries of their lands. God did this so that they would seek him and perhaps reach out for him and find him, though he is not far from any one of us. "For in him we live and move and have our being." As some of your own poets have said, "We are his offspring."
>
> ACTS 17:25-28

This is more correction from Paul: The true God isn't part of the world as the Greek gods were. The true God *made* the world and everything in it, including all people. The Greeks thought Zeus gave us our being, but Paul said His God did that and even quoted two of their own poets to make his point more palatable (the Cretan philosopher Epimenedes and the Cilician stoic philosopher Aratus).

Only after bringing the Athenians along incrementally does Paul actually talk about idolatry, repentance, and the Resurrection:

> Therefore since we are God's offspring, we should not think that the divine being is like gold or silver or stone—an image made by human design and skill. In the past God overlooked such ignorance, but now he commands all people everywhere to repent. For he has set a day when he will judge the world

with justice by the man he has appointed. He has given proof
of this to everyone by raising him from the dead.

ACTS 17:29-31

Now imagine how this conversation would go if it happened today.
Do you think it would happen the same way? Would most Christians
first emphasize what Zeus and the Christian God have in common, or
would they immediately accuse Zeus followers of worshiping a false god?
Would Christians ask questions to discover why the Athenians believe
what they believe? (That's something Paul appears to have done when
he reasoned with both Jews and God-fearing Greeks in the synagogue;
see Acts 17:17.)

Persuasion is a forgotten art in our culture today, with so many of
us posting snarky insults online rather than truly engaging with people
and seeking to understand them. As Christians, it is our responsibility
to engage people as Jesus and the apostles did. We don't want to "win"
arguments but lose people.

Paul's tactical approach in Athens illustrates how we hope you will
use this book. In modern terms, Paul knows the "movies" of his day.
Despite being a foreigner, he is familiar with the culture and beliefs of
those to whom he is speaking. He knows that he must find common
ground rather than just tell them what's wrong with their beliefs. He's
unlikely to get anywhere with the Athenians if he goes into the debate
with a fire-and-brimstone speech filled with condemnation.

Instead, Paul offers points of agreement and then shows how those
points apply better to the Christian God than to Zeus. Now of course,
Paul tries to show them where they are wrong as well, but not without
first telling them what they've gotten right. Likewise, we have to know
where people are before we can try to take them where God wants them
to be.

But that's not the only reason why we bring this passage up. The
stories of Greek gods like Zeus and Athena form a large part of the

foundation for modern heroic storytelling. The DC Extended Universe (DCEU) that forms the new DC storyline that started with Zack Snyder's 2013 movie *Man of Steel* has a mythical air to it—exploring many themes related to gods and men. In fact, there is a direct connection between the Bible, Greek mythology, and the DCEU. Paul makes a direct reference to Zeus in the verses above, and almost 2,000 years later a daughter of Zeus—Wonder Woman—shows up on the silver screen.

Wonder Woman

Wonder Woman, a.k.a. Diana Prince, was one of the first female comic book heroes with widespread popular appeal. She was created by William Moulton Marston, and her first comic book appearance was in October of 1941. (Trivia buffs may also know that Marston was one of the inventors of the polygraph and the originator of the DISC personality profile.)

Part of the reasoning behind the creation of the character was Marston's desire for a superhero who didn't win by being stronger or more powerful than an adversary but instead won with love. As his wife, Elizabeth, suggested, they decided to make their superhero a woman. Marston later wrote that the idea behind the character was to change the feminine archetype, which at the time emphasized weakness and fragility. Writing in the 1943 issue of *American Scholar*, he observed that:

> Not even girls want to be girls so long as our feminine archetype lacks force, strength, and power. Not wanting to be girls, they don't want to be tender, submissive, peace-loving as good women are. Women's strong qualities have become despised because of their weakness. The obvious remedy is to create a feminine character with all the strength of Superman plus all the allure of a good and beautiful woman.

As we'll see, these qualities are highlighted in the movie versions of Wonder Woman, particularly *Wonder Woman 1984* (released on Christmas Day 2020).

There's an extensive Wonder Woman history and a variety of story-lines in the comic books. Our more seasoned readers may also recall the popular 1970s live-action TV show *Wonder Woman* starring Lynda Carter. But prior to 2016, the majority of her on-screen appearances have been in cartoons. Since the recent DCEU movies are the only version of the character most people have seen, we'll focus on the story told in those films.

Wonder Woman's first appearance on the big screen occurs in *Batman v Superman: Dawn of Justice* (2016). As we saw in the last chapter, that's where Wonder Woman helps Batman and Superman defeat the monstrosity Doomsday, costing Superman his life in the process. Superman's sacrifice starts a chain of events that eventually leads to an invasion of earth led by Steppenwolf, one of Darkseid's chief lieutenants. Darkseid, by the way, is one of the most powerful villains you'll ever come across. He is one of the main inspirations for Thanos (yes, it was the MCU that borrowed from DC this time).

Zack Snyder's Justice League (2021) shows this invasion and how Batman, Superman, Aquaman, Wonder Woman, and Cyborg come together to stop it. Wonder Woman plays a key role in the film, both in bringing the team together and also being the one to ultimately kill Steppenwolf. The movie ends with Diana helping Batman set up the Hall of Justice (the meeting place for the Justice League).

The first complete movie about the character is 2017's *Wonder Woman*. That movie set a record for the highest-grossing film with a solo female director, Patty Jenkins, and is the highest-grossing film in the DCEU to date. Gal Gadot's portrayal of the character has drawn almost ubiquitous praise.

Wonder Woman is the daughter of Zeus and the Amazonian queen Hippolyta. Her given name is Princess Diana of Themyscira, though she later uses the name Diana Prince to blend in while living in the world of men. The Amazons are female warriors who were created by the Olympian gods to protect mankind. The story in the movie tells of a divide between the gods—Zeus on one side and Ares, the god of war, on the other. Ares is jealous of mankind and desires to destroy them.

In the ensuing war, Ares kills all the other gods, including Zeus. But before dying, Zeus uses the last of his power to deliver a terrible wound to Ares and shroud the Amazon home island of Themyscira in a mist, preventing Ares or the world of men from being able to find it. He also leaves the Amazons a weapon capable of defeating Ares, the so-called "god-killer." Initially we are led to believe this weapon is a sword, but later we find out the weapon is Diana herself—and as Ares himself points out, only a god can kill another god. Diana, as a daughter of Zeus, certainly fits that bill.

The Courage to Do What's Right

The first part of *Wonder Woman* shows this history and includes a montage of Diana growing up and training to become a warrior in preparation for Ares's inevitable return. We are also introduced to several of the weapons that have come to define the character over the years. The Lasso of Truth compels all those who come in contact with it to tell the truth. The Lasso appears indestructible. Diana's bracelets were formed from the goddess Athena's legendary shield, the Aegis. They are able to absorb energy and can be slammed together to release a concussive shockwave.

While Diana appears to be young, she is actually several thousand years old at the start of *Wonder Woman*. She has all of the knowledge and experience we would expect from someone her age. She speaks hundreds of languages and has an extensive knowledge of both math and science. In 1918, Diana rescues an American spy named Steve Trevor who crashes a stolen German aircraft into the water just off the island of

Themyscira. She pulls him from the wreckage, which is the first instance of a "gentleman-in-distress" inversion of traditional roles that occurs often between the two characters. Steve then immediately joins Diana and the Amazon ladies of Themyscira in fighting off a group of invading German sailors who have pursued Steve to the island.

Soon after, Steve explains to Diana that there's a war going on where millions are dying (World War I). It's supposed to be the "war to end all wars." Diana concludes that Ares is behind the war and that she needs to stop him. She accompanies Steve to London, where he wants to report the intelligence he's stolen from the evil German scientist developing lethal weapons—the masked Dr. Isabel Maru.

This is the first time in her life Diana is off her idyllic island. She's not impressed with the factories belching out dark black smoke as they sail up the river Thames:

STEVE: Welcome to jolly old London.

DIANA: It's hideous!

STEVE: Yeah, it's not for everybody.

When she gets off the boat, she is thrust into a world where men dominate and women are relegated to the sidelines. She is at best marginalized and at worst objectified. This in spite of being smarter and stronger than all of them. Diana is constantly told throughout the movie that *she* is the one who needs to change when, in reality, she is going to be the one to change the world.

When she is introduced to members of the British High Command, it becomes clear that no one is taking her seriously. In fact, they don't even think she should be allowed in the room much less allowed to speak. Despite that, she is immediately able to decode Dr. Maru's journal, which was written in both Ottoman and Sumerian, and she is able to explain the science behind the poison gas that Dr. Maru has invented with Ares's help. One of the generals asks who she is, and Steve responds:

STEVE: She is my secretary, sir.

GENERAL: And she can understand Ottoman and Sumerian?

STEVE: She's a very good secretary.

At this point, it's apparent that Diana is in a league of her own, and Steve is starting to realize it as well. But they still have a ways to go before everyone else notices who she is and acknowledges her capabilities.

As they move to the front lines of the war in Belgium, Diana begins to assert herself. Steve wants to proceed to their objective, where they will be able to cross enemy lines unnoticed, but Diana sees that the people they are walking by need help:

DIANA: We cannot leave without helping them. These people are dying. They have nothing to eat, and in the village . . . enslaved!

STEVE: I understand that.

DIANA: Women! Children!

STEVE: We need to make our next position by sunset.

DIANA: How can you say that? What is the matter with you?

STEVE: This is No Man's Land, Diana! It means no man can cross it, alright? This battalion has been here for nearly a year, and they barely gained an inch. Alright? Because on the other side, there are a bunch of Germans pointing machine guns at every square inch of this place. This is not something you can cross. This is not possible.

DIANA: So, what? So, we do nothing?

STEVE: No, we are doing something. We are, we just . . .

DIANA: Steve.

STEVE: We can't save everyone in this war.

DIANA: Steve.

STEVE: This is not what we came here to do.

DIANA: No, but it's what I'm going to do.

What follows next is probably the most iconic scene in the entire DCEU. Diana, with nothing but a sword, shield, and lasso, crosses No Man's Land under heavy enemy machine gun and artillery fire (in slow motion, we might add). She then proceeds to almost singlehandedly liberate an entire village from the Germans, despite the fact she was told she would be walking into certain death. And she doesn't even know any of the people she's saving.

If you're familiar with the history of World War I, you know that generals on both sides were not prepared to deal with the new lethal weaponry, such as machine guns and artillery, that were introduced in this war. The French, for example, showed up on the battlefield with their traditional swords and caps (not helmets) and lost 75,000 men *in one day* of the war![1] (To put that in perspective, the US lost about 58,000 in the entire Vietnam war.) If we follow the actual historical numbers, by the time Steve and Diana get to the front lines, roughly eight million men have already been killed, many of them by trying to cross No Man's Land in a futile attempt to breach enemy lines.

Now, can you blame Steve for trying to stop Diana? But imagine what would have happened in the movie if she had just bowed her head, did what she was told, and went to the next checkpoint like Steve wanted. How many more people would have died if she let people who "knew better" control what she did? This was a choice only she could make, and she did so despite everyone else telling her she was wrong. (One Internet meme summarized the entire *Wonder Woman* plot as Steve yelling, "Diana, NO!") Diana has the courage to do what is right, and she inspires others who then follow her across the battlefield.

Courage is most important among virtues because without it you won't do anything else. Too many Christians today lack courage to do something far less dangerous than crossing No Man's Land: crossing the culture to stand with Christ. Despite the clear teachings of Christ and His apostles on the divinity of Jesus, His substitutionary atonement for our sins, the authority of the Bible, the sanctity of marriage, the dangers of sexual immorality, His resurrection from the dead, the reality of hell, and many other doctrines, people claiming to be Christians are disagreeing with Jesus and trying to satisfy the crowd rather than Christ. Tragically, they are like the Roman governor Pilate, who, "*wanting to satisfy the crowd* . . . had Jesus flogged, and handed him over to be crucified*" (Mark 15:15, emphasis added).

By what standard do people disagree with Jesus? Do we really think we know better? Don't we realize that culture changes continuously, that what may be fashionable and popular now could be unfashionable and unpopular just a few decades from now? In fact, several cultures around the world disagree *right now* with American culture on issues such as marriage, sexual immorality, and the reality of hell. Why do we think we have it right? By what standard? Only God is the true and good standard, and He never changes.

Not What You Deserve but What You Believe

One of the most attractive aspects of the Wonder Woman character is her idealism. She genuinely wants to save innocent lives; she can't just stand by and do nothing. But being isolated for so long makes her a little naive to the ways of the world and human nature. In that sense, she is much like Captain America.

Her devotion and naivete are brought out clearly by her mother when Diana is about to leave the island with Steve for London:

DIANA: I'm going, Mother. I cannot stand by while innocent lives are lost. If no one else will defend the world from Ares, then I must. I have to go.

QUEEN HIPPOLYTA: I know. Or at least I know I cannot stop you. [*dismounts from horse*] There's so much . . . so much you do not understand.

DIANA: I understand enough that I'm willing to fight for those who cannot fight for themselves. Like you once did.

QUEEN HIPPOLYTA: You know that if you choose to leave, you may never return.

DIANA: Who will I be if I stay?

QUEEN HIPPOLYTA: [*holding up a tiara*] This belonged to the greatest warrior in our history, our beloved Antiope. Make sure you are worthy of it.

DIANA: I will.

QUEEN HIPPOLYTA: [*shakes her head*] Be careful in the world of men, Diana. They do not deserve you. [*gently cupping her daughter's face*] You have been my greatest love. [*releases her*] Today, you are my greatest sorrow.

People don't deserve Diana's service and idealism. She's unwaveringly good, but people are not. Their nature is such that they will disappoint you.

But Diana doesn't realize that. She believes that if she can kill Ares, the war will end because Ares is the one completely responsible for the war. People are just pawns in his scheme. When Diana eventually kills German General Ludendorff—whom she thinks is Ares in disguise— she is stunned to find out that the war doesn't stop. People keep killing one another, even loading a plane with lethal gas to wipe out innocent people in London. Steve tries to explain the truth about human nature, even blaming himself:

DIANA: I killed [Ares]; why are they doing this? Why are they still fighting?

STEVE: Because maybe it's them! Maybe people aren't always good, Ares or no Ares. Maybe it's just who they are.

DIANA: No. . . . After everything I saw, it can't be. It cannot be! They were killing each other! Killing people they cannot see! Children. Children! No, it had to be him; it cannot be them!

STEVE: Diana, people . . .

DIANA: [*in tears*] She was right, my mother was right. . . . She said the world of men do not deserve you; they don't deserve our help. . . .

STEVE: It's . . . it's not about *deserve*. Maybe, maybe we don't. But it's not about that; it's about what you believe. You don't think I get it, after what I've seen out there? You don't think I wish I could tell you that it was one bad guy to blame? It's not! We're all to blame!

DIANA: I'm not!

STEVE: But maybe I am.

Lesson number one should be obvious: Mama is always right! She knows human nature because she has survived the terrible twos with you (at least).

Another lesson for us is that unlike many other religious texts, the Bible nails the truth about human nature. As we've seen throughout this book (and you can see by looking at the news or your own heart), people are bent toward evil, not good.

More than 2,500 years ago, Jeremiah wrote, "The heart is deceitful above all things, and desperately wicked" (Jeremiah 17:9, NKJV). A proverb from Solomon says, "A person's own folly leads to their ruin, yet their heart rages against the LORD" (Proverbs 19:3). Jesus said, "For out of the heart come evil thoughts—murder, adultery, sexual immorality, theft, false testimony, slander" (Matthew 15:19) and "No one is good—except God alone" (Mark 10:18). Paul revealed, "I know that good itself does not dwell in me, that is, in my sinful nature. For I have the desire to do what is good, but I cannot carry it out" (Romans 7:18). There are many more passages we could cite as well. And just from our own experience, we know it's easy to be bad and hard to be good.

Wonder Woman and *Wonder Woman 1984* explicitly reveal this biblical truth about human nature. No character does this more than the real Ares, who is disguised as British politician Sir Patrick Morgan. When

Ares confronts Diana after she has killed Ludendorff, he unloads on humanity for their evil:

> You're right, Diana. They don't deserve our help. They only
> deserve destruction. . . . You blame me, but the truth is *[motions*
> *to the airfield where the bombs are being loaded]* . . . all of this—
> I did none of it. . . . All these years, I've struggled. Whispering
> into their ears. . . . Ideas. Inspiration. For weapons. Formulas.
> But I don't make them use them. . . . They start these wars on
> their own. . . . They have always been and always will be weak,
> cruel, selfish, and capable of the greatest horror. . . . All I ever
> wanted was to show my father (Zeus) how evil his creation was.
> But he refused.

The accusations mirror those of Satan, whose name means "accuser." Ares then urges Diana to join him in annihilating human beings to create paradise:

> All the suffering. All the pain and destruction they create. You
> could join me. We could return the world to the paradise it
> was before them. And there would be absolute peace, Diana.
> Forever.

Satan could not have said it better. Neither could Lenin, Mao, Hitler, or the MCU's Thanos. Tyrants always justify murdering innocent people under the guise of doing good—creating a paradise on earth. As Paul warns us, "Satan himself masquerades as an angel of light" (2 Corinthians 11:14).

Diana, of course, refuses and fights Ares on the airfield. Meanwhile, Steve commandeers the plane loaded with Dr. Maru's poison gas to prevent it from being dropped on London. The only way he can stop the gas from harming people is to blow the plane up at altitude, effectively sacrificing himself. Diana sees the plane explode, which triggers her to explode on Ares.

At one point in the battle, she has a chance to kill Dr. Maru, who is defenseless while kneeling on the tarmac. Maru is unmasked, revealing her deformed face. As Diana stands over the evil Maru, ready to slam down a tank on her for her crimes, Ares entices Diana to go through with it.

"She is the perfect example of these humans. And unworthy of your sympathy in every way," says Ares. "You know she deserves it. They all do!"

Ares is right. We all deserve punishment for the evil we've done, just as the Bible teaches. While we probably haven't made lethal gas intended to kill millions, we have committed other moral crimes that an infinitely just Being must punish (otherwise He wouldn't be *infinitely* just, and justice itself wouldn't exist).

According to the Bible, on Judgment Day, each and every one of us will be kneeling before Jesus unmasked. All of our evil deeds will be exposed, showing how our sins deformed our lives and that of others. His infinitely just nature will require Him to punish us as our deeds deserve *unless* we have accepted the grace made possible by Christ's sacrifice.

Diana is about to bring heavy justice down on Dr. Maru when she has a flashback to Steve saving the day by his sacrifice and saying "I love you" to her. Suddenly, Diana realizes humans are not all bad. They also display love. She throws aside the tank, providing grace to Dr. Maru, and reengages Ares:

> **WONDER WOMAN:** They're everything you say they are. But they're capable of so much more.

> **ARES:** Lies! They do not deserve your protection!

> **WONDER WOMAN:** It's not about *deserve*; it's about what you believe. And I believe in love.

She then turns her power on Ares, eventually destroying the evil tempter and ending the war. As Steve put it, he saved the day, but she saved the world.

Through His infinite love, Christ saved the real world, making Diana's maxim possible: "It's not what you deserve, but what you believe." Those who believe and put their trust in Christ will not get what they deserve. They will get grace. As Jesus said in one of the more famous verses in the Bible, "For God so loved the world that he gave his one and only Son, that whoever believes in him shall not perish but have eternal life" (John 3:16).

Your Best Life Now?

If Diana has one regret at the end of the first movie, it's that she was unable to save Steve Trevor. Despite saving mankind from Ares, she couldn't save the man she loved. As a result, she largely withdraws from the world. She still saves people when she can, but at the start of *Wonder Woman 1984*, you can tell that even after more than sixty years have passed, Diana still hasn't recovered from losing Steve.

Enter the Dreamstone—a powerful artifact created by a god called the Duke of Deception (Dolos in Greek mythology). The Dreamstone is capable of granting wishes to those who ask—but not without a price. Diana, of course, has one wish—to bring Steve back from the dead—which she makes without knowing how the artifact works. She's overjoyed when he shows up again in her life, even though she can't explain why.

What follows is a reversal of the first movie. It's now Diana's turn to show Steve how to integrate into a modern society, which leads to some 1980s lessons on fashion, the utility of fanny packs, and parachute pants:

STEVE TREVOR: Parachute pants?

DIANA PRINCE: Yeah.

STEVE TREVOR: Does, does everybody parachute now?

We quickly find out that the Dreamstone can be used for evil as well. A failed businessman, Maxwell Lord, steals the stone and cleverly uses his wish to *become* the stone. This allows him to become a sought-after king maker who also takes advantage of those making wishes. In virtually every case, Max takes some power or resources from people in exchange for granting their wish.

Maxwell Lord is the perfect name to communicate someone whose god (or lord) is maximizing their personal wellness here on earth, particularly by pursuing their material and sensual desires. But there's a catch.

As more and more people ask Max for wishes, it becomes increasingly apparent that the very fabric of society is being torn apart. People wish for whatever is on their hearts without thinking through the negative implications on their own lives and the lives of others. People die when a person simply says, in a moment of frustration, "I wish you were dead." Legal immigrants are harmed when people wish they'd "go back where they came from." Those who wish for fame and fortune quickly see their lives destroyed.

As the proverb put it, "A faithful person will be richly blessed, but one eager to get rich will not go unpunished" (Proverbs 28:20). Paul provides a similar warning. "Those who want to get rich fall into temptation and a trap and into many foolish and harmful desires that plunge people into ruin and destruction. For the love of money is a root of all kinds of evil. Some people, eager for money, have wandered from the faith and pierced themselves with many griefs" (1 Timothy 6:9-10).

People wish for power as well, with equally disastrous results. Diana's shy friend Barbara (played by Kristen Wiig) wishes so much to be beautiful, popular, and powerful like Diana that the pursuit goes to her head. She eventually loses her humanity after wishing to become an "apex predator." Even the president of the United States gets enticed into the madness. He wishes for more nuclear weapons to be closer to the Soviet Union, not realizing that such a wish could inflame tensions and cause a war rather than keep the peace.

Max, played by Pedro Pascal, resembles those gaudy and greedy TV prosperity teachers who are "Dukes of Deception" themselves, twisting the truth for their own benefit. As the prosperity teachers do—ignoring Jesus' command to deny yourself and serve others—Max appeals to *our* lusts to get what *he* wants, exuberantly declaring:

"Everything you've been waiting for, it's all yours!"

"Why not wish for more! We want what we want!"

"Say the word: you can have it all!"

Meanwhile, Max himself can't even have it all. He sees his health deteriorate with each wish, and he begins to lose his relationship with his young son, Alistair, because of his all-consuming quest for money and power. At one point, Alistair starts to wish that his dad would spend more time with him, but Max stops him before he can finish. (Kids spell love T–I–M–E.)

This tension reflects an important truth about our own lives. Real life requires a series of tradeoffs. You can't live as if everything or everyone is at the top of your priority list. You can't achieve optimum health or deep relationships if you're working eighty hours per week. You can't be at your kid's ball game *and* be on a business trip at the same time. We each have limited time, energy, and opportunity, which lays bare the lie that we can have it all. (In fact, Steve Trevor's wish to Diana at the end of *Wonder Woman* was, "I wish we had more time.")

If you've ever wondered why God doesn't answer some, maybe even most, of your prayers, this movie (along with the Jim Carrey film *Bruce Almighty*) can help you see why. As we saw when we discussed why God allows certain evils, there's a ripple effect at play. No matter what God does in response to your prayers, there's a ripple effect of outcomes that you can't foresee. But God can. God may say no to your requests so that the best long-term outcome is achieved.

Much of the time we don't know what is good for us. And what we mean by "good" is not short-term comfort but long-term character. God is more interested in our character than our comfort. His mission is to make us more like Jesus, and that often requires Him to say no to our prayers and wishes. In fact, if you look back at your own life, you might be able now to see why God said no to some of your previous requests. When you were younger, perhaps you thought a certain spouse or profession was right for you. But now you realize *you* had it wrong and should thank God for the prayers He *didn't* answer.

God isn't interested in you living your best life now. He's interested in making you best for eternity (2 Corinthians 4:16-18).

Diana Puts Facts over Feelings

The choices we make in life, even beneficial choices, normally involve some kind of price. Diana begins to realize this with Steve. The price of Steve's return from the dead is the loss of some of her powers, making her unable to stop Max from tearing the world apart. In order to save the world, Diana decides she must be the first to renounce her wish, which means she will lose Steve back to the dead. Steve realizes this as well and, just like at the end of the first movie, agrees to sacrifice himself:

> STEVE: I had a great life, and you only made it better. But you know what you need to do. The world needs you.

Diana is smart enough and strong enough not to let her feelings for Steve get in the way of the truth. The world needs her to renounce her wish and let Steve go. She knows that she can't always follow her feelings but must sometimes suffer for the truth. She also knows she doesn't get her identity from Steve or her feelings for him.

Diana completely contradicts our culture on this point. Our culture tells us that we should "follow our heart," that our identity and worth are found in our feelings and we should, therefore, chase our feelings at all costs. This is well-intended advice. But it rarely works long term because our feelings and desires change and our hearts can lead us down the wrong path.

To see this, Pastor Tim Keller asks you to reflect on your own life. He points out that as we mature, our feelings and desires often change so we wind up lamenting our younger selves. When you're fifteen, you probably think you were an idiot when you were ten. When you turn twenty, you say the same about your fifteen-year-old self. Reach thirty, and you look at your twenty-year-old self the same way. Do you know what this means? No matter what age you are now, as Keller put it, "You're always an idiot!" because your feelings, desires, knowledge, and priorities change over time. (These changes had one man admit to Keller, "My wife has been married to five men, and they have all been me!") The bottom line is that it makes little sense to follow temporary feelings and desires at all costs.

By the end of the movie, Max thinks his younger self was an idiot for putting material pursuits above his son. His thoughts, feelings, and priorities about his son changed for the better after Diana lassoed him with truth.

Another problem with slavishly following our hearts is that our feelings can lead us to make morally wrong choices. A married man may feel desire for another woman, but leaving his wife and kids for her would violate his vow to love his wife and their children. Love is not a feeling. (If it were, we couldn't love our enemies.) Love seeks the good of the other person even when you don't feel like doing so. In fact, marriage vows wouldn't be possible if love was purely a feeling. How can anyone vow to *feel* a certain way for fifty years? You can't. All you can vow is to behave in a loving way. In fact, you only need a vow because times will come when you *don't* feel like loving your spouse!

All freedom requires restraint. If you want the freedom to enjoy an intact family, you have to restrain yourself from following your impulsive heart that's urging you to run off with the latest person you find attractive. If you want to have the freedom to drive safely somewhere, you have to restrain yourself to follow the rules of the road. If you want the freedom to enjoy good health, you have to restrain yourself from eating everything and anything.

C. S. Lewis points out the dangers awaiting us when we follow our feelings and desires without restraint:

> Surrender to all of our desires obviously leads to impotence, disease, jealousies, lies, concealment, and everything that is the reverse of good health, good humor, and frankness. For any happiness, even in this world, quite a lot of restraint is going to be necessary. . . . For 'nature' (in the sense of natural desire) will have to be controlled anyway, unless you are going to ruin your whole life.[2]

Solomon warns, "There is a way that appears to be right, but in the end it leads to death" (Proverbs 14:12). Indeed, we often ruin our lives and the lives of others when we put no restraints on our desires and blindly follow our fallen and fickle hearts. We rarely think that our hearts might be leading us astray. Since they do, we should follow God's heart rather than our own.

Jesus claimed to be the truth and said, "The truth will set you free" (John 8:32; see also 14:6). This of course implies that if you don't have the truth, you're in bondage—bondage to the same fallen human nature that made Max's victims such easy targets.

A moment's reflection on Christ's point shows He's right. Ask the person who has followed their desires into drug, alcohol, or pornography addiction, "Are you free or in bondage to your addiction?" How about asking those who have followed their desires and spent beyond their means, "Are you free or in bondage to debt and the dollar?"[3] If Diana had denied the truth and selfishly followed her desire to keep Steve, do you think she would be free or in bondage, knowing she allowed millions to die?

Love as a Superpower

After bravely and selflessly following the truth and renouncing her wish, Diana's next task is to make sure the rest of the world understands the danger of their wishes as well. But Max is working hard to make things much worse. He uses the stone's power to become the president of the United States so that he can access a secret US satellite broadcast network to reach the entire world. He wants to grant wishes to the rest of the world in exchange for more power.

After defeating "apex predator" Barbara—who is defending Max has assumed her final form as the Cheetah—Diana infiltrates the broadcast network. But what follows is not the typical physical confrontation that happens between the hero and villain at the climax of a movie. In fact, up to this point, Diana has had more than one opportunity to kill Max but has never elected to do so. Why not? Because she believes that in order for love to triumph over evil, men must be willing to be redeemed and must choose that for themselves.

Besides, a physical victory will solve nothing. What Diana needs to achieve is a mental and moral victory. To save the world, minds and moral choices need to change. Why? Because Diana is not really fighting a typical supervillain; she's actually fighting the lustful heart of humanity. She must get Max and the rest of the world to renounce their selfish wishes voluntarily.

Diana initiates the following exchange with Max and the world, which is broadcast over the satellite network. (We encourage you to read this quote slowly, sentence by sentence. You might even want to find the clip on YouTube. It takes Diana almost three and a half minutes of screen time in the movie to finish the speech, which is accompanied by a montage of people realizing their mistakes and Max finally realizing his own.)

> DIANA: I've never wanted anything more [Steve]. But he's gone, and that's the truth. And everything has a price. One I'm not willing to pay. Not anymore. This world was a beautiful place just as it was, and you cannot have it all. You can only have the truth. And the truth is enough. The truth is beautiful. So look at this world, and look at what your wish is costing it. You must be the hero. Only you can save the day. Renounce your wish if you want to save this world.

> MAX LORD: Why would I? When it's finally my turn? The world belongs to me! You can't stop me. No one can.

> DIANA: I wasn't talking to you. I was talking to everyone else. Because you're not the only one who has suffered. Who wants more. Who wants them back. Who doesn't want to be afraid anymore. Or alone. Or frightened. Or powerless. 'Cause you're not the only one who imagined a world where everything was different. Better. Finally. A world where they were loved and seen and appreciated. Finally. But what is it costing you? Do you see the truth?

As the Soviets are about to launch a nuclear attack, and sirens wail, Alistair begins calling out, "Daddy! Daddy! Daddy! Help me!" Meanwhile, Diana is using the Lasso of Truth to persuade Max to come to his senses. While Max has long believed he needs to be financially successful in order for his son to love him, he finally comes to realize that his son needs a father more than anything else. He renounces his wish, averts a nuclear disaster, and runs to apologize to Alistair.

MAX: You don't ever have to make a wish for me to love you. I'm here because I love you. I just . . . I just wish and I pray that, one day, I'll be able to make you proud enough that you'll be able to forgive me. And love me. Because I'm nothing to be proud of, Alistair.

ALISTAIR: I don't need you to make me proud. I already love you, Daddy. You're my dad.

We know our loved ones should take priority over our selfish desires, but we often need to be reminded. Most parents would die for their children if ever put in that position. But too often, we won't live for them.

Now how many other movies have you ever seen where the hero appeals to love to get the villain to give up? Diana's approach shows that Wonder Woman is a different kind of superhero. Yes, she's strong, but she's not trying to emulate the men. (As one reviewer put it, "She's not Superman with a wig.")

Wonder Woman 1984 follows what William Marston intended for the character: a hero who overcomes evil with truth and love. We don't see much of that from Hollywood. Imagine the Avengers trying to show Thanos how much they love and care about him. *Wonder Woman 1984* is so committed to these themes that Diana rarely uses her sword and shield; her primary weapon throughout the movie is her Lasso of Truth.

In a fallen world, there will always be times when the use of force is necessary to restore peace or protect the innocent. But force rarely changes hearts. Love does. Had Diana simply dope-slapped Max with superhero power, not much would have changed. The world would have still been destroyed. Instead, like Paul on the Hill of Ares in Athens, Diana sought to persuade and redeem Max and the world rather than just condemn or overpower them.

Diana showed that the world doesn't become a better place if we get what we want or even get what we deserve. It gets better if we love each other. Diana's closing narration in *Wonder Woman* illustrates this idea better than any other:

> I used to want to save the world. To end war and bring peace to mankind. But then I glimpsed the darkness that lives within their light. I learned that inside every one of them, there will always be both. The choice each must make for themselves— something no hero will ever defeat. I've touched the darkness that lives in between the light. Seen the worst of this world, and the best. Seen the terrible things men do to each other in the name of hatred, and the lengths they'll go to for love. Now I know. Only love can save this world. So I stay. I fight, and I give . . . for the world I know can be. This is my mission, now. Forever.

Love really is a superpower. And unlike superstrength or the ability to fly, it's a superpower that's accessible to each of us. Love is the reason Christ died for us, and it's the motivation Christians have to live for Him. Love is the way He chose to stop evil.

But let's be clear about what love truly is. Contrary to what our culture says, loving someone doesn't mean that you approve of everything they do. Diana doesn't approve of what Max is doing. In fact, she shows love for him and those she's trying to save *by opposing his behavior*. Parents and their children know this truth as well. Any parent who approves of everything his or her child wants to do is not loving but unloving. Love requires that we protect people by opposing evil behaviors.

Paul calls the way of love "the most excellent way" (1 Corinthians 12:31) and then goes on to describe the selfless behaviors that comprise love:

If I speak in the tongues of men or of angels, but do not have love, I am only a resounding gong or a clanging cymbal. If I have the gift of prophecy and can fathom all mysteries and all knowledge, and if I have a faith that can move mountains, but do not have love, I am nothing. If I give all I possess to the poor and give over my body to hardship that I may boast, but do not have love, I gain nothing.

Love is patient, love is kind. It does not envy, it does not boast, it is not proud. It does not dishonor others, it is not self-seeking, it is not easily angered, it keeps no record of wrongs. Love does not delight in evil but rejoices with the truth. It always protects, always trusts, always hopes, always perseveres.

Love never fails. But where there are prophecies, they will cease; where there are tongues, they will be stilled; where there is knowledge, it will pass away. For we know in part and we prophesy in part, but when completeness comes, what is in part disappears. When I was a child, I talked like a child, I thought like a child, I reasoned like a child. When I became a man, I put the ways of childhood behind me. For now we see only a reflection as in a mirror; then we shall see face to face. Now I know in part; then I shall know fully, even as I am fully known.

And now these three remain: faith, hope and love. But the greatest of these is love.

I CORINTHIANS 13:1-13

Again, these are behaviors, not feelings. Notice as well that "love rejoices in the truth" and "always protects." That's Diana's mission, and it's ours as well. In a world full of anger and hate, we are called to love—to rejoice in the truth and to protect. That's how Christ saved us from death. With love and truth, we are to take that message to the world—even a world of enemies.

For Personal Reflection or Family/Small Group Discussion

1. What is the most attractive/unattractive characteristic of Wonder Woman to you? Why?

2. Wonder Woman has to sacrifice something important to her (her relationship with Steve) to uphold the truth. Is there something in your life you need to give up as well? What is it?

3. Why is "following your heart" often a bad idea?

4. Wonder Woman is unique in that she does not defeat Maxwell Lord in physical combat. Much like the apostle Paul in Athens, she relies on the art of persuasion to convince him to stop. What type of application does this have in your life?

5. How does the concept of love we see in Wonder Woman differ from the concept of love we see in society today?

8

THE ULTIMATE HERO

Jesus is the ultimate superhero, the model for all other heroes.

MAX McLEAN

IF YOU WERE MAKING UP YOUR OWN SUPERHERO, what kind of qualities would your hero have? Imagine you could create someone who had:

- Captain America's righteous idealism
- Iron Man's genius
- Harry Potter's willingness to sacrifice
- Luke Skywalker's discipline
- Sam's loyalty
- Frodo's humility
- Aragorn's courage
- Gandalf's wisdom
- Batman's focus
- Superman's power
- Wonder Woman's love

You would have Jesus, right? Actually, you would have someone closer to Jesus than any of these heroes individually, but you would still be a long way from the real Jesus.

The person of Jesus is unique in all of history and literature. No one rivals Him. There are commonalities, as we have seen, but there is no perfect match because there is no one with the perfect credentials of Jesus. Let's take a look at some of the many truths about Jesus that make Him the most unique and influential human being ever to walk the earth.

No Other Person in History or Fiction Is Perfect Like Jesus

Not only did Jesus claim to be sinless, His enemies even had a hard time finding fault in Him. "Can any of you prove me guilty of sin?" Jesus challenged the Pharisees, who were all too eager to find a way to get rid of Him (John 8:46). Jesus was a threat to their power, yet they couldn't name any real sins He'd committed. All they could come up with was the charge that Jesus was "demon-possessed" because He was a miracle worker who claimed to be God (John 8:48). They didn't want to consider the option that Jesus actually *was* God!

No other person can measure up, not even fictional Hollywood heroes. For all their incredible talents and admirable attributes, they all have flaws. Captain America, whether he admits it or not, can come off as a little self-righteous, and his uncompromising nature often causes rifts in his team; Tony Stark is a sarcastic, selfish playboy; Spider-Man is young, and his selfishness costs his uncle his life; and we all know the Hulk has anger-management issues. Batman can be cruel; Luke Skywalker is headstrong and rushes off to help his friends before he's ready; Superman can be manipulated and creates a lot of collateral damage; Frodo gives in to temptation at the easiest point of the journey; and Wonder Woman's naivete gets her into trouble more than once.

If we are honest with ourselves, we are flawed in multiple ways too.

We struggle with self-centeredness, pride, fear, inadequacy, addiction, loneliness, and an inability to do what we know we should do—and that's just for starters.

In other words, no one is perfect . . . except Jesus.

But it's not just what He didn't do (sin) that makes Him unrivaled; it's what He did do and how He did it. And we're not just talking about His miracles. You can't know who Jesus is apart from His miracles because they authenticate the fact that He is the divine Savior who can fix the problems we have in this broken world. His miracles demonstrate that He has power over sin, nature, sickness, and death. But even if you set His miracles aside, Jesus remains unique in all of human history.

Jesus Is the First and Only World Religious Figure to Make Himself the Message

Most religious leaders offer a new philosophy on how to live. Buddha offers an eightfold path to enlightenment. Muhammad offers a series of works to show you how to please Allah. But Jesus is not offering new teachings designed to help you work your way to God; Jesus claims that *He is the way to God* because He actually is God who has worked His way to you. His perfect life is offered to save yours. As Tim Keller put it, "The founders of every other major religion said, 'I'm a prophet who shows you how to find God,' but Jesus taught, 'I'm God, come to find you.'"[4]

This is not a philosophy but news—good news. Being the perfect sacrifice, Jesus has accomplished something that only He could accomplish, and He did so for your benefit. Just like in the movies we've been reliving, we can't save ourselves. Only Iron Man could save the universe from Thanos, and only Superman could save the world from Doomsday. People living in the Marvel and DC universes couldn't have followed a philosophy or series of rules to defeat those villains. Like us, they each needed a savior to do the work for them.

There Has Not Been a Person in History More Other-Centered Than Jesus

While Jesus makes Himself the message, it is because He is remarkably focused on others. Jesus states His mission clearly: "For even the Son of Man did not come to be served, but to serve, and to give his life as a ransom for many" (Mark 10:45). He knows that He was born to be a servant, a sacrificial Lamb who will be killed for the benefit of others.

Does He ever waver? Certainly, people want Him to waver. His family wants Jesus to back off. In fact, Jesus is so devoted to God that His family said, "He is out of his mind" (Mark 3:21). His own brothers don't believe in Him (John 7:5). These are just two of several details about Jesus' life that seem too embarrassing to be invented (more on that soon).

Jews in the Nazareth synagogue want to murder Him after He suggests that His ministry extends to non-Jews (Luke 4:24-29). "But he walked right through the crowd and went on his way" (Luke 4:30). The Jewish ruling council called the Sanhedrin plots to kill Jesus. Meanwhile, others want to make Him King, and great crowds follow Him everywhere.

Does He get diverted by the popularity on one side or the persecution on the other? No, Jesus never loses focus on His mission. Any normal man would have succumbed to the many distractions and diversions and then bailed out when the mission required Him to suffer an excruciating death.

There Is Not Another Person in History as Humble as Jesus

Earlier in the book we used a famous quote from Lord Acton, "Power tends to corrupt, and absolute power corrupts absolutely." There's a second part of the quote that few people cite but is relevant here: "Great men are almost always bad men." Indeed, most great world figures have monster egos. But not Jesus.

Almost every hero we've talked about in this book goes on a journey to obtain power to defeat evil. But the inverse is true of Jesus. *He gives up power* and becomes a servant in order to save the world. Here is how the apostle Paul describes Jesus to the church at Philippi:

Who, being in very nature God,
did not consider equality with God
something to be used to his own
advantage;
rather, he made himself nothing
by taking the very nature of a servant,
being made in human likeness.
And being found in appearance as a man,
he humbled himself
by becoming obedient to death—
even death on a cross!

PHILIPPIANS 2:6-8

Despite being the Creator of the universe, Jesus comes in weakness, not power—exactly the opposite of every hero not modeled on Jesus. He takes the form of a servant, leaving the privileges of heaven behind. While on His earthly mission, He takes the more modest title of King of the Jews. And even then, when He makes His triumphal entry into Jerusalem, He rides on the back of a donkey. (Anyone else would have come on a white stallion escorted by an army!)

When Jesus is being tempted by Satan, He doesn't pull rank. He doesn't display His divine power but human humility. He responds by simply quoting the Word of God.

When Jesus prays, He doesn't pray for His will but for His Father's will. Even when He knows He will soon be taken away to a torturous death, Jesus prays, "Father, if you are willing, take this cup from me; yet *not my will*, but yours be done" (Luke 22:42, emphasis added).

When He does miracles, there's no fanfare. There's no, "Hey, look at me!" or "Watch this!" Any fallen human being would draw attention to Himself. Jesus never does. He humbly goes about healing people, even raising them from the dead, without grandstanding or asking for anything in return. In fact, He does exactly the opposite of what you'd expect a normal person blessed with the ability to do miracles would do. Instead of broadcasting it and using the ability for His own benefit, Jesus tells people to keep quiet about it!

Telling people to keep quiet is partially motivated by His desire to complete His mission to die for our sins (which itself requires humility). If more people learn about His power too soon, His mission will be in jeopardy. Too many people might want to make Him a political king, and the authorities might be prevented from carrying out His execution—the reason He came to earth in the first place. It is only after His mission is complete, after He's resurrected, that He tells His disciples to proclaim what He's done to the world.

Even the way Jesus sacrifices Himself is different from other heroes. When Iron Man, Superman, or Harry Potter sacrifice themselves, they do so to great admiration. Everyone readily acknowledges the good in what they have done. Jesus, on the other hand, dies as a Lamb in the most humiliating way possible. He is denied three times by one of His closest disciples (Peter), flogged, and then crucified as a criminal—the most shameful type of death in that culture. In fact, the Jews believed that anyone hung on a tree was under God's curse (Deuteronomy 21:23). There is no virtue attached to His passing, and all but a few of His followers desert Him.

It's been said that humility is not thinking less of yourself but thinking of yourself less. Do you know any other great person who thinks about himself less than Jesus? Jesus is completely other-focused to His own detriment. We win when He dies, and that's what He wants. No one in the history of the world has been like Him.

There Is Not Another Person in History as Brilliant as Jesus

We are not talking here about academic brilliance. We are talking about His brilliance in dealing with people. Those who wanted to trap Him, such as the chief priests and teachers of the law, left feeling trapped themselves. Luke 20 records a couple examples of this:

> "Tell us by what authority you are doing these things," they said. "Who gave you this authority?"
>
> He replied, "I will also ask you a question. Tell me: John's baptism—was it from heaven, or of human origin?"
>
> They discussed it among themselves and said, "If we say, 'From heaven,' he will ask, 'Why didn't you believe him?' But if we say, 'Of human origin,' all the people will stone us, because they are persuaded that John was a prophet."
>
> So they answered, "We don't know where it was from."
>
> Jesus said, "Neither will I tell you by what authority I am doing these things."
>
> LUKE 20:2-8

Then they tried again:

> "Is it right for us to pay taxes to Caesar or not?"
>
> He saw through their duplicity and said to them, "Show me a denarius. Whose image and inscription are on it?"
>
> "Caesar's," they replied.
>
> He said to them, "Then give back to Caesar what is Caesar's, and to God what is God's."

They were unable to trap him in what he had said there in public. And astonished by his answer, they became silent.

LUKE 20:22-26

Since the Pharisees rejected that Jesus, a man, could actually be God, Jesus challenged them to explain why their Scriptures (the Old Testament) said the Messiah would be both the Lord of David and a descendant of David. Here's what happened:

While the Pharisees were gathered together, Jesus asked them, "What do you think about the Messiah? Whose son is he?"

"The son of David," they replied.

He said to them, "How is it then that David, speaking by the Spirit, calls him 'Lord'? For he says,

"'The Lord said to my Lord:
"Sit at my right hand
until I put your enemies
under your feet."'

If then David calls him 'Lord,' how can he be his son?" No one could say a word in reply, and from that day on no one dared to ask him any more questions.

MATTHEW 22:41-46

In addition to silencing His enemies with mere words, Jesus never seems flustered or unsure in an interaction with anyone. Do you ever see Him corrected? Does He ever have to deliberate a point or get advice from anyone? But how many times do you walk away from a conversation or debate and later think, *"Oh, I should have said that!"*? Never seems to happen to Jesus. And unlike fallible human beings, He doesn't improve or need to improve over the course of His ministry. His brilliance is on display from the beginning.[5]

Somehow Jesus knows how to teach those who are open to His message while hiding the truth from those opposed to it. His parables are simple on the one hand but complex on the other. They can slap receptive people upside their heads with profound life-changing truths while leaving the closed-minded in full-throated rebellion.

Jesus Never Allows His Good Qualities to Lead Him into Sin

Everyone has good qualities. But some of our good qualities turn into bad behavior when we fail to hold them with the proper tension. For example, Captain America is usually right, but when he splits hairs or is unkind when expressing what is right, he fails to hold the tension between righteousness and humility. Iron Man wants to defeat evil, but when he insists that he must be in charge, he fails to defeat the evil in his own heart.

The same may be true in our own lives. We may be warriors for truth, but our zeal for truth often causes us to speak without humility or grace. Conversely, we may be champions of compassion and grace for people struggling with sin, but when we lack the courage to speak the truth that can actually help them, our cowardice enables them to continue down the path of destruction. The great economist Thomas Sowell nails this point, saying, "When you want to help people, you tell them the truth. When you want to help yourself, you tell them what they want to hear."

None of us holds the tension between truth and grace perfectly like Jesus did. Jesus is, at the same time, both a Lion and a Lamb. He is someone who walks and talks the absolute truth—in fact, He's the embodiment of truth. And while He totally exposes people with His insight, He somehow delivers the message without adding offense. (Yes, those already opposed to Him—the Pharisees—are offended by the truth He proclaims, but Jesus doesn't *add* offense.)

He tells the Samaritan woman at the well that she has had five husbands and that the man she's now living with is not her husband. That would normally be perceived as intrusive and "none of your business!" but the grace and love of Jesus wins her over. Even though Jews and Samaritans hate one another, she tells her entire village that Jesus could be the Messiah. Then many come to believe He is "the Savior of the world" (John 4:42).

Now, you'll have to read the biographies of Jesus (called Matthew, Mark, Luke, and John in the New Testament) in order to fully appreciate how these amazing qualities are displayed by one person. After reading them, we think you'll see that this quote from Tim Keller is spot on:

It is this paradox—that he is both God and human—that gives Jesus an overwhelming beauty. He is the Lion and the Lamb. Despite his high claims, he is never pompous; you never see him standing on his own dignity. Despite being absolutely approachable to the weakest and broken, he is completely fearless before the corrupt and powerful. He has tenderness without weakness. Strength without harshness. Humility without the slightest lack of confidence. Unhesitating authority with a complete lack of self-absorption. Holiness and unending convictions without any shortage of approachability. Power without insensitivity.[6]

Marinate in these seemingly opposed characteristics. Do you see all of these displayed in any other human being from history, literature, or in your own personal experience? Maybe someone you know can hold the tension between one or two of these characteristics, but all of them? Jesus did. This Jesus, who is perfectly full of grace and truth (John 1:14), is a character who could not have been invented.

Jesus Is the Only Person in History to Die for His Enemies

Dr. Gary Habermas, who has probably written more on the evidence for the resurrection of Jesus than any other person in history, points out several ways in which Jesus is unique. One of them is that "of the major world religious founders, only Jesus taught that his death would provide the means by which salvation would be available for the world."[7]

As we've seen in both history and fiction, there are people who will sacrifice themselves to save their loved ones. Michael Monsoor's selfless act to smother a grenade to save the lives of his teammates is above and beyond any call of duty. Nobody would have blamed him if he had leapt through the door behind him to save himself. We praise the way he demonstrated his love for his friends, but how would we explain why anyone would jump on a grenade to save his enemies?

Jesus voluntarily went to the cross to save His enemies; those who had rebelled against Him; those who tortured and later killed Him; those who continue to rebel against Him to this day. That kind of love can't be anything but divine.

Jesus Is the Only Person in History Who Proved to Be God by Rising from the Dead

Imagine a friend of yours utters these statements to you:

"Before Abraham was born, I Am."
"Your sins are forgiven."
"I and the Father are one."
"All authority in heaven and on earth has been given to me."
"Whoever obeys my word will never see death."
"I am the resurrection and the life."

"I am the way and the truth and the life. No one comes to the
   Father except through me."
"I am the light of the world. Whoever follows me will never walk
   in darkness."
"[I am the] Lord of the Sabbath."
"I am the bread of life."
"Anyone who has seen me has seen the Father."
"Can any of you prove me guilty of sin?"
"I am with you always, to the very end of the age."
"Whatever you ask in my name the Father will give you."
"Father, glorify me in your presence with the glory I had with you
   before the world began."[8]

What conclusion would you draw about your friend? You would
either conclude your friend is nuts or that he really is God (but you'd
ask for proof). The one thing you wouldn't do is conclude your friend is
just a good moral teacher! Yet this is what so many people today blindly
say about Jesus. They clearly don't know the true Jesus.

As we've seen throughout this book, C. S. Lewis has wonderful
insights into so many aspects of Christianity. Here's what he writes about
this issue in his classic work *Mere Christianity*:

I am trying here to prevent anyone saying the really foolish
thing that people often say about Him: I'm ready to accept
Jesus as a great moral teacher, but I don't accept his claim
to be God. That is the one thing we must not say. A man
who was merely a man and said the sort of things Jesus said
would not be a great moral teacher. He would either be a
lunatic—on the level with the man who says he is a poached
egg—or else he would be the Devil of Hell. You must make
your choice. Either this man was, and is, the Son of God, or
else a madman or something worse. You can shut him up for

a fool, you can spit at him and kill him as a demon or you can fall at his feet and call him Lord and God, but let us not come with any patronizing nonsense about his being a great human teacher. He has not left that open to us. He did not intend to.[9]

This is now known as the Lord, Liar, Lunatic trilemma. Jesus can't be a good teacher if He claims to be God but really isn't. Dr. Peter Kreeft makes it even simpler. If Jesus was a good man, then He's God:

There are only two possible interpretations: Jesus is God, or Jesus is not God. The argument in its simplest form looks like this: Jesus was either (1) God, if his claim about himself was true, or (2) a bad man, if what he said was not true, for good men do not claim to be God. But he was not a bad man. (If anyone in history was not a bad man, Jesus was not a bad man.) Therefore, he was (and is) God.[10]

You may be thinking, *"Okay, but all of this assumes that the New Testament documents are telling us the truth about Jesus. How do we know they're not fiction?"*

I (Frank) have written about the evidence for New Testament documents and the entire Bible in *I Don't Have Enough Faith to Be an Atheist*. Please take a look at that because, obviously, we don't have room to cover all that evidence here. But allow us to make four quick points by asking four questions:

1. **Why would the observant Jews who wrote down most of the New Testament documents invent a resurrected Jesus?** Observant Jews believed they were God's chosen people and thought it was blasphemy for a man to claim to be God. They also had no expectation that a resurrection would occur before the end of history. Those who chose to follow Jesus had no motive to write falsehoods—they

didn't get money, sex, or power by inventing such a story. In fact, they got exactly the opposite: they got kicked out of the synagogue and then beaten, tortured, and killed. Certainly not a list of perks! They had every earthly motive to say the Resurrection was *not* true and no motive to invent it.

2. **If they were inventing it, why would they make themselves look so bad?** If you're trying to get people to accept a false story, would you invent embarrassing details about yourself and the hero you're trying to get people to follow? Then why are there so many embarrassing details in the accounts? Here are just a few:

- The disciples depict themselves as dimwitted, slow to understand Jesus and His mission.

- Their leader, Peter, denies Christ three times after saying he never would.

- The disciples run away when Jesus is crucified, while the women are the brave ones who stay at the cross.

- Then the women—whose testimony was not considered as credible as that of men—discover the empty tomb and the resurrected Jesus while the men are hiding for fear of the Jews.

- Even after Jesus is resurrected and is standing in front of them, giving them the Great Commission, they report that "they worshiped him; but some doubted" (Matthew 28:17)!

Jesus is also depicted in embarrassing ways:

- He's called "a drunkard" and "demon-possessed."

- His own family thinks He's out of His mind, and His brothers don't believe in Him.

- He has His feet wiped with the hair of a prostitute, and there are two prostitutes in His bloodline.

- He seems not to know when He's coming back.

- He cries out on the cross, "My God, My God, why have you forsaken me?" (Matthew 27:46).

There are explanations for why these seemingly embarrassing details about the disciples and Jesus are true and not problematic. What certainly isn't a good explanation is that the New Testament writers made them up.

3. **Do you realize there were thousands of Christians before a single sentence of the New Testament was written?** We erroneously tend to think that Christianity originated with a book, the Bible. It did not. In fact, Christianity would be true even if the Bible never existed. We wouldn't know much about it, but it would still be true. How so? Because Christianity did not originate with a book; it originated with an event—the resurrection of Jesus.

Paul became a Christian before he wrote a word of the New Testament. So did Matthew, John, James, Peter, etc. They became Christians not because they had read a book but because they had witnessed the risen Jesus. As we just saw, there would be no New Testament documents written by observant Jews in the first century unless Jesus rose from the dead. The New Testament writers didn't create the Resurrection; the Resurrection created the New Testament writers!

Before you assume miracles can't occur, keep in mind that the Resurrection is certainly possible because the greatest miracle in the Bible has already occurred—the creation of the universe from nothing (see the *Star Wars* chapter). Since God created the universe, He can certainly raise Jesus from the dead.

The key to everything, including salvation, is the Resurrection. If Christ rose from the dead, then Jesus is Lord and the essential teachings of Christianity are true on His authority. On the other hand, as the first-century eyewitness Paul admitted, if Jesus did not rise from the dead, then Christianity is false (1 Corinthians 15:17). But those who deny the Resurrection despite the abundant evidence have the added problem of explaining the perfect character of Jesus.

4. **How could ordinary men have invented the perfect character of Jesus?** As we have seen, Jesus is unparalleled in all of human history, fiction included. Thomas Griffith observes, "Poets, novelists, dramatists, philosophers, essayists have given the world wonderful creations and yet no writer has ever attempted to portray a perfect man or woman. . . . And yet in the Gospels, written by ordinary men, not literary geniuses, we have a perfect character depicted. How did the Evangelists accomplish what no writer has ever attempted with success?"[11]

David Limbaugh, in his fine book *The True Jesus*, asks, "Is it more likely that these four men created a literary miracle or that their presentation of Christ is true?"[12] It takes tremendous faith to believe these ordinary men somehow created a literary miracle that no one in history has ever accomplished before or since, especially when those ordinary men had every motive *not* to create a forgery that would get them beaten, tortured, and killed. And even if they, for some unknown reason, attempted to invent Jesus, the character would have lacked authenticity and the fullness of the real Jesus we read in the Gospels. If Jesus had never lived, no one would have been able to invent Him.

Jesus Is the Most Influential Human Being in History

In his book of sweeping scope called *Person of Interest*,[13] Detective J. Warner Wallace shows that even if someone burned every Bible and manuscript in existence, you could reconstruct the person of Jesus and His teachings from the monumental impact Jesus has had in the following six areas: literature/movies, art, music, education, science, and religion. Here is a short summary of his findings:

In Literature/movies: Jesus has been written about more than any other figure in history. To date, there are more than 109 million books written about Jesus (George Washington is a distant second at nearly 59 million books). Christ figures—parallels to Jesus—populate not just classical literature but even popular fiction, including movies (a few we've seen in this book). In fact, no other person has been the subject of more movies or inspired more movie characters. And the movie seen by the most people in history is not any of the blockbusters we've mentioned in this book. It is a 1979 movie called *Jesus*, based on the Gospel of Luke. *Jesus* has been seen by more than 8.1 billion people, making it the most watched movie of all time.[14]

In Art: No other figure in history has inspired more art than Jesus. The master of every genre of art has painted or sculpted Jesus. In every period of the last two millennia—from the early centuries, through the middle ages, to the Renaissance, all the way to the modern era—Jesus dominates art in the West, and He has even inspired art in non-Christian regions of the world. Wallace writes of other religious figures, "Indra, Thakur Jiu, Zoroaster, Krishna, and Buddha had a dramatic head-start on Jesus, yet *combined* they haven't had the global impact on art that Jesus has had. Jesus is not just the most inspirational historical figure in the West, he's the most inspirational figure in the history of the *world*."[15]

In Music: Nearly every style of music created since Jesus walked the earth has been created by a follower of Jesus. In addition, almost every popular band or singer in the modern era—those you find on the *Billboard* and *Rolling Stone*—have at least one song about Jesus. You can't say that about any other figure in history, religious or otherwise.

In Education: Since Christians are "people of the book" and are reproduced through education, reading, and discipleship, more libraries, schools, and universities have been founded by Christians than by any other group. Wallace writes, "Even though Hindus had a 2,300 to 1,500–year advantage, Jews had a 2,000 to 1,800–year lead, and Buddhists and Zoroastrians had a 600-year head start, Christians established more universities than all the other groups (combined) by a magnitude of 10 to 1."[16] If you had no Bible and just read the charters and bylaws of the top fifty universities in the world, you would know the history of Jesus and His essential teachings.

In Science: The founders and fathers *of every major discipline of science* have been Christians (Wallace lists 228!). Why? Because Christians believe that God provides us with two books: the book of Scripture (the Bible) and the book of nature and that the book of nature is orderly because God created the universe and sustains orderly natural laws to govern it. Johannes Kepler, the German mathematician, astronomer, and theologian who was a key figure in the scientific revolution, described his work this way: "I was merely thinking God's thoughts after him. Since we astronomers are priests of the highest God in regard to the book of nature, it benefits us to be thoughtful, not of the glory of our minds, but rather, above all else, of the glory of God."[17]

In Religion: Jesus is so influential that He's not only the central figure of the world's largest religion, He's even been made a part of *other* world religions. Many of the world's religions or mythical figures—even those that predate Christianity—have been modified to merge Jesus into their beliefs in some way. These include Hinduism, Buddhism, Krishna, the cult of Attis, Hercules, Mithras, Islam, Bahai, New Age, and several others. Everyone wants a piece of Jesus. He's too special to ignore. Yet the influence is only one way. As Wallace put it, "While these worldviews all acknowledged Jesus in some way, Christianity didn't modify its claims to embrace their prophets, 'manifestations,' or deities. The religions of the world made room for Jesus, but Christianity never budged."[18]

And the seismic impact of Jesus in those six areas is in addition to the billions of people who have worshiped Him over the last two thousand years! How has this single man—a man on whom we measure time itself—been so influential?

Dr. James Allan Francis asks the same question in this famous short sermon he gave in 1926 called "One Solitary Life":

He was born in an obscure village, the child of a peasant. He grew up in another village, where he worked in a carpenter shop until he was 30. Then, for three years, he was an itinerant preacher.

He never wrote a book. He never held an office. He never had a family or owned a home. He didn't go to college. He never lived in a big city. He never traveled 200 miles from the place where he was born. He did none of the things that usually accompany greatness. He had no credentials but himself.

He was only 33 when the tide of public opinion turned against him. His friends ran away. One of them denied him. He was turned over to his enemies and went through the mockery of a trial. He was nailed to a cross between two thieves. While he was dying, his executioners gambled for his garments, the only property he had on earth. When he was dead, he was laid in a borrowed grave, through the pity of a friend.

[Twenty] centuries have come and gone, and today he is the central figure of the human race. I am well within the mark when I say that all the armies that ever marched, all the navies that ever sailed, all the parliaments that ever sat, all the kings that ever reigned—put together—have not affected the life of man on this earth as much as that one, solitary life.[19]

How can this one solitary life from a remote corner of the ancient Roman Empire be the most influential life in human history? Jesus is certainly a compelling man. But if He had just died—if there had been no resurrection—do you think He would have the impact He has?

Look how historian Philip Schaff sums up the influence of Christ:

This Jesus of Nazareth, without money and arms, conquered more millions than Alexander, Caesar, Muhammad, and Napoleon; without science and learning, he shed more light on matters human and divine than all philosophers and scholars combined; without the eloquence of schools, he spoke such words of life as were never spoken before or since and produced effects which lie beyond the reach of orator or poet; without writing a single line, he set more pens in motion and furnished themes for more sermons, orations, discussions, learned volumes, works of art and songs of praise than the whole army of great men of ancient and modern times.[20]

The most important point of everything we've discussed so far is that the world's most influential human is actually the perfect God-man who sacrificed Himself to offer you an eternal relationship with Him.

Jesus Is the Only Hero or World Religious Figure Who Wants a Relationship with *You*

The reason we love Hollywood heroes so much is that, deep down, we all want someone to save us from the evil and suffering in the world today. Your family and friends can love you and your spouse might be your soulmate, but they can't completely stop evil in the world. Someone else has to do that—a hero. Only then, we think, can we live happily ever after.

A number of stories in this book have led to happy endings. Captain America ends up with his long-lost love, Peggy Carter. Harry Potter, nineteen years after defeating Voldemort, takes his children to the Hogwarts Express and is able to give them an experience he never had— being sent off to school by loving parents. Middle-earth returns to peace after the Ring is destroyed. Luke redeems his father and then sees him transfigured in the afterlife.

In all the happy endings, though, there's something that's missing— a real connection with us personally. We see those endings and wish them for ourselves, but there's nothing in them that gives you or me that happy ending too. No Hollywood hero saves us.

Of course, the Hollywood heroes we've been discussing don't really exist. But what if they did? What if Superman knew *your* name and wanted to be friends with you? What if *you* were the one whom Tony Stark died to save? What if it was *you* Luke Skywalker would stop at nothing to redeem?

The truth is, that Someone already exists. If there's one point we're trying to make with this book, it's this: The happily-ever-after that we're all searching for is within our grasp because Jesus—the Ultimate Hero— exists in our world. In fact, He made our world and you, too. And He also wants to know and save *you*. You and I are the reason He came in the first place.

Jesus declares, "Come to me, all you who are weary and burdened, and I will give you rest. Take my yoke upon you and learn from me, for I am gentle and humble in heart, and you will find rest for your souls. For my yoke is easy and my burden is light" (Matthew 11:28-30).

Unlike other religious founders who want us to work our way to God, Jesus, who is God, works His way to us. This God enters creation and experiences suffering on our behalf. He's the hero of the story and now desires to have a personal relationship with you.

How many of the heroes we've seen can you say that about? Tony Stark might have died to save the universe, but he had other concerns first—namely protecting his family and friends. Jesus' first and only concern was us. There was no ulterior motive.

Remember, this is the transcendent, infinite Being who created and sustains this vast and beautiful universe of stars as numerous as the grains of sand on 100,000 earths. In light of that, you might be tempted to think you are insignificant. But the exact opposite is true. The universe isn't made in the image of God, but you are! That's why He came to save you and me. His sacrificial love for us should motivate us to love others the same way and to share with them the salvation He offers everyone.

Jesus says, "My command is this: Love each other as I have loved you. Greater love has no one than this: to lay down one's life for one's friends. You are my friends if you do what I command" (John 15:12-14).

Imagine if you were one of the two SEALs Michael Monsoor died to save. If he somehow resurrected from the dead and wanted to have a relationship with you, if he also wanted you to help him spread his message of sacrifice and urge people to love others the same way, would you do it?

Will You Be a Star or a Hero?

Nietzsche wrote, "The strength of a person's spirit could be . . . measured by how much truth he could tolerate, or more precisely, to what extent he *needs* to have it diluted, disguised, sweetened, muted, falsified."[21] The famous atheist was right: many people will not tolerate the truth about God or Christianity. At best, they will dilute, sweeten, or mute it.

That's one reason I (Frank) often ask atheists who attend my college talks this question: "If Christianity were true, would you become a Christian?"

How would you answer that question?

Some atheists will answer no publicly and then privately admit their atheism isn't so much about the *existence* of God but about their *resistance* to God. While this is not true of all atheists, many people don't want there to be a God because they want to be the god of their own lives. They are not on a truth quest but on a happiness quest. They think God's moral demands will get in the way of their quest to be happy, not realizing that His moral commands are guardrails designed to help them flourish in a dangerous world.

Satan is a liar and a deceiver.[22] He wants to deceive us into thinking we will never be happy if we follow and obey Christ. But as we've seen in the Scriptures and reflected in some of the movies we love, the only way to get long-lasting contentment is to go straight through truth. Jesus is the Truth. We can deny the truth. We can suppress the truth. We can run from the truth. But in the end, we will all succumb to the Truth either as adopted sons and daughters saved by the Ultimate Hero or as rebels quarantined by Him. God will not force any rebels into heaven against their will.

In the meantime, Christians are on a mission to love God and one another and to make disciples of all nations. If you've decided to join this great adventure, keep in mind that you will probably be called to be a hero yourself as the culture continues to become more anti-Christian.

When you're asked to renounce your Christian beliefs to adopt the latest cultural trend, how will you respond? Will you be a hero or a star? There's a big difference.

Stars are popular. They satisfy the crowd. Heroes often do not. Author Walter Truett Anderson writes, "Today, our leaders are stars, not heroes. Stars are surrounded by crowds; heroes walk alone. Stars consult focus groups; heroes consult their conscience."[23]

Jesus went to the cross alone to save you. When the time comes, will you satisfy the crowd or your Savior? "How can you believe," asks Jesus, "since you accept glory from one another but do not seek the glory that comes from the only God?" (John 5:44).

While many who claim the name of Christ abandon Him to seek

glory from one another, we pray that you will stand with Jesus as you love your enemies. A true hero's glory comes from God—the God who entered this dangerous world and sacrificed Himself to save us all. The Ultimate Hero.

For Personal Reflection or Family/Small Group Discussion

1. If you are not a Christian, why not? If you are, think of someone close to you who is not. Why is that person not a Christian? How do you think they would answer the question: "If Christianity were true, would you become a Christian?" Ask them.

2. Which of the Hollywood heroes that we have discussed do you most identify with? Why? What personal qualities do they have that are strengths for you? How can you use those strengths to build God's Kingdom?

3. Which of the truths about Jesus presented in this chapter are most convincing to you that Jesus was not just another man? Why?

4. Which of the reasons given that Jesus was not invented are most persuasive to you? Why?

5. When persecution comes to Christians, will you be prepared to be a hero rather than a star? What do you need to do to get prepared?

ACKNOWLEDGMENTS

This father-and-son project was really a Turek all-family affair. Stephanie (Frank's wife), Lili (Zach's wife), and sons/brothers Spencer and Austin gave us many helpful insights on the draft chapters. Illustrator Keith Carter, who is part of the CrossExamined.org family, not only reviewed the manuscript but also came up with the great idea for the cover (he's so good at this that his clients have included Marvel, Disney, Paramount, and Lucasfilm).

The NavPress/Tyndale team has been an enthusiastic supporter of *Hollywood Heroes* from the second Wes Yoder of the Ambassador Agency sent them the idea (thanks, Wes!). Publisher David Zimmerman took on this unusual project and assembled a team of superheroes to refine the manuscript and get it into your hands. They include John Greco, Erin Healy, Olivia Eldredge, Danny Nicklin, Robin Bermel, and Mariah Franklin.

Our friend Detective J. Warner Wallace shared his personal plan for raising awareness about his phenomenal *Person of Interest* book—a plan that took months to develop. Without Jim, you might have never heard of this book.

Finally, thanks to all those wonderful authors, artists, producers, directors, and actors who have brought superheroes to life from the comics to the silver screen. Although many of them probably had little intention to advance any kind of Christian message, the historical accounts of the Ultimate Hero are so compelling that their mythical hero stories can't help but imitate history—His story.

NOTES

PREFACE

1. While Iron Man/Tony Stark doesn't appear in this movie, his father, Howard Stark, plays an important role.
2. You can forgo watching the original *Justice League* in favor of this one if you have not seen either movie yet.

INTRODUCTION

1. Official citation, Master-at-Arms Second Class (Sea, Air, and Land), Michael A. Monsoor, United States Navy, https://www.navy.mil/MEDAL-OF-HONOR-RECIPIENT-MICHAEL-A-MONSOOR/#:~:text=Official%20Citation,-MASTER%2DAT%2DARMS&text=CITATION%3A,FREEDOM%20ON%2029%20SEPTEMBER%202006.
2. C. S. Lewis, *Mere Christianity* (London: Macmillan, 1952), 120.
3. Michael S. Heiser, *The Unseen Realm* (Bellingham, WA: Lexham Press, 2015).
4. See Psalm 82:1; see also Deuteronomy 32:7-9, where verse 8 should read, "sons of God," according to the Dead Sea Scrolls, not "sons of Israel." (Israel wasn't yet a nation when God confused the languages of the people at Babel, the incident being described in this passage.) See also www.thedivinecouncil.com.
5. See Greg Koukl's excellent book *The Story of Reality: How the World Began, How It Ends, and Everything Important That Happens in Between* (Grand Rapids, MI: Zondervan, 2017).
6. Craig Keener, *Miracles: The Credibility of the New Testament Accounts* (Grand Rapids, MI: Baker Academic, 2011). See also two interviews with Dr. Keener and one with Lee Strobel from March and April 2018 on the *I Don't Have Enough Faith to Be an Atheist* podcast, which can be found in the Cross Examined App.
7. We abbreviated and paraphrased the actual interaction due to brevity and clarity requirements here. If you want to see the complete exchange, go to the Cross Examined YouTube channel for the video called "Is God a Bad Parent?": https://www.youtube.com/watch?v=Hg6N3t57-cM.

8. God doesn't say everything is good, but He promises that all things will work together for good to those who love God and are called according to His purpose (see Romans 8:28).

9. The writer of Hebrews put it this way: "During the days of Jesus' life on earth, he offered up prayers and petitions with fervent cries and tears to the one who could save him from death, and he was heard because of his reverent submission. Son though he was, he learned obedience from what he suffered and, once made perfect, he became the source of eternal salvation for all who obey him and was designated by God to be high priest in the order of Melchizedek" (Hebrews 5:7-10).

10. See Peter Kreeft's fine book, *Making Sense Out of Suffering* (Ann Arbor, MI: Servant Books, 1986).

11. God's Kingdom arrived when Jesus came the first time, but it will not be fully completed until Christ comes the second time. In the meantime, we are left in a world where suffering exists because of Adam's sin and our own.

12. Paul says that the stories surrounding the idolatry of the Israelites during the wilderness wanderings serve "as examples to keep us from setting our hearts on evil things as they did" (1 Corinthians 10:6). He says that "everything that was written in the past was written to teach us, so that through the endurance taught in the Scriptures and the encouragement they provide we might have hope" (Romans 15:4).

13. Gisela Kreglinger as quoted in Michael T. Jahosky, *The Good News of the Return of the King: The Gospel in Middle-earth* (Eugene, OR: Wipf & Stock Publishers, 2020), 103.

14. Richard Dawkins, *The God Delusion* (New York: Houghton Mifflin, 2006), 53.

15. Why do natural laws exist? Laws come from lawgivers. Why are the natural laws that govern the universe consistent, precise, and goal-directed? As Aristotle and then Aquinas argued, they are best explained by a mind directing and sustaining them every moment. For a more detailed explanation, see chapter 3 in Frank Turek, *Stealing from God: Why Atheists Need God to Make Their Case* (Colorado Springs, CO: NavPress, 2015).

16. For philosophical arguments for the existence of a theistic God with these attributes, see Edward Feser, *Five Proofs of the Existence of God* (San Francisco: Ignatius Press, 2017).

17. For popular arguments for the truth of Christianity, see Norman Geisler and Frank Turek, *I Don't Have Enough Faith to Be an Atheist* (Wheaton, IL: Crossway, 2004). Also visit Crossexamined.org and its YouTube channel for hundreds of short videos.

18. Peter Kreeft, quoted in Michael T. Jahosky, *The Good News of the Return of the King: The Gospel in Middle-earth* (Eugene, OR: Wipf & Stock Publishers, 2020), 87.

19. C. S. Lewis to Arthur Graves, October 18, 1931, in *The Collected Letters of C. S. Lewis*, vol. 1: Family Letters 1905–1931, ed. Walter Hooper (San Francisco: Harper, 2004), 977.

NOTES

CHAPTER 1: CAPTAIN AMERICA

1. See, for example, John 8:46 and 1 John 3:5.
2. See 1 Corinthians 9:24-27 and 2 Timothy 3:2.
3. For a detailed and insightful look at the supernatural worldview described in the Bible—a worldview often overlooked even by Christians—read Michael Heiser, *The Unseen Realm* (Bellingham, WA: Lexham Press, 2015). You can also get more by visiting http://www.moreunseenrealm.com/ and by listening to his *The Naked Bible* podcast.
4. See Philippians 2.
5. Sierro Burrell, "Why Captain America Retires in 'Avengers: Endgame,'" *ScreenGeek*, May 18, 2019, https://www.screengeek.net/2019/05/18/avengers-endgame-captain-america-retirement/.
6. As we're writing this, the Disney+ series *The Falcon and the Winter Soldier* is about to be released, so we'll see if and how this changes.

CHAPTER 2: IRON MAN

1. Eric Eisenberg, "Jon Favreau Details His Fight with Marvel Studios to Cast Robert Downey Jr. as Iron Man," CinemaBlend, June 3, 2014, https://www.cinemablend.com/new/Jon-Favreau-Details-His-Fight-With-Marvel-Studios-Cast-Robert-Downey-Jr-Iron-Man-43293.html.
2. Mike Lee, "Stan Lee Admitted He Created Iron Man to Be Completely Unlikable," *ScreenRant*, July 5, 2021, https://screenrant.com/stan-lee-iron-man-unlikable-hero-creation-marvel/.
3. "Nobody Had the Chance to Be Tony Stark: RDJ's Brutal Honesty on Screen Test," YouTube video, 8:09, July 19, 2019, https://youtu.be/kG1254jSZw8.
4. "Robert Downey Jr. on Addiction," *I Am Sober*, February 19, 2019, https://iamsober.com/blog/robert-downey-jr-sober-story/.
5. Carrie Bryson, "Kevin Feige: On Iron Man 3, Pepper Potts, and Marvel's Family Appeal," WebCite, April 24, 2013, https://www.webcitation.org/6G7kXDjMk?url=http://kidstvmovies.about.com/od/IronMan3/a/Kevin-Feige-On-Iron-Man-3-Pepper-Potts-And-Marvels-Family-Appeal.htm.
6. "Robert Downey Jr. on Addiction."
7. See Paul C. Vitz, *Faith of the Fatherless: The Psychology of Atheism* (San Francisco: Ignatius Press, 2013). See also "Faith of the Fatherless," Beliefnet, June 2000, https://www.beliefnet.com/love-family/2000/06/faith-of-the-fatherless.aspx.

CHAPTER 3: HARRY POTTER

1. Shawn Adler, "'Harry Potter' Author J. K. Rowling Opens Up about Books' Christian Imagery," MTV News, October 17, 2007, http://www.mtv.com/news/1572107/harry-potter-author-jk-rowling-opens-up-about-books-christian-imagery/.
2. Ibid.
3. While Christians are certainly free to disagree, Connie Neal agrees with this point in her book *What's a Christian to Do with Harry Potter?* (Colorado Springs, CO:

Waterbrook Press, 2001), published when only the first four books of the series had been written.

4. For additional prophecies and explanation, see chapter 13 in Norman Geisler and Frank Turek, *I Don't Have Enough Faith to Be an Atheist* (Wheaton, IL: Crossway, 2004).

5. "Conversation between J. K. Rowling and Steve Kloves (2011)," YouTube video, 47:28, November 15, 2016, https://www.youtube.com/watch?v=Me3SbSWhICg.

6. "J. K. Rowling 2012 Interview—Harry Potter: Beyond the Page [Hi-Res]," YouTube video, 50:47, January 21, 2020, https://www.youtube.com/watch?v=aA_QYZBWQ88.

7. J. K. Rowling, *Harry Potter and the Sorcerer's Stone* (New York: A.A. Levine Books, 1998), chapter 12.

8. In this way, the New Testament provides the boxtop to the prophetic jigsaw puzzle of the Old Testament. Once you see the boxtop of a jigsaw puzzle, you can see how the pieces were designed to fit together. Those pieces were designed before you recognized they were designed. Likewise, Old Testament prophecy came from the mind of God long before anyone recognized the prophecies were fulfilled in Jesus.

9. See Norman Geisler and Frank Turek, *I Don't Have Enough Faith to Be an Atheist* (Wheaton, IL: Crossway, 2004); see also Frank Turek, *Stealing from God: Why Atheists Need God to Make Their Case* (Colorado Springs, CO: NavPress, 2015).

CHAPTER 4: STAR WARS

1. These quotes are from an interview Bill Moyers conducted with George Lucas in 1999, the transcripts of which are available here: https://billmoyers.com/content/mythology-of-star-wars-george-lucas/.

2. Some may claim that by "balance" Lucas means the moderation between extremes that pantheists often advocate (signified by the yin and yang symbol). But if that's the case, why would he claim we should want compassion and greed to be in balance?

3. C. S. Lewis, *Mere Christianity* (London: Macmillan, 1952), 50–51.

4. James Harleman, "The Gospel for Han Solo," *Cinemagogue*, December 21, 2015, http://cinemagogue.com/2015/12/21/the-gospel-for-han-solo/.

5. Ibid.

6. C. S. Lewis, *The Screwtape Letters* (San Francisco: HarperSanFrancisco, 1996), 60–61.

7. George Lucas, in an interview with Bill Moyers, around the time of the release of *The Phantom Menace*, "The Mythology of 'Star Wars' with George Lucas," June 18, 1999, https://billmoyers.com/content/mythology-of-star-wars-george-lucas/ (transcript); https://www.imdb.com/title/tt0458432/ (video).

8. It's interesting to note that the quest to be rational contradicts Obi-Wan's instructions to Luke that he must trust his feelings.

9. "Understanding the Tragedy of Darth Vader (The Chosen One)," YouTube video, 15:06, September 2, 2017, https://www.youtube.com/watch?v=4Bq_0-a9WJE.

10. Our culture not only does evil but also cheers it on. The killing of babies in the womb is now being promoted and paid for by our government. Young girls and boys who are not old enough to make life-altering decisions are being given drugs and hormones that will change their bodies forever. Our government is sponsoring seminars that call people racist not because of any racist behavior but because of their race. And if you oppose any of it, you will likely be canceled by those who say they are fighting for inclusion, tolerance, and diversity.

CHAPTER 5: THE LORD OF THE RINGS

1. Michael S. Heiser, interview with Michael Jahosky, "Naked Bible 351: The Good News of the Return of the King," November 22, 2020, *The Naked Bible* podcast, produced by Trey Strickland, podcast audio, 01:16:35, https://nakedbiblepodcast .com/podcast/naked-bible-351-the-good-news-of-the-return-of-the-king/.
2. J. R. R. Tolkien, *The Letters of J. R. R. Tolkien*, ed. Humphrey Carpenter and Christopher Tolkien (New York: Houghton Mifflin Harcourt, 2000), 246, quoted in Peter Kreeft, *The Philosophy of Tolkien: The Worldview Behind* The Lord of the Rings (San Francisco: Ignatius Press, 2005), loc. 1267–69, Kindle.
3. Ibid., 201, quoted in Kreeft, *Philosophy of Tolkien*, loc. 878, Kindle.
4. Michael T. Jahosky, *The Good News of the Return of the King: The Gospel in Middle-earth* (Eugene, OR: Wipf & Stock Publishers, 2020), 11.
5. C. S. Lewis, quoted in Kreeft, *Philosophy of Tolkien*, 12.
6. J. R. R. Tolkien, quoted in Jahosky, *The Good News of the Return of the King*, 85–86.
7. C. S. Lewis, *Broadcast Talks* (London: The Centenary Press, 1942), 36, https:// www.fadedpage.com/showbook.php?pid=20140875. These were originally broadcasts that Lewis gave on BBC radio during WWII. These talks later served as much of the material for *Mere Christianity*, which was published in 1952.
8. We won't spend much time on their history prior to *The Lord of the Rings* or etymology here, but those who are interested should check out *The Silmarillion*, which covers the First and Second Ages of Tolkien's world; *The Lord of the Rings* covers the Third.
9. *Letters of J. R. R. Tolkien*, 202, quoted in Kreeft, *Philosophy of Tolkien*, 52.
10. In the books, this happens in the Shire before Frodo leaves; in the movies, this conversation happens in Moria.
11. Stratford Caldecott, "The Horns of Hope: J. R. R. Tolkien and the Heroism of Hobbits," in *The Chesterton Review* 28, no. 1/2 (February/May 2002), 37; quoted in Kreeft, *Philosophy of Tolkien*, loc. 2432, Kindle.
12. *Letters of J. R. R. Tolkien*, 201, quoted in Kreeft, *Philosophy of Tolkien*, 47.
13. J. R. R. Tolkien, *The Return of the King* (Ballantine/Del Rey, 2018), 266.

CHAPTER 6: BATMAN

1. For more on what the law can and can't do, and the fact that all laws legislate morality, see a book I (Frank Turek) cowrote with Norman Geisler entitled

Legislating Morality: Is It Wise? Is It Legal? Is It Possible? (Eugene, OR: Wipf & Stock Publishers, 1998).

2. Matthew Rosa, "'Batman v. Superman' isn't a flop: A superhero movie that questions absolute power is tailor-made for 2016," *Salon*, March 29, 2016, https://www.salon.com/2016/03/29/batman_v_superman_isnt_a_flop_a_superhero_movie_that_questions_absolute_power_is_tailor_made_for_2016/.

3. See Austin Gentry, "Superman Parallels Jesus in 11 Ways," *Austin Gentry* blog, June 15, 2013, https://www.austingentry.com/superman-parallels-jesus-in-11-ways/.

4. For more, see my (Frank's) book, *Stealing from God: Why Atheists Need God to Make Their Case* (Colorado Springs, CO: NavPress, 2015).

5. Since evil is a privation in good, the ultimate Being, God, cannot be evil. And there cannot be two coequal opposing forces of good and evil. In chapter two of *Mere Christianity* (London: Macmillan, 1952), C. S. Lewis writes: "To be bad, [the devil] must exist and have intelligence and will. But existence, intelligence and will are in themselves good. Therefore he must be getting them from the Good Power: even to be bad he must borrow or steal from his opponent. And do you now begin to see why Christianity has always said that the devil is a fallen angel? That is not a mere story for the children. It is a real recognition of the fact that evil is a parasite, not an original thing. The powers which enable evil to carry on are powers given it by goodness. All the things which enable a bad man to be effectively bad are in themselves good things—resolution, cleverness, good looks, existence itself. That is why Dualism, in a strict sense, will not work."

6. This quotation is attributed to Jacques-Marie-Louis Monsabré.

7. Chris Begley, interview with Ben Affleck, "Ben Affleck talks 'Batman v Superman' and what it was like in the 'heavy' armored Batsuit (video)," Batman News, March 18, 2016, https://batman-news.com/2016/03/18/ben-affleck-batman-v-superman-armored-suit/.

8. Here are just a few examples: Isaiah warns about calling good evil and evil good (Isaiah 5:20); the book of Proverbs contains many warnings about indulging in or doing evil; Paul tells us that if we suppress the truth long enough, we'll be given over to a depraved mind that actually encourages evil (Romans 1:18-32); John tells us not to love the evils in the world (1 John 2:15-17).

9. Deep Talks: Exploring Theology & Meaning-Making, "Snyder Cut | Batman v Superman Is Deeper Than You Think | Symbolism. Philosophy. Theology," YouTube video, 26:45, July 22, 2020, https://www.youtube.com/watch?v=_eZkgte8Tx4.

10. While there certainly has been much evil done in the name of religion, it is a myth that most wars have been caused by religion. According to *The Encyclopedia of War*, less than 7 percent of more than 1,700 known wars since 8000 BC have had religion as the primary cause (take Islam out, and the figure drops to only about 3 percent). For more on this, see Andrew Holt, "Counting 'Religious Wars'

in *The Encyclopedia of Wars*," APHolt.com, December 26, 2018, https://apholt
.com/2018/12/26/counting-religious-wars-in-the-encyclopedia-of-wars/.
Moreover, you don't judge a religion by its heretics. Using violence to settle
theological differences was prohibited by Christ. Such violence is the illogical
outworking of Christianity, while it could certainly be seen as the logical
outworking of atheism. For if there is no real right or wrong, and if there will
be no final judgment, then why not lie, steal, and murder to get what you want
if you can get away with it?

11. Friedrich Nietzsche, *Daybreak: Thoughts on the Prejudices of Morality* (1881; repr.,
Cambridge: Cambridge University Press, 1997), 14, https://archive.org/details
/daybreakbook/page/n7/mode/2up.

12. C. S. Lewis, *Mere Christianity* (London: Macmillan, 1952), 13–14.

CHAPTER 7: WONDER WOMAN

1. August 22, 1914. See Dan Carlin's in-depth series of podcasts that cover major
battles in fascinating detail. This fact comes from episode 51: https://www.podgist
.com/dan-carlins-hardcore-history/show-51-blueprint-for-armageddon-ii/index
.html.

2. C. S. Lewis, *Mere Christianity* (London: Macmillan, 1952), 93.

3. You hear it said time and time again that when it comes to addiction, the first
step to overcoming it is admitting you have a problem. What's the problem? That
whatever you are addicted to has enslaved you.

4. Timothy Keller, *Encounters with Jesus: Unexpected Answers to Life's Biggest Questions*
(New York: Dutton, 2013), 46.

5. For more on this, see the excellent book by Tom Gilson, *Too Good to Be False:
How Jesus' Incomparable Character Reveals His Reality* (Tampa, FL: DeWard
Publishing, 2020).

6. Keller, *Encounters with Jesus*, 51–52.

7. Gary Habermas, *The Uniqueness of Jesus Christ among the Major World Religions*
(self pub., 2016), PDF. Available for free download at http://www.garyhabermas
.com.

8. See (in the order listed) John 8:58; Matthew 9:2; John 10:30; Matthew 28:18;
John 8:51; 11:25; 8:12; Matthew 12:8; John 6:35; 14:9; 8:46; Matthew 28:20;
John 15:16; 17:5.

9. Lewis, *Mere Christianity*, 55–56.

10. Peter Kreeft, "Why I Believe Jesus Is the Son of God" in *Why I Am a Christian:
Leading Thinkers Explain Why They Believe*, eds. Norman L. Geisler and Paul K.
Hoffman (Grand Rapids, MI: Baker Books, 2006), 228–29.

11. Thomas Griffith, quoted in David Limbaugh, *The True Jesus: Uncovering the
Divinity of Christ in the Gospels* (Washington: Regnery Publishing, 2017), 51.

12. Limbaugh, *The True Jesus*, 51.

13. J. Warner Wallace, *Person of Interest: Why Jesus Still Matters in a World That Rejects
the Bible* (Grand Rapids, MI: Zondervan Reflective, 2021).

14. "Official Jesus Film Project Ministry Statistics—May 27, 2020," August 16, 2021, https://www.jesusfilm.org/about/learn-more/statistics.html. *Jesus* is also the most translated movie of all time, according to the Guinness World Records (https://www.guinnessworldrecords.com/world-records/85523-most-translated-film).

15. Wallace, *Person of Interest*, 135.

16. Ibid., 170.

17. Ibid., 188.

18. Ibid., 244.

19. For more on the background of this sermon, visit https://www.celebratingholidays.com/?page_id=4456.

20. Philip Schaff, quoted in Paul E. Little, *Know Why You Believe*, 4th ed. (Downers Grove, IL: InterVarsity Press, 2000), 45.

21. Friedrich Nietzsche, *Beyond Good and Evil* (1886; repr., Cambridge: Oxford University Press, 1998), 37.

22. See John 8:44; 2 Corinthians 11:3, 14; and 1 Timothy 4:1, which points out that demons are deceivers.

23. Walter Truett Anderson, quoted in a sermon by Timothy Keller called "Hero of Heroes," available at https://gospelinlife.com/downloads/the-hero-of-heroes-3.

ABOUT THE AUTHORS

Frank Turek is a world-renowned apologist and award-winning author. He has written or cowritten several books, including *I Don't Have Enough Faith to Be an Atheist*. He hosts a weekly TV program broadcast to 32 million homes and an apologetics podcast. Frank speaks over 100 times per year to youth and college students. He has debated several prominent atheists, including Christopher Hitchens, Michael Shermer, and David Silverman. Frank is the founder and president of CrossExamined.org and runs OnlineChristianCourses.com and ImpactApologetics.com.

Captain Frank Zachary Turek is assistant director of operations for the United States Air Force with a specialization in intelligence. Zachary earned his master's degree in philosophy from Southern Evangelical Seminary.

THE NAVIGATORS® STORY

T HANK YOU for picking up this NavPress book! We hope it has been a blessing to you.

NavPress is a ministry of The Navigators. The Navigators began in the 1930s, when a young California lumberyard worker named Dawson Trotman was impacted by basic discipleship principles and felt called to teach those principles to others. He saw this mission as an echo of 2 Timothy 2:2: "And the things you have heard me say in the presence of many witnesses entrust to reliable people who will also be qualified to teach others" (NIV).

In 1933, Trotman and his friends began discipling members of the US Navy. By the end of World War II, thousands of men on ships and bases around the world were learning the principles of spiritual multiplication by the intentional, person-to-person teaching of God's Word.

After World War II, The Navigators expanded its relational ministry to include college campuses; local churches; the Glen Eyrie Conference Center and Eagle Lake Camps in Colorado Springs, Colorado; and neighborhood and citywide initiatives across the country and around the world.

Today, with more than 2,600 US staff members—and local ministries in more than 100 countries—The Navigators continues the transformational process of making disciples who make more disciples, advancing the Kingdom of God in a world that desperately needs the hope and salvation of Jesus Christ and the encouragement to grow deeper in relationship with Him.

NAVPRESS was created in 1975 to advance the calling of The Navigators by bringing biblically rooted and culturally relevant products to people who want to know and love Christ more deeply. In January 2014, NavPress entered an alliance with Tyndale House Publishers to strengthen and better position our rich content for the future. Through *The Message* Bible and other resources, NavPress seeks to bring positive spiritual movement to people's lives.

If you're interested in learning more or becoming involved with The Navigators, go to navigators.org. For more discipleship content from The Navigators and NavPress authors, visit thedisciplemaker.org. May God bless you in your walk with Him!

NavPress

navpress.com

CP1308